Stanislav Grof, M.D.

REALMS OF THE HUMAN UNCONSCIOUS

Observations from LSD Research

A CONDOR BOOK
SOUVENIR PRESS (E & A) LTD.

First published in the U.S.A. 1975 by The Viking Press, New York

First British Edition published 1979 by
Souvenir Press (Educational & Academic) Ltd,
43 Great Russell Street London WC1B 3PA
Reprinted 1993, 1996

Acknowledgement is made to The Bobbs-Merrill Company, Inc., for:
Illustrations on pages 84–87 from *The Use of LSD in Psychotherapy
and Alcoholism,* Copyright © 1967 by Harold A. Abramson, reprinted by
permission of the publisher, The Bobbs-Merrill Company, Inc.

ISBN 0 285 64881 0 casebound
ISBN 0 285 64882 9 paperback

Printed in Great Britain by
The Guernsey Press Co Ltd, Guernsey, Channel Islands

To Joan and my parents

Preface

This volume is the first of a series of books in which I plan to summarize and condense in a systematic and comprehensive way my observations and experiences during seventeen years of research with LSD and other psychedelic drugs. Exploration of the potential of these substances for the study of schizophrenia, for didactic purposes, for a deeper understanding of art and religion, for personality diagnostics and the therapy of emotional disorders, and for altering the experience of dying has been my major professional interest throughout these years and has consumed most of the time I have spent in psychiatric research.

In 1965, I was invited to participate in an international conference on LSD psychotherapy in Amityville, Long Island, and gave a paper on the experiences I had gathered during almost a decade of LSD research in Prague, Czechoslovakia. During a lecture-journey in the United States after this conference, I was offered an invitation to come to the West on a one-year fellowship from the Foundations' Fund for Research in Psychiatry in New Haven, Connecticut. After my return to Prague, I received a letter from Dr. Joel Elkes, Chairman of the Department of Psychiatry and Behavioral Sciences at the Johns Hopkins University in Baltimore, inviting me to come to Baltimore and continue my LSD work as a clinical and research fellow at the Henry Phipps Clinic and in the Research Unit of Spring Grove State Hospital.

When this unusual opportunity occurred, I was deeply

involved in my research activities in Prague. I had accumulated detailed records from many hundreds of LSD sessions and was in the process of analyzing the data, trying to formulate a theoretical framework for understanding the striking observations that I had encountered during my work. By then I had completed the first outline of a conceptual model that seemed to account for most of the findings in my LSD research; this model allowed for the creation of several partial hypotheses that could be put to a more rigorous test. In addition, I became intrigued by the possibilities that LSD psychotherapy seemed to offer for the alleviation of the emotional suffering of cancer patients facing the prospect of imminent death. On the basis of some preliminary observations, I was preparing a special project to explore this new area in a more systematic way.

Dr. Elkes' generous offer was too tempting to refuse; I decided to pursue this possibility and ask the Czech authorities for a one-year leave of absence and permission to go to the United States. After many administrative difficulties, this permission was finally granted. When I arrived at Kennedy Airport in March 1967, more than half of my forty pounds of luggage consisted of the records from LSD research that I had conducted at the Psychiatric Research Institute in Prague. My intention, at that time, was to complete the analysis of my data and to perform a controlled clinical study of the efficacy of the technique of LSD psychotherapy that I had developed during many years of therapeutic experimentation. My secret hope was that, in addition, I might be able to carry out at least one of the more theoretical studies testing some aspects of my new conceptual framework.

After my arrival in the United States, it soon became obvious that my plans were highly unrealistic, to say the least. I was astounded by the situation regarding psychedelic drugs that had developed in this country since my first visit in 1965. In Czechoslovakia at the time of my departure, LSD was being legally manufactured by the leading pharmaceutical company sponsored by the government. It was listed in the official medical pharmacopoeia as a therapeutic agent with specific indications and contraindications, together with such reputable drugs as penicillin, insulin, and digitalis. LSD was freely available to qualified professionals as an experimental and therapeutic agent, and its distribution was subject to special regulations. The training required for each LSD therapist more or less followed the psychoanalytic model; it involved a minimum of five training LSD sessions for the applicant and his conducting at least thirty sessions with selected patients under the supervision of an experienced LSD therapist. The general public knew almost nothing about psychedelic drugs, since the reports concerning research with such substances were published almost exclusively in scientific journals. At the time of my departure, there was no black-market traffic in psychedelics and no nonmedical use of them. Anyone interested in self-experimentation could have an LSD session provided it was conducted by an approved professional and in a medical facility.

The situation I found in the United States contrasted sharply with the one described above. Psychedelics had become an issue of general interest. Black-market LSD seemed to be readily available in all parts of the country and for all age groups. Self-experimentation with psychedelics flourished on university campuses, and many large cities had their hippie districts with distinct drug subcultures. The casualties from the psychedelic scene were making newspaper headlines; almost every day one could read sensationalist reports about psychotic breakdowns, self-mutilations, suicides, and murders attributed to the use of LSD. At the same time, the psychedelic movement was profoundly influencing contemporary culture—music, painting, poetry, design, interior decorating, fashion, movies, theater, and television plays.

The legislative measures undertaken with the intention of suppressing dangerous self-experimentation proved rather ineffective in curbing nonmedical use of LSD but had adverse direct and indirect consequences for scientific research. Only a handful of projects survived under these complicated circumstances. As a result, LSD research was reduced to a minimum and, paradoxically, very little new scientific information was being generated at a time when it was most needed. LSD and other psychedelics had become a serious national problem; it was difficult to imagine how effective measures could be undertaken without a real understanding of the nature of this problem.

The information about psychedelic drugs spread by the mass media and various agencies was mostly superficial, inaccurate, and one-sided. This situation can be attributed, in part, to ignorance and emotional bias and to a desire to discourage and deter the lay experimentation that was flourishing in spite of all of the repressive legislative measures. Such distorted information, since it was unbalanced, disproportional, and frequently obviously incorrect, was regarded with suspicion by young people, many of whom found it easy to laugh it off, reject it totally, and ignore the real dangers associated with psychedelics.

Under these circumstances, the prestige of mental-health professionals started deteriorating, especially among members of the younger generation and counterculture. Many psychiatrists and psychologists found themselves in situations in which they were called on as experts to handle various emergencies related to psychedelic-drug use; they were expected to intervene with authority in crisis situations and treat casualties from the psychedelic scene. At the same time, they did not have adequate training and experience in this area, nor was the opportunity available for them to increase their theoretical understanding of psychedelics because of the critical dearth of scientific research.

The situation I encountered in 1967 has not changed substantially in the following years. Hundreds of thousands of people in the United States alone have been experimenting with LSD and other psychedelic drugs; many of them have had frequent, multiple exposures. This self-experimentation has been accompanied by many extraordinary experiences and has often resulted in profound changes in the personality structure, hierarchy of values, and world view of the experiencer. The phenomena observed in psychedelic sessions are manifestations of deep areas of the unconscious unknown to and unacknowledged by contemporary science. The application of existing theoretical concepts and practical procedures to the problems related to psychedelic-drug use has been, therefore, inappropriate, inadequate, and ineffective.

Since my arrival, I have been lecturing in various parts of the

United States, Canada, and Europe for universities, psychiatric hospitals, research institutes, growth centers, colleges, and church communities. During these lecture tours, I have found that heterogeneous audiences consistently manifested a deep, vivid interest in the data I was presenting. On many occasions, I was approached by people who wanted more detailed information and asked for book references and reprints of papers from which they could learn more about the problems related to serial LSD sessions. A considerable number of these people were psychiatrists, psychologists, psychiatric nurses, and social workers concerned about patients who had problems related to psychedelic-drug use. They wanted to know more about LSD in order to understand the world of these patients, establish better rapport with them, and help them more effectively. I encountered, however, an equal demand for more honest information in many desperate parents, who felt the need to bridge the ever-widening generation gap and gain more insight into the problems of their children. Similarly, a number of teachers and guidance counselors, puzzled by and alienated from their pupils and clients, have expressed interest in unbiased information about LSD. Clerics have also shown a sincere need to fathom the nature of religious and mystical experiences triggered by psychedelic drugs. They hoped that such an understanding, in addition to its philosophical and spiritual relevance, would also help them to be more sensitive counselors for their communities, which are so often vexed by drug problems. On occasion, I have also been approached by lawyers who harbored serious doubts about the adequacy and efficacy of the existing drug laws and wanted to have a clearer understanding of the problems involved. Specialists from various disciplines have asked me for specific details of my observations, because they felt that these data may have important implications for such diverse areas as personality theory, psychology of religion, psychotherapy, genetics, psychology and psychopathology of art, anthropology, the study of mythology, education, psychosomatic medicine, and obstetric practice. Last but not least, most requests for more systematic and comprehensive information have come from people who have had LSD experiences and were looking

...or clarification of problems they encountered. I have found an unusually vivid and serious interest among members of the younger generation, especially among students.

As I mentioned earlier, my original plan at the time of my arrival in the United States was to complete the analyses of the LSD research data from Prague and to conduct controlled studies that would test some of the new concepts I had developed. I considered the ten years of LSD research in Prague to be a continuing pilot study. This period of time might seem excessively long for orientation in a new field; it has to be taken into consideration, however, that the task involved was nothing less than to draw the first maps of new, unknown, and uncharted territories of the human mind.

My decision to write a series of books at this stage of research was brought about by several sets of circumstances. I soon realized that it would be difficult to replicate my European study under better-controlled circumstances at a time when the existing hysteria concerning psychedelic drugs was growing rapidly and was further aggravated by the alarming reports of possible genetic damage related to LSD use. Another important factor was the increasing number of people suffering from serious complications associated with LSD self-experimentation. It seemed that more clinical information about LSD and better understanding of its effects were urgently needed for a more effective approach to such problems. Moreover, the intensity of interest expressed by mental-health professionals as well as by a cross-section of the general public indicated that there was a critical demand for honest and objective information in the area of psychedelic drugs. In addition, some of the unusual experiences that typically occur in psychedelic sessions have been observed and described with increasing frequency in the context of the new psychotherapeutic techniques and experimental laboratory procedures, among them bioenergetics, marathon sessions, encounter groups, Gestalt therapy, biofeedback, sensory isolation and sensory overload. It seemed that the maps of consciousness developed with the help of a powerful facilitating agent such as LSD could prove useful for organizing and integrating the data from these related areas. My final reason for writing this series of books is based on the conviction that the material from serial LSD sessions even in its present form is of crucial theoretical significance and represents a serious challenge to the existing concepts of contemporary science. I feel that these data should be made available for consideration and evaluation to researchers from various scientific disciplines. For this purpose, I have tried to present the material with much emphasis on actual clinical observations and on illustrative case histories. In this form, it can, I hope, provide an incentive and basis for speculations even for those readers who will not accept the theoretical framework I have suggested for the conceptualization of the observed phenomena.

After much consideration, I have decided to present the findings from my LSD research in five separate volumes. In this book, which is the first part of the intended series, I have summarized the basic information about LSD, briefly outlined various stages of my own psychedelic research, and focused primarily on the "cartography of inner space" or a phenomenological description of the various levels and types of experiences manifested in psychedelic sessions. The second volume of this series, to be called *The Human Encounter with Death* and co-authored by my wife, Dr. Joan Halifax-Grof, and myself, will describe the use of psychedelic therapy in terminal cancer patients and discuss the problem of dying and death from historical, cross-cultural, clinical, philosophical, and spiritual perspectives. The third volume will focus on the practical aspects of LSD psychotherapy, such as the preparation of the patient, techniques of conducting the sessions, indications and contraindications, the therapeutic results, and the problem of side effects and complications. The fourth book will cover some of the heuristic aspects of LSD research and its implications for personality theory, the etiology of emotional disorders, the practice of psychotherapy, and the understanding of human culture. The last volume of the series will focus on the philosophical and spiritual dimensions of the LSD experience, with special emphasis on ontological and cosmological issues. It will describe in detail the surprisingly consistent metaphysical system that seems to be emerging from the experimentation with psychedelic substances.

Acknowledgments

I would like to use this opportunity to express my deep gratitude to at least some of the many preceptors and friends to whom I owe thanks for invaluable help or guidance during various stages of the research work that has resulted in the publication of this book. I first became acquainted with LSD in 1955 in the department of Dr. George Roubíček, former Associate Professor of the Department of Psychiatry, Charles University School of Medicine in Prague; it was Dr. Roubíček who introduced this compound into Czechoslovak psychiatry. During the last two years of my medical studies, when I was working as a volunteer in the faculty psychiatric hospital, I had the opportunity of observing and interviewing some of the LSD subjects in Dr. Roubíček's pioneering experiments. In his department and under his auspices, I had, in 1956, my own first LSD session; this experience deepened and intensified my already existing interest in psychedelic drugs to the extent that it has become my life's work.

During the early years of my research, I received inestimable help from Dr. Miloš Vojtěchovský; at that time, he headed the interdisciplinary team in which I began my LSD explorations, focusing on the relationship between the effects of various psychedelic drugs and the symptomatology of schizophrenia. After several years of exciting and fruitful cooperation with his research group, I shifted my interest from the "model psychosis" approach to diagnostic and therapeutic experimentation with psychedelics. Although our professional cooperation had been relatively shortlived, our personal friendship continued far beyond the point of our intellectual parting. I remember with gratitude and appreciation the basic training in scientific thinking and methodology that I received during this period.

In this context, I am particularly indebted to Dr. Lubomír Hanzlíček, Director of the Psychiatric Research Institute in Prague, where I carried out most of the research on which this book is based. The LSD study could not have been conducted and completed without his unusual openmindedness, understanding, and support during the years of my unconventional explorations of this new scientific frontier. I also wish to thank in this connection my two former colleagues from the same institute, Dr. Julia Sobotkiewicz and Dr. Zdeněk Dytrych, both of whom participated in the LSD research in Prague of which I was the principal investigator. In our everyday discussions, these two kindly shared with me the experiences from the LSD sessions of their patients and made their records readily available for my studies. Although partially based on their clinical material, the theoretical concepts described in this book have been developed independently of the concepts and approaches of these two colleagues; the ideas expressed in this volume are entirely my responsibility. I owe words of gratitude to Dr. Thomas Dostál, whose understanding, encouragement, and friendly help were essential at a time when I was exploring uncharted territories of the human mind in relative isolation from most of my professional colleagues.

In addition to the above, I would like to mention the nurses of my department in the Psychiatric Research Institute in Prague, whom I found to be extremely cooperative and helpful during the years of my LSD research. They demonstrated unusual interest and trust by volunteering for their own LSD training sessions in order to understand the drug experiences of our patients and their therapeutic impact. In everyday clinical work, they patiently tolerated the often dramatic circumstances of the new experimental treatment program and with unrelenting enthusiasm and dedication carried out all the extra duties imposed on them by the LSD program.

A decisive factor in the inception and completion of this book was my two-year fellowship in the United States (1967–1969), which gave me the necessary time and proper frame of mind to write the first version of the manuscript summarizing my LSD research. I am especially indebted to the Foundations' Fund for Research in Psychiatry in New Haven, Connecticut, whose generous financial support made my stay in the United States possible. I would also like to express my deep appreciation to Dr. Joel Elkes, Professor and Chairman of the Department of Psychiatry and Behavioral Sciences at Johns Hopkins University School of Medicine in Baltimore, Maryland. Dr. Elkes extended to me the invitation to come to Johns Hopkins Hospital as a clinical and research fellow and granted me invaluable help and guidance during my stay.

Special words of gratitude are deserved by Dr. Albert A. Kurland, Director of the Maryland Psychiatric Research Center and Assistant Commissioner for Research of the Maryland State Department of Mental Hygiene. It was under Dr. Kurland's auspices that I have been able to continue my LSD research work from my arrival to the present. I would also like to mention in this connection the members of the Maryland Psychiatric Research Center and their families. The friendly atmosphere of mutual respect and understanding that they created, not only in the Center but also during many of our jointly spent evenings and weekends, helped me considerably to adjust to my new life in the United States. I especially appreciate the friendship of Robert Leihy and his wife, Karen, whose house became for many years my second home.

This book probably would not have been written and published without the encouragement and support of many of my American friends, who kept reassuring me about the importance of the information that I had to offer. My special thanks belong here to Huston Smith, Joseph Campbell, Walter Clark, Margaret Mead, Alan Watts, Laura Huxley, Anthony Sutich, Gaby and Sonja Margulies, and, particularly, Abraham Maslow.

I am deeply grateful to Esalen Institute at Big Sur, Hot Springs, California, and the increasing network of affiliated growth centers in the United States and Canada for offering me the opportunity to give lectures, seminars, and workshops in which I could test the early formulations of my ideas in contact with understanding and sympathetic audiences. Esalen Institute has also generously offered to my wife and me extraordinary and congenial conditions that have made it possible for us to work on a long-planned series of books.

Over the years, one encounters certain people who become close friends as well as primary catalysts of important changes in one's life. In this regard, I am deeply indebted to Robert Schwartz and Lenore Schwartz for the role they have played in my personal as well as professional life. It was through their generosity that my wife and I have been able to free ourselves temporarily from administrative duties and research activities in order to concentrate our efforts on writing. I want to mention in this context Michael Murphy, Richard Price, Julian Silverman, Andrew Gagarin, and Richard Grossman, all close friends of ours, who, along with the Schwartzes, have created ideal conditions for our work.

My brother, Dr. Paul Grof, has contributed to this book in a unique combination of roles. His background in research psychiatry gave him the necessary qualifications and knowledge and the nature of our lifelong relationship made it possible for him to be my most determined supporter and my most candid and unrelenting critic.

It is hard to find adequate words of thanks and gratitude for the contributions to this volume made by my wife, Dr. Joan Halifax-Grof. During our joint lectures, seminars, and workshops, and in many of our private discussions, she has helped me to put the LSD findings in a broad cross-cultural perspective, crystallize new concepts, and find the proper formulations for my ideas. As a co-therapist in the research project using LSD-assisted psychotherapy with individuals dying from cancer, her anthropological background as well as personal sensitivity added many new and relevant dimensions to research and treatment. In our home, she created an atmosphere conducive to rich intellectual crossfertilization and productive writing. Her enthusiasm, energy, and deep emotional commitment have been a powerful remedy during periods of creative diastole and inertia. Her constant encouragement and assistance have been the necessary ingredients for the completion of this text.

Those who have played the most important role in the development of the concepts described in this book and who have brought the greatest personal sacrifice have to remain anonymous—the hundreds of patients and LSD subjects who were part of the research. These people found enough trust and courage for repeated journeys to the unknown and shared with me their experiences from the most fascinating of all frontiers. I am deeply grateful to all of them for their participation in this study and for their unique individual contributions that have made this book possible.

Big Sur, California
December 1973

Contents

Preface vii

Acknowledgments xv

1 General Introduction 1
The LSD Controversy 1
LSD and Its Effects in Human Beings 6
Empirical Basis for a New Theoretical Framework 14
Heuristic Value of LSD Research 25

2 Abstract and Aesthetic Experiences in LSD Sessions 34

3 Psychodynamic Experiences in LSD Sessions 44
COEX Systems (Systems of Condensed Experience) 46
Origin and Dynamics of COEX Systems 60
Manifestation of COEX Systems in LSD Sessions 77
Dynamic Interaction between the COEX Systems and
Environmental Stimuli 88

4 Perinatal Experiences in LSD Sessions 95

Perinatal Matrix I. Primal Union with the Mother (Intra-uterine Experience before the Onset of Delivery) 104

Perinatal Matrix II. Antagonism with the Mother (Contractions in a Closed Uterine System) 115

Perinatal Matrix III. Synergism with the Mother (Propulsion through the Birth Canal) 123

Perinatal Matrix IV. Separation from the Mother (Termination of the Symbiotic Union and Formation of a New Type of Relationship) 138

Significance of Basic Perinatal Matrices in LSD Psychotherapy 149

5 Transpersonal Experiences in LSD Sessions 154

Experiential Extension within the Framework of "Objective Reality" 158

TEMPORAL EXPANSION OF CONSCIOUSNESS 158

Embryonal and Fetal Experiences 158

Ancestral Experiences 162

Collective and Racial Experiences 167

Phylogenetic (Evolutionary) Experiences 171

Past-Incarnation Experiences 173

Precognition, Clairvoyance, Clairaudience, and "Time Travels" 177

SPATIAL EXPANSION OF CONSCIOUSNESS 178

Ego Transcendence in Interpersonal Relationships and the Experience of Dual Unity 178

Identification with Other Persons 179

Group Identification and Group Consciousness 180

Animal Identification 180

Plant Identification 181

Oneness with Life and with All Creation 183

Consciousness of Inorganic Matter 184

Planetary Consciousness 185

Extraplanetary Consciousness 185

Out-of-Body Experiences, Traveling Clairvoyance and Clairaudience, "Space Travels," and Telepathy 186

SPATIAL CONSTRICTION OF CONSCIOUSNESS 191

Organ, Tissue, and Cellular Consciousness 191

Experiential Extension beyond the Framework of "Objective Reality" 194

Spiritistic and Mediumistic Experiences 194

Experiences of Encounters with Suprahuman Spiritual Entities 196

Experiences of Other Universes and Encounters with Their Inhabitants 197

Archetypal Experiences and Complex Mythological Sequences 198

Experiences of Encounters with Various Deities 199

Intuitive Understanding of Universal Symbols 201

Activation of the Chakras and Arousal of the Serpent Power (Kundalini) 202

Consciousness of the Universal Mind 203

The Supracosmic and Metacosmic Void 204

Significance of Transpersonal Experiences in LSD Psychotherapy 205

Transpersonal Experiences and Contemporary Psychiatry 208

6 Multidimensional and Multilevel Nature of the LSD Experience 215

Environmental Stimuli and Elements of the Setting 219

Personality of the Therapist and the Therapeutic Situation 220

Present Life Situation 221

Past Life History 221

Early Childhood and Infancy 221

Biological Birth and the Perinatal Period 222

Embryonal and Fetal Existence 222

Transindividual (Transpersonal and Transhuman) Sources 222

Epilogue 241

Bibliography 245

Index 247

REALMS OF THE HUMAN UNCONSCIOUS

1 General Introduction

The LSD Controversy

More than a quarter of a century has elapsed since the Swiss chemist Albert Hofmann accidentally discovered the potent psychoactive properties of diethylamide of d-lysergic acid, better known as LSD-25.[17]* Shortly afterward, this substance became the subject of considerable controversy, which over the years has reached unprecedented dimensions. It seems pertinent to start the discussion of LSD by a brief review of its stormy history.

The discovery of the properties of LSD became a sensation in scientific circles and had a stimulating effect on researchers from many different disciplines. Many of the early papers emphasized the similarities between the LSD-induced "experimental" or "model psychosis" and naturally occurring psychoses, especially schizophrenia. The possibility of simulating schizophrenic symptoms in normal volunteers under laboratory conditions and of conducting complex laboratory tests and investigations before, during, and after this transient "model psychosis" seemed to offer a promising key to the understanding of the most enigmatic disease in psychiatry. As a drug that could provide a short, reversible journey into the world of the schizophrenic, LSD was also recommended as an unrivaled tool for the training of psychiatrists, psychologists, medical students, and psychiatric nurses. It was repeatedly reported in this context that a single

*Superior numbers refer to the Bibliography, pp. 241–242.

LSD experience could considerably increase the subject's ability to understand psychotic patients, approach them with more sensitivity, and treat them more effectively.

The LSD controversy started when the concept of the LSD state as "model schizophrenia" was seriously attacked by many phenomenologically and psychoanalytically oriented psychiatrists and was eventually rejected by most clinical researchers. It became obvious that, in spite of certain superficial similarities, there were also very fundamental differences between the two conditions. The hope that research with LSD would result in a simple test-tube solution of the mystery of schizophrenia gradually faded and was finally given up entirely.

The "psychotomimetic" (psychosis-simulating) emphasis in LSD research was soon overshadowed by an increasing number of enthusiastic papers indicating that LSD might have undreamed-of therapeutic potential. According to many clinical researchers, LSD-assisted psychotherapy seemed to allow a considerable shortening of the time required for treatment. In addition, therapeutic success was repeatedly reported in various categories of psychiatric patients who were considered to be poor prognostic prospects or were unresponsive to conventional treatment; these included chronic alcoholics, narcotic-drug addicts, criminal psychopaths, sexual deviants, and severe character neurotics. These claims did not remain unchallenged. Many clinicians, knowing how difficult it is to change deep-rooted psychopathological symptoms, not to mention the personality structure, were incredulous of the dramatic effects achieved in a matter of days or weeks. Critics of these reports pointed to the lack of controlled studies demonstrating the usefulness of LSD psychotherapy; however, similar objections were raised at that time in regard to psychoanalysis and other types of widely accepted and practiced drug-free psychotherapy. Most of the criticisms were mainly of a methodological nature, and none of the skeptics seriously questioned the safety of this approach. In this regard, Sidney Cohen's paper published in 1960 demonstrated that the risks associated with the responsible and professional use of LSD in normal volunteers were minimal.[2] They were slightly higher when LSD was used in psychiatric patients but, in general, LSD psychotherapy appeared to be much safer than many other procedures commonly used in psychiatric therapy, such as electric shock therapy, insulin coma treatment, and psychosurgery. By and large, in the early 1960s, LSD seemed to have a firm position in psychiatry as a valuable tool for basic research, psychiatric training, and therapeutic experimentation.

In addition, there were at least two other areas in which the use of LSD opened exciting new perspectives and interesting possibilities. Many LSD subjects reported in their sessions unusual aesthetic experiences and insights into the nature of the creative process; they frequently developed a new understanding of art, in particular modern art movements. Painters, sculptors, and musicians were able to produce under the influence of LSD most interesting and unconventional pieces of art which differed considerably from their usual modes of expression. It became obvious that experimentation with LSD had important implications for the psychology and psychopathology of art.

Another area in which the use of LSD appeared to be rather revolutionary was the psychology of religion. It had been observed that some LSD sessions had the form of profound religious and mystical experiences quite similar to those described in the holy scriptures of the great religions of the world and reported by saints, prophets, and religious teachers of all ages. The possibility of triggering such experiences by means of a chemical instigated an interesting and highly controversial discussion around the issue of "chemical" or "instant mysticism" and the validity and spiritual genuineness of these phenomena. The debates carried on by behavioral scientists, philosophers, and theologians oscillated among three extreme points of view. Many experimenters felt that the observations from psychedelic sessions made it possible to take religious phenomena from the realm of the sacred, produce them at will in the laboratory, study them, and eventually explain them in scientific terms. Ultimately, there would be nothing mysterious and holy about religion, and it would be explained in terms of brain physiology and biochemistry. Some theologians tended to view LSD and other psychedelic substances as sacred and the sessions as sacraments, because they could bring the individual in touch with transcendental realities. The opposite trend was to deny that the LSD experiences were genuine religious phenomena comparable to those that come as "God's grace" or are the result of discipline, abnegation, devotion, or austere practices; in this framework, the apparent easiness with which these experiences could be triggered by a chemical entirely disqualified their spiritual value.

In the mid-1960s, when LSD became widely available on the black market and "street acid" was used by masses of young people as a tool for uncontrolled lay experimentation, new dimensions were added to the LSD controversy. The situation that arose was much different from the rather passionate but basically scientific and academic atmosphere of the discourses of preceding years. Sober and rational arguments almost completely disappeared from the scene, and it was dominated by an emotionally charged hostile encounter between two irreconcilable groups. On one hand, LSD proselytes announced the era of a new religion whose messiah had the form of a chemical. For them, LSD was a panacea for desperately sick mankind, offering the only reasonable alternative to mass suicide in a nuclear holocaust. It was recommended that everybody without exception should take LSD as frequently as possible and under any circumstances; the risks were denied or underestimated and, if admitted, were considered worth taking in view of the final goal. On the other hand, an atmosphere close to mass hysteria was created in the public, which was frightened by this new movement and violently opposed to it. Almost every day sensation-hungry journalists would bring new reports about the horrors and disasters due to unsupervised self-experimentation: people walking out of windows of highrise buildings into the setting sun, killed while trying to stop automobiles with their bodies, blinded by staring into the sun for hours, wounded by cutting fat from their bodies with kitchen knives, murdering their lovers and mothers-in-law, or ending up in locked wards of state mental hospitals in a permanently psychotic state. These reports created an image of LSD as a diabolic drug and provided sufficient background for a witch-hunting response from parents, teachers, ministers, police authorities, and legislators.

Unfortunately, many mental-health professionals participated to some extent in this irrational approach; although the reports of two decades of scientific experimentation with LSD were available in the psychiatric and psychological literature, they allowed their image of this drug to be formed by newspaper headlines.

The association of the drug scene with the "hippie" movement and the revolt in the counterculture added an important sociopolitical dimension to the already existing problems. The issue was further exacerbated by the conflicting reports about the possible association of LSD with chromosomal and genetic damage, leukemia, and cancer. The view of LSD has thus covered a wide range, from a spiritual, emotional, and social panacea for mankind and a powerful therapeutic tool for individuals suffering from serious mental and psychosomatic disorders to a vicious enemy causing organic brain impairment and serious physical and mental damage to the individual and endangering the well-being of future generations. To complete the controversial picture of LSD, it should be mentioned that this drug had been seriously considered as an effective adjunct to brainwashing techniques and a powerful means of chemical warfare.

The atmosphere of hysteria, together with the lack of serious research, has made it very difficult to realize the scientific importance of many of the phenomena involved in this controversy. Lay self-experimenters with LSD frequently enter realms of experience that totally bewilder and puzzle practicing psychiatrists and psychologists who are called in to handle emergency situations related to that drug. On one hand, the LSD experiences do not fit any existing theoretical system; on the other hand, many sensitive clinicians realize that it is inaccurate and inappropriate to label LSD experiences simply as psychotic. In addition, as a result of such experimentation, many people have undergone dramatic personality changes, involving the hierarchy of values and religious and philosophical beliefs, as well as general life style. Lacking a theoretical framework to explain the mechanisms involved, professionals who occasionally have had the opportunity to witness these transformations have found them incomprehensible. Even some of the negative occurrences following the ingestion of LSD, such as psychotic breakdowns or attempts at suicide, could provide important data about the dynamics of these phenomena if approached scientifically rather than emotionally.

If we consider the nature and scope of the LSD controversy, it seems obvious that it reflects something much more fundamental than the pharmacological effects of a single chemical agent. Although all the discussions appear to be about LSD, other issues implicit in such exchanges give them their emotional charge. Several decades of LSD research have uncovered much evidence concerning the nature of the common denominator responsible for this situation. As will be illustrated in the following chapters, careful analysis of the LSD data strongly indicates that this substance is an unspecific amplifier of mental processes that brings to the surface various elements from the depth of the unconscious. What we see in the LSD experiences and in various situations surrounding them appears to be basically an exteriorization and magnification of the conflicts intrinsic to human nature and civilization. If approached from this point of view, LSD phenomena are extremely interesting material for a deeper understanding of the mind, the nature of man, and human society.

LSD and Its Effects in Human Beings

In recent years, LSD has become increasingly well known. Information has been fed to the general public through the daily press, articles in various magazines, books, antidrug propaganda pamphlets, radio broadcasts, television programs, and movies, as well as hearsay. Most adults and young people have been exposed to the LSD lore. However, most of this information has not been very systematic, to say the least, and much of it has been biased and distorted by commercial and political interests. For this reason, I will give a brief synoptic review of the basic data on LSD as a general descriptive background for further discussions. Such an introduction should be useful for a better understanding of some of the more specific, dynamic aspects of the LSD experience, which constitutes the major contribution of this study.

LSD-25, or diethylamide of d-lysergic acid, is a semisynthetic chemical compound; its natural component is lysergic acid, which is the basis of all major ergot alkaloids, and the diethylamide group is added in the laboratory. According to Stoll, Hofmann, and Troxler,[18] it has the following chemical formula:

LSD, as such, has not been identified in any known organic substances although the natural production of LSD has been suspected to occur in the brains of animals infected by toxoplasmosis.[19] The synthesis of various other amides of lysergic acid has been demonstrated in submerged cultures of the fungus *Claviceps paspali*.[1] Similar amides have also been found in morning-glory seeds *(Rivea corymbosa)*, which, for centuries, have been used in Mexico for ritual purposes in the form of ointments and potions called *ololiuqui*.[3]

It is interesting to recall that LSD was first synthesized in 1938 in the Sandoz laboratories in Switzerland by Stoll and Hofmann as a drug possibly useful for obstetrics and gynecology and in the treatment of migraine headache. It was subjected to routine laboratory testing in animals and found to be uninteresting, and its study was discontinued. The hallucinogenic properties of LSD were discovered by Albert Hofmann approximately five years later, in April 1943.[17] Reviewing the results of the early research with this substance, Hofmann concluded that the data suggested the possibility of an interesting stimulating effect on the central nervous system. While synthesizing a new sample of LSD for further studies, he accidentally intoxicated himself during the purification of the condensation products and experienced very dramatic psychological changes. He was able to make the hypothetical link between his abnormal mental condition and the drug he was working with; later, he intentionally ingested 250 micrograms of LSD to put his suspicion to a solid scientific test. His reaction to this dose was very similar to his first experience but much more intense and dramatic. A minute quantity of LSD drastically changed Hofmann's mental functioning for a period of several hours; he spent this time in a fantastic world of intense emotions, brilliant colors, and undulating forms. Hofmann then described his unusual experiment to Stoll, of the psychiatric clinic in Zurich, who was sufficiently interested to run the first scientific study of LSD in normal volunteers and mental patients.[17] His observations of the LSD effects in these two categories of subjects were published in 1947; this communication evoked enormous interest and stimulated further research in many countries of the world. Subsequent studies confirmed Stoll's findings that LSD was the most powerful psychoactive drug ever known. In incredibly minute dosages, starting from 10 to 20 micrograms (1 microgram or gamma = one millionth of a gram), it could produce very profound and variegated mental changes lasting several hours. Thus, LSD was approximately five thousand times more effective than the already-known mescaline and one hundred and fifty times more effective than the later-discovered psilocybin.

It was established by further research that LSD can be administered by any of the common routes. It can be taken orally and injected intramuscularly, intravenously, intraperitoneally, or directly into the cerebrospinal fluid in the vertebral canal. There seems to be an unusually wide range within which LSD can be used safely. Acute and chronic toxicity studies of animals indicated that LSD has a low toxicity level and a large safety range; in clinical experiments, the dosages administered without any detectable biological side effects ranged between 10 and 2000 micrograms.

The onset of the LSD reaction follows a latency period, the duration of which can vary in the extremes between ten minutes and three hours, depending on the individual, mode of administration, dose, degree of psychological resistance, and other variables. This latency period does not exist when LSD is administered directly into the cerebrospinal fluid. In this case, its action is almost immediate. An uncomplicated LSD session can last between four and twelve hours; the most important factors determining its duration are the personality of the subject, the nature and dynamics of the unconscious material activated during the experience, and the dosage used. Prolonged reactions, which occasionally occur during LSD work, can last for days or weeks. The intensity of the LSD experience can be mitigated by opening the eyes and moving around and can be deepened by staying in a reclining position, using eyeshades, and listening to stereophonic music. The LSD phenomena cover an extremely wide range and occur in almost all areas of mental and physical functioning. They will be only briefly outlined here.

Physical symptoms are a typical, standard aspect of the LSD reaction; most of them can be understood in terms of the stimulation of the vegetative (autonomic), motor, and sensitive nerves. Vegetative manifestations can be of a sympathetic nature, a parasympathetic nature, or both. Sympathetic effects involve acceleration of the pulse rate; increase in blood pressure; dilation of the pupils; blurring of vision and problems in focusing; secretion of thick saliva; profuse sweating; constriction of arteries in the periphery, resulting in coldness and blue color of hands and feet; and erection of body hair. Parasympathetic effects are retardation of the pulse rate, lowering of the blood pressure, hypersalivation, secretion of tears, diarrhea, nausea, and vomiting. Also frequent are symptoms of a more general nature, such as malaise, flu feelings, fatigue, and alternating chills and hot flushes. The most common motor phenomena include increased muscular tension; a variety of tremors, twitches, and jerks; or complex twisting movements. Although the above phenomena are more common, some subjects can also experience a total and complete relaxation of all muscles in the body. Besides the vegetative and motor manifestations, a number of different changes in neurological reflexes have been described in LSD subjects. Symptoms associated with the activation of sensitive nerves are headache, pains in various other parts of the body, feelings of heaviness in the extremities, a variety of strange sensations, and sexual feelings.

Perceptual changes are the most frequent and constant part of the LSD reaction. Although they can occur in any sensory area, there seems to be a definite predominance of visual phenomena. They range from elementary visions of flashing lights, geometrical figures, and illusory transformations of the environment to complex images involving groups of persons, various animals, and specific scenery. Less frequent are perceptual changes in the acoustic area. Typical are hypersensitivity to sounds, difficulty in differentiating among various auditory stimuli, acoustic illusions, and pseudohallucinations. Olfactory and gustatory changes are rather common in normal subjects and psychiatric patients; they can dominate the sessions of people with congenital blindness, who usually do not experience optical phenomena after the administration of LSD. Typically, smell and taste are inhibited during the culmination period of the session but are extraordinarily enhanced in the termination period of sessions with a good resolution. Olfactory and gustatory illusions or pseudohallucinations are particularly frequent during deep regression into early childhood. Perceptual distortions in the tactile area involve a decrease as well as an occasional increase in sensitivity of various parts of the body; unusual sensations of all kinds are also rather frequent in LSD sessions. Especially interesting are complex and often bizarre changes of the body image.

Distortions in the perception of time and space are one of the most striking and constant aspects of LSD sessions. The perception of time is quite regularly altered; most commonly a short time interval is experienced as being much longer, although sometimes the opposite is true. In the extreme case, minutes can be experienced as centuries or millennia, or, conversely, a long time period in the session can be perceived as lasting only several seconds. Occasionally, time is changed not only quantitatively but also as a dimension. It can stop completely, so that the sequential nature of events disappears; past, present, and future are experienced as juxtaposed. A special category of time change is the experience of regression to various periods in the individual's history.

The perception of space is also typically modified; distances can seem greater or be underestimated; objects are perceived as larger or smaller than they actually are; and space can appear horizontally or vertically compressed. Subjects can have the feeling of loss of perspective or experience fluctuations of consistency of space, such as its rarefaction or condensation. They can also create any number of subjective spaces and individual microworlds that are autonomous and unrelated to our time-space continuum. Experiences of melting into space occur frequently; they can give way to feelings of ecstasy or be associated with the fear of death and annihilation. An extreme in the experience of changed time and space is the awareness of infinity or eternity.

Emotional changes appear as one of the first manifestations of the LSD reaction and represent a very regular and constant part of sessions. Early reports on LSD emphasized euphoria, which is quite typical for medium-dose sessions of normal subjects. It can take several different forms—exhilarated elation with unmotivated laughter, exuberant joy, deep feelings of peace, serenity, and relaxation, orgiastic ecstasy, hedonistic pleasure, or feelings of voluptuousness and sensuality. If psychiatric patients are subjects and higher dosages are administered, the incidence of negative mood qualities increases considerably. Anxiety can dominate the sessions and culminate in absolute panic and a profound fear of death. Depressions can have the form of quiet sadness, tearless melancholy, or an agitated despair with rather dramatic manifestations. In some sessions, serious suicidal ideation or even tendencies can occur and make strictest supervision of the subject indispensable. Agonizing inferiority and guilt feelings are frequent, especially in therapeutic sessions with mental patients. Affective lability, or, on the contrary, apathy, are common occurrences. In some sessions, excruciating ambivalence and irresolution are the most typical characteristic. Although aggressive feelings are quite frequent, aggression usually is not acted out in an uncontrollable and destructive way and does not present serious problems; there are, of course, exceptions to this rule.

Changes in thinking, intellect, and memory are rather distinct, although not always clearly demonstrable in psychological tests. In some types of the LSD experience, thought processes are accelerated; in others, retarded. Logical and abstract thinking usually is possible, but it is subjectively more difficult; alogical and freely associating pictorial thinking of a dreamlike quality comes to the foreground. Occasionally, this can result in a sudden simplification and resolution of certain problems, not dissimilar to artistic inspiration or the creative illumination of a scientist or inventor. Such basic intuitive insights can at times integrate information from various areas in a productive way. Equally frequent, however, is a distorted perception of events and their delusional interpretation in terms of ideas of persecution, grandeur, or reference.* In any case, practical judgment should not be trusted in an LSD session and no serious, irrevocable decisions made by an individual who is under the influence of the drug.

Investigation of intellectual functioning and memory during the sessions by standard psychological tests has usually revealed a slight impairment of performance. The interpretation of these results is, however, difficult; it is not clear whether this is a result of regression of the intellectual functions to an earlier developmental level, of toxic impairment of the brain, or of the subject's lack of interest and motivation and of his preoccupation with his fascinating inner experiences.

As far as the memory of the LSD experience itself is concerned, there is usually a more or less clear memory of everything that was distinctly perceived and experienced at the time of the session. Amnesia is rather infrequent, unless high dosages are used or excessively charged emotional material is involved. Occasionally, the LSD experience can be so overwhelming that the subject is not able clearly to discriminate its various facets even at the time of the session. In this case, it is the general atmosphere that is remembered rather than specific details.

Psychomotor changes are usually quite striking, but they do not all go in one specific direction. Some LSD subjects show a definite inhibition of activity, with a lack of spontaneity and

---

*A person who has *ideas* or *delusions of reference* tends to interpret various accidental events and neutral remarks as having deep significance and direct reference to himself.

initiative. Others manifest marked psychomotor excitement, occasionally with an element of inadequate behavior, such as unmotivated laughter, diffuse aggression, theatrical performance, or acting out of various impulses.

Changes of consciousness are of a rather specific nature. There are usually no signs of quantitative impairment in the direction of somnolence, stupor, and coma. Typically, there is also none of the confusion and disorientation in regard to personal identity, time, and place of the session that can be seen after the administration of common delirogens such as atropine, scopolamine, or benactyzine. Consciousness after the ingestion of LSD manifests a characteristic qualitative transformation of a dreamlike nature. It can transcend its usual limits and encompass phenomena from the deep unconscious not accessible under normal circumstances. This is frequently referred to as expansion of consciousness.

Sexuality can be influenced in several different ways. Sometimes, it is so inhibited that nothing seems more alien than sex. However, it can also be considerably enhanced so that long episodes in the sessions are dominated by intense sexual feelings and imagery. Sexual experiences in LSD sessions occasionally have a rather unusual flavor; they can involve sadistic or perverse elements or take the form of satanic, oceanic, or tantric sex. In the termination period of sessions with good resolution, the orgastic ability of an individual is usually greatly increased, in both male and female subjects. Sexual intercourse on the session day can become the most powerful experience of this sort in the subject's life.

The experience of art is often an important aspect of the LSD session. The unique perception of colors and forms, as well as the overwhelming impact of music, frequently mediate a new understanding of art and artistic movements. This ability to experience unusual aspects of art can persist after a single session for an indefinite period of time. Occasionally, a striking increase of creativity has been observed in and after an LSD session; however, this is not a general rule.

Religious and mystical experiences represent the most interesting and challenging category of LSD phenomena. Their incidence seems to be directly related to the dosage and number of previous sessions of the subject. They can also be facilitated by the special preparation, set, and setting of the psychedelic treatment technique.* The experience of death and rebirth, union with the universe or God, encounters with demonic appearances, or the reliving of "past incarnations" observed in LSD sessions appear to be phenomenologically indistinguishable from similar descriptions in the sacred scriptures of the great religions of the world and secret mystical texts of ancient civilizations.

It has been a puzzling problem since the early years of experiments with LSD to understand how a single drug can produce such an enormous range of different experiences appearing in various combinations and seemingly on the same continuum. It was obvious that the long-term systematic investigation of the LSD procedure in a large number of individuals would be required in order to develop a typology of experiential patterns and sequences, to relate them to each other and to the personality of the subject, and to discover the principles underlying this seemingly chaotic situation. The research described in this book has been characterized by a constant effort to obtain a sufficient amount of experimental data, analyze them carefully, and develop new conceptual frameworks for the observed clinical realities.

Empirical Basis
for a New Theoretical Framework

The concepts presented in this book are based on my own clinical research of LSD covering a period of seventeen years. During this time, I have used this drug in different categories of subjects and in several dosage levels; also, the set and setting of the sessions varied to a considerable degree. My understanding of LSD and my concepts of how it should be used therapeutically underwent fundamental changes during these years of clinical

---

*The expression "set and setting" is a technical term referring to a complex of non-pharmacological factors occurring in the LSD reaction. "Set" includes the psychological expectations of the subject, the sitter's or guide's concept of the nature of the LSD experience, the agreed-upon aim of the psychedelic procedure, and the preparation and programing for the session. "Setting" refers to the actual environment, both physical and interpersonal, the concrete circumstances in which the drug is administered.

experimentation. I will briefly describe the most important stages of this development.

As I have mentioned in the discussion of the LSD controversy, the early years of LSD research were characterized by the so-called "model psychosis" approach. The accidental discovery of LSD and the pioneering research of its effects demonstrated that incredibly minute quantities of this substance could produce dramatic and profound changes in the mental functioning of an individual. Many researchers felt at that time that LSD could mimic the symptoms of schizophrenia and believed that the study of LSD would provide a key to the understanding of this disease as basically a biochemical deviation. It was conceivable that the human body could produce, as a result of a metabolic error, infinitesimal quantities of LSD or a similar psychoactive substance; if that were the case, schizophrenia could actually be a manifestation of an abnormal function of the brain reflecting a general autointoxication of the organism.

This tempting concept strongly influenced the early research on hallucinogenic drugs in Czechoslovakia. In 1956, I joined a team of researchers who were conducting a multidimensional comparative study of various psychedelics. This group consisted of psychiatrists, psychologists, internists, and biochemists; the experimental project was conducted in a complex of coordinated research institutes in Prague-Krč under the direction of Dr. Miloš Vojtěchovský. The basic idea was to administer different psychoactive drugs to normal volunteers and use a standard set of examinations and laboratory tests at regular intervals to assess the effects of the various substances. The selection of these tests was such that they reflected the changes in a variety of clinical, physiological, psychological, and biochemical parameters. The aim of this part of the research effort was to find the similarities and differences between the effects of diverse psychedelic drugs, such as LSD, mescaline, psilocybin, dimethyl- and diethyltryptamine, and the adrenaline derivatives adrenochrome and adrenolutine. Another part of the study used the same laboratory tests in a group of selected schizophrenic patients, with the idea of assessing the similarities and differences between the clinical picture of "model psychoses" and the symptomatology of schizophrenia.

During this study, it soon became obvious that with the exception of adrenochrome and adrenolutine, the psychedelic drugs we tested showed much more basic similarities than differences when compared to each other. Nevertheless, we failed to demonstrate any significant parallels between the phenomenology of the states induced by these drugs and the symptomatology of schizophrenia. When we arrived at these conclusions, there were already several other teams in Europe and in the United States who had serious objections against the concepts that equated LSD intoxication with schizophrenia.

Abandoning in theory and practice the "model psychosis" approach, I found it increasingly difficult to share the opinion of the critics who considered the LSD-induced state as simply an unspecific reaction of the brain to a noxious chemical, or "toxic psychosis." At that time, I was discovering more and more striking differences in the reaction of various individuals to LSD, differences that reflected their basic personality characteristics. The observations concerning these specificities represented for me an important milestone indicating the beginning of the next stage of my research.

The most astonishing and puzzling aspect of the LSD sessions which I observed in the early years of experimentation was the enormous variability among individuals; using the same dose of the same drug and under relatively constant conditions, we obtained an extraordinary range of individual responses in various subjects. The LSD literature available at that time seemed to suggest that there existed a standard, common pattern of LSD reaction. The classical description involved a latency period of about thirty to fifty minutes; then the so-called "autonomic" or "vegetative phase" with various physical manifestations, mostly unpleasant; and finally the "psychotic phase." Dramatic changes in the optical area, such as intensification of color perception, abstract imagery, illusions, and pseudohallucinations, were considered uniquely characteristic of the LSD state. In my experience, this classical pattern could be observed only in some of our subjects. On occasion, the concept of the "vegetative" and "psychotic" phases following each other did not apply at all; vegetative symptoms could be completely missing, dominate the whole course of the session, or appear and disappear at any point of the experience. In some individuals, there were no optical changes whatsoever, and the LSD session took a very different form from the prescribed "orgies of vision." There were persons who experienced the entire LSD session only as a period of extreme physical discomfort or even somatic illness. For several of the subjects, sessions consisted of sequences of enormous erotic excitement and sexual tension alternating with feelings of orgastic relief; there were no other perceptual changes. When asked about the nature of the LSD reaction, these individuals were convinced that the drug was the world's most potent aphrodisiac. Others had a reaction that seemed to justify the "model psychosis" hypothesis; they experienced episodes of overwhelming anxiety or homosexual panic, had delusions of grandeur or reference, and showed a strong tendency to interpret the experiment in paranoid terms. Not infrequently, the entire LSD session or a part of it took the form of depth psychological self-exploration; individuals regressed into various periods of their life, relived traumatic events from childhood, and gained interesting insights into their basic psychodynamic processes. There were several subjects who, under the same circumstances, had what appeared to be a profound mystical or religious experience involving elements of death and rebirth, cosmic unity, or communication with God. In addition, whenever the drug was administered repeatedly to the same subject, it became obvious that there also existed a unique intraindividual variability that was no less striking than the interindividual differences.

With the increasing number of sessions I observed, I became more and more aware that many of the LSD phenomena seemed to have an interesting psychodynamic meaning and could be understood in psychological terms. The next logical step was an attempt to explore whether some general principles, or at least regularities, could be discovered with regard to the content, character, and course of LSD sessions. It seemed plausible at this point that the phenomenology of the LSD experience might be related to the personality structure of the subject and to his clinical diagnosis if he happened to be a psychiatric patient. Two other variables to be considered were biographical data from the past and the present life situation. I had a general idea of how the problem should be approached but could not imagine how it could be done without an enormous investment of time and energy.

A unique opportunity came to me and made it possible to explore this issue without having to design a special expensive research project. At that time, I worked in the Psychiatric Research Institute in Prague in the Department for the Study of Psychogenic Disorders. Our task was to study the problem of maladjustive interpersonal patterns in various life periods of neurotic patients. This required a detailed study of each patient's history as well as the circumstances of his current life situation. Hundreds of hours were spent in individual exploratory and therapeutic interviews with these patients and with their parents, siblings, spouses, children, friends, superiors, and coworkers. Ongoing transactional group sessions with these patients represented an additional source of valuable data on their interpersonal behavior and interactional patterns. When the study was terminated, we had a group of seventy-two patients with various psychogenic disorders, mostly fixated chronic neuroses and psychosomatic diseases, about whom we had a considerable amount of detailed information. This was an ideal situation for exploratory research of the problem of psychodynamic and situational determinants of the LSD reaction. After signing informed consents, these patients were given from 100 to 200 micrograms of LSD in a protective and supportive but unstructured environment; the therapist was present in these sessions for the whole period of the drug action (six to eight hours). On the days following the sessions, the patient and therapist discussed the experience in great detail. Typewritten records were kept about each patient; these included a summary of the information obtained before the session, the therapist's and patient's detailed report about the LSD experience itself, and a description of all the important changes observed immediately after the session and during the follow-up.

The analysis of these records indicated clearly that the LSD reaction is highly specific for the personality of the subject.

Rather than causing an unspecific "toxic psychosis," LSD appeared to be a powerful catalyst of the mental processes activating unconscious material from various deep levels of the personality. Many of the phenomena in these sessions could be understood in psychological and psychodynamic terms; they had a structure not dissimilar to that of dreams. During this detailed analytical scrutiny, it soon become obvious that LSD could become an unrivaled tool for deep personality diagnostics if its specific effects and symbolic language were better understood.

I also attempted to assess whether these sessions, which did not have an explicit therapeutic goal and structure, had some detectable effect on the patients' clinical symptoms. I found that only three out of seventy-two patients showed a dramatic and lasting improvement of their clinical condition after this single LSD exposure. There were many others in whom various degrees of improvement could be observed; however, these beneficial results were only temporary, and after several days or weeks, patients returned to their previous symptoms and behavior. Conversely, several individuals manifested an intensification of psychopathology and a temporary worsening of the clinical condition. The rest of the patients had only insignificant and transient changes limited to the day immediately following the session; these involved hangover feelings, fatigue, drowsiness, and distractibility, or feelings of unusual calmness and relaxation. In this group, there was, by and large, no great difference from pre- to postsession clinical condition.

For several of the patients included in this exploratory study, the LSD procedure was not limited to one exposure, and additional sessions were scheduled at a later time. Sometimes this happened at the request of the patient, who liked the experience or found it valuable; at other times, because the therapist observed something that seemed worth pursuing. It thus happened that for one reason or another a few individuals received over a period of several months five to eight consecutive sessions. The analysis of the records of these serial sessions brought to light very interesting facts that represented a decisive and crucial step toward a deeper understanding of the LSD experience and indicated the direction of further research. When I was studying the material from several consecutive LSD sessions of the same person, it became evident that there was a definite continuity between these sessions. Rather than being unrelated and random, the experiential content seemed to represent a successive unfolding of deeper and deeper levels of the unconscious. It was quite common that identical or very similar clusters of visions, emotions, and physical symptoms occurred in several consecutive LSD sessions. Patients often had the feeling that they were returning again and again to a specific experiential area and each time could get deeper into it. After several sessions, such clusters would then converge into a complex reliving of traumatic memories. When these memories were relived and integrated, the previously recurring phenomena never reappeared in subsequent sessions and were replaced by others. It soon became clear that this observation might have important implications for the practice and theory of dynamic psychotherapy. The use of repeated LSD sessions in a limited number of subjects suddenly appeared to be much more promising than the study of single sessions in large groups of individuals.

This sequence of observations was the basis on which I developed, independently of several other European therapists, the concept of a therapeutic series of LSD sessions, usually referred to as *psycholytic therapy*.* On the basis of the preliminary findings we started a new exploratory study, this time focusing on the systematic investigation of the therapeutic potential of serial LSD sessions in the framework of psychoanalytically oriented psychotherapy. The basic idea of this approach was that consecutive sessions might make it possible for patients gradually to confront various levels of their unconscious and resolve deep conflicts underlying their psychopathological symptoms.

There were several guiding principles influencing the selection of potential candidates for the LSD procedure. First, it seemed important that all major diagnostic categories be represented in the research sample, from depressive disorders, psychoneuroses, and psychosomatic diseases to character disorders

---

*The term "psycholytic therapy" was coined by Ronald A. Sandison, an English therapist of Jungian orientation and pioneer of clinical LSD research. The root *lysis* suggests dissolving or releasing of tensions and conflicts in the human mind.

and borderline cases, as well as clearcut psychoses of the manic-depressive and schizophrenic type. The reason for this was to find not only the specific differences in the therapeutic response of patients with various emotional disorders but also to determine the characteristics of their reaction to LSD and the nature of their sessions. Second, all the patients selected for this study had more than average intelligence, as measured by their educational level and performance in psychological tests. This was an important requirement, since LSD experiences are rather difficult to verbalize; in order to obtain high-quality research data, it was necessary to have patients with a gift for introspection and a good level of intellectual functioning. Third, there was a definite bias toward a dim clinical prognosis. Most of the patients had serious and fixated emotional disorders that had lasted for many years and proved unusually unresponsive to a variety of conventional therapies. This seemed to provide a moral justification for exposing them to this experimental venture involving repeated administration of a new and insufficiently explored powerful psychoactive drug.

Before the commencement of LSD therapy, each patient had several weeks of drug-free psychotherapy. During this time, the therapist explored with the patient his past history and tried to help him understand the nature of his problems, as well as the connection between his symptoms and his life situation. An equally important goal of this initial period was to establish a good therapeutic relationship. Quite early during this therapeutic experimentation, it became obvious that the element of trust was the single most important variable of successful LSD therapy. After the objectives of the preparatory period were achieved, patients started a series of LSD sessions; the intervals between the sessions ranged from one to two weeks. The usual procedure was to start with 100 micrograms and to increase the dose in each subsequent session until an optimum dosage was found. Criteria for the optimum dose were an adequate depth of self-exploration, the overcoming of important psychological defenses, the emergence of a sufficient amount of unconscious material, and, at the same time, the ability to maintain a good therapeutic contact. Once such a dose was established for a particular patient, it was then repeated in future sessions, unless special circumstances required its increase or reduction. The average dose in my therapeutic experiments was around 200 micrograms, but, on occasions, it reached 400 or 500 micrograms. It was typically low for hysterical patients, who are very sensitive to the effect of LSD, and very high for obsessive-compulsive neurotics, whose excessive psychological resistances represent the opposite extreme. The total number of sessions per patient ranged between fifteen and one hundred.

In each session of the series, the therapist would spend several hours with the patient, providing human support and all the necessary security measures, as well as professional assistance and guidance. The approach to all treatment situations in the initial phase of this research closely resembled the techniques of psychoanalytically oriented psychotherapy; in the LSD session *per se*, it was similar to Frieda Fromm-Reichmann's methods for psychotherapy with psychotic patients.* Later, when we became increasingly familiar with the LSD state and sensitive to its specific characteristics, more and more modifications of the original techniques seemed indicated; the most important of them were the use of physical contact, the introduction of various experiential techniques, listening to stereophonic music, and, particularly, the full appreciation of the therapeutic potential of the mystical and religious dimension of the LSD experience. The final result was a unique treatment modality that represented a considerable departure from its early psychoanalytic model.

When the major effects of the drug subsided, the therapist discussed with the patient the most important events of the day and helped him to integrate the session. He then left the subject in the company of his fellow patients, who were familiar with the LSD state from their own therapy. Trained psychiatric nurses who were in attendance knew the nature of the LSD experience because they themselves had had training sessions. There was an explicit rule in the experimental ward that a person who had ingested LSD should not be left without supervision for the next twenty-four hours.

*Frieda Fromm-Reichmann, *Principles of Intensive Psychotherapy* (Chicago: University of Chicago Press, 1950).

Between LSD sessions, the therapist saw the patients in drug-free interviews; they discussed and analyzed the material from the preceding session and worked on any transference problems that might have occurred. In addition to their therapeutic function, these interviews were the source of valuable research data. Both the therapist and the patient kept detailed records about the experiences in the LSD sessions, as well as the events and relevant developments in the free intervals between sessions. The basic objective was to identify typical patterns and characteristic experiential sequences and relate them to the patient's personality, clinical problems, and therapeutic progress. The exploratory focus was not only on the variables determining the content and course of the sessions but also on the dynamic laws underlying the postsession changes, whether they were the frequently observed dramatic clinical improvements or the equally enigmatic negative aftereffects, such as prolonged reactions, "flashbacks," and other complications. After completion of the psycholytic series with a particular patient, all the collected material was retrospectively analyzed; an effort was made to understand what had occurred during the entire treatment procedure and to find for it an appropriate conceptual framework. During my work at the Psychiatric Research Institute, fifty-two psychiatric patients were treated by serial LSD sessions. Although this research project was primarily my responsibility, two other psychiatrists, Dr. Julia Sobotkiewicz and Dr. Zdeněk Dytrych, conducted the treatment of approximately one-third of these patients. The records from psycholytic therapy have been the most important source of data on which I have based the assumptions and theoretical speculations presented in this book.

From 1967 to 1973, after my arrival in the United States, I continued my research at Spring Grove in Baltimore. There I joined a group of psychiatrists and psychologists who were conducting controlled studies of LSD psychotherapy. This work had begun some years earlier in the Research Unit of the Spring Grove State Hospital and was later transferred into the newly built Maryland Psychiatric Research Center. The therapeutic use of LSD in these studies differed considerably from the psycholytic treatment described above. Instead of a gradual unfolding of different levels of the unconscious such as was observed in my European approach, the goal here was to facilitate the occurrence of a deep religious and mystical experience, sometimes at the expense of bypassing areas of conflicts on the psychodynamic level. Clinical data suggested that these experiences had a unique therapeutic potential in the treatment of various emotional disorders; changes were frequently so dramatic that they seemed to warrant systematic exploration. The dosages used in this approach were rather high, ranging between 300 and 500 micrograms. Patients were encouraged to stay in a reclining position for most of the session, keep their eyes covered with eyeshades, and listen to selected stereophonic music through headphones. The therapist and a specially trained nurse or co-therapist* stayed with the patient for the entire duration of the drug action, sometimes as many as twelve to sixteen hours. The total number of sessions was limited to three in number because of the research design and other special circumstances. During the drug-free preparation period, which usually lasted between fifteen and twenty-five hours, the therapist explored the patient's life history, helped him understand his symptoms, and discussed his philosophical and spiritual orientation. He gave him basic information about the effects of LSD and explained the rationale of the treatment. There were also several drug-free interviews in the period following the session in which the patient's written account of the LSD experience was discussed in detail. The major purpose of these talks was to help the individual integrate the LSD experience into his everyday life. In contrast to the psycholytic treatment described earlier, this form of LSD-assisted psychotherapy is usually referred to as *psychedelic therapy*.** In the Spring Grove research we systematically explored the efficacy of this kind of treatment with alcoholic patients, neurotics, heroin addicts, and terminal cancer patients.

My clinical experience with LSD is based on more than twenty-five hundred LSD sessions that I have conducted or in which I was present for more than five hours. In addition, I have also

---

*It is very important that both sexes be represented on this team.

**The term *psychedelic* was invented by Humphrey Osmond, one of the leading pioneers in LSD research. It literally means mind manifesting or revealing the psyche.

had access to records from over thirteen hundred sessions run by several of my colleagues in Czechoslovakia and in the United States. The majority of the subjects in these sessions were patients with a wide variety of disorders, such as severe psychoneuroses, psychosomatic diseases, borderline psychoses, and various forms of schizophrenia, sexual deviations, alcoholism, and narcotic drug addiction. Another rather large category of subjects was that of "normal" volunteers—psychiatrists, psychologists, students, and nurses, who had LSD sessions for training purposes; painters, sculptors, and musicians seeking artistic inspiration; philosophers and scientists from various disciplines interested in the insights that often emerge in the session; as well as priests and theologians wishing to explore the mystical and religious dimensions of psychedelic experiences. A small number of the sessions was conducted with patients suffering from a terminal disease and facing impending death—especially with cancer patients. The fact that during the seventeen years of my research, I was able to administer LSD to many different subjects and in various sets and settings has made me aware of the complexity of the LSD experience and of all the major variables involved. This awareness has helped me to crystallize my ideas regarding the nature of the LSD effect and to develop a more general theory of LSD psychotherapy and the human unconscious.

Heuristic Value of LSD Research

Before we discuss the theoretical implications of LSD research, it is necessary to justify the heuristic value of LSD as a tool for the exploration of the human unconscious and the legitimacy of drawing more general conclusions from the work with this compound. There has been a tendency among many professions to discard the experiences in LSD sessions as manifestations of a toxic alteration of the brain function (toxic psychosis) that have little, if any, relevance for the understanding of the human mind as it functions under more natural circumstances. This is a rather basic and serious objection that deserves special attention and careful consideration. The pivotal question that has to be dealt with in this context is whether there exist invariant, constant, and standard effects of LSD that are purely pharmacological in nature, are unrelated to the personality structure of the subject, and occur without exception in every subject who takes a sufficient dose of this drug.

The phenomena that can occur in the course of LSD sessions cover an enormous range; there exist hardly any perceptual, emotional, or psychosomatic manifestations that have not been observed and described as part of the LSD experience. The extreme multiformity and interindividual variability of the LSD state is complemented by its equally striking intraindividual variability. If the same person takes LSD repeatedly, each of his consecutive sessions is usually very different from the others in its content, general character, and course. This variability certainly is in itself a serious objection to the idea that the LSD reaction has simple chemical and physiological determinants. The proportion to which various extrapharmacological factors participate in the LSD experience is both interesting and theoretically important.

The search for the typical, mandatory pharmacological effects of LSD was an important aspect of my analytical work on the LSD data. The result of this quest was rather surprising; after analyzing over thirty-eight hundred records from LSD sessions, I have not found a single symptom that would be an absolutely constant component in all of them and could thus be considered truly invariant. Changes of optical perception are usually presented as a typical manifestation of the LSD state and thus were a serious candidate for pharmacological invariants. Although they occurred rather frequently in our records, there were a number of high-dose sessions where alterations in the optical realm were not present at all even though, in some of these sessions, the dosage amounted to 500 micrograms. Several of the LSD reactions without any visual phenomena had the form of intense sexual experiences; others were characterized by massive somatization manifested in various parts of the body, by feelings of general malaise and physical illness, or by experiences of excruciating pain. Special examples of sessions without optical perceptual changes were observed in advanced stages of psycholytic treatment and in some psychedelic sessions. These involved either a brutal and primitive biological experiential complex described by various subjects as reliving of their own birth or transcendental experiences with a paradoxical quality of being "contentless yet all-containing."

Physical manifestations of the LSD state deserve special notice in this context, since, in the early reports, they were considered simple pharmacological effects and a result of direct chemical activation of the vegetative centers in the brain. Careful observations of a large number of sessions and analysis of the records did not support this explanation. The spectrum of the so-called "vegetative symptoms" is very broad and exceeds that of any known drug with the exception of some other psychedelics. Strangely enough, these symptoms include both sympathetic and parasympathetic phenomena, and they appear in clusters involving various combinations thereof. The physical concomitants of the LSD reaction vary considerably from session to session. They are practically independent of the dosage used, and there is no demonstrable dose-effect relationship. In many high-dose LSD sessions, physical manifestations were entirely absent, or they occurred intermittently and in close association with difficult and strongly defended unconscious material. Another aspect of these symptoms that could be mentioned here is their unusual sensitivity to various psychological factors; they can often be modified or even terminated by various external influences and specific psychotherapeutic interventions. One of the physical manifestations of the LSD reaction deserves special emphasis—namely, dilation of the pupils (mydriasis). It is so common that its presence has been used by many experimenters and therapists as a reliable indicator that the person is still under the influence of the drug. For a long time, mydriasis was also a serious candidate for an invariant manifestation of the LSD effect in my investigations. Later, I witnessed several LSD sessions, some of them very dramatic, in which the pupils of the subject appeared constricted, or in which they oscillated rapidly between extreme dilation and constriction. A situation similar to that of the vegetative symptoms existed in the area of gross physical manifestations, such as muscular tonus, tremors, twitches, seizure-like activities, and various twisting movements. None of these symptoms was standard and predictable enough to be considered a specific pharmacological effect of LSD. This does not mean that LSD *per se* does not have any specific physiological effects; these can be clearly demonstrated in animal experiments, which use incomparably higher dosages. My experience, however, indicates that, within the range of doses commonly used in human experiments or in psychotherapeutic practice, physical manifestations are not the result of a direct pharmacological stimulation of the central nervous system. They seem to reflect chemical activation of psychodynamic matrices in the unconscious and have a structure similar to those of hysterical conversions, organ-neurotic phenomena, or symptoms of psychosomatic disorders.

As unpredictable as the content of the LSD reaction is its intensity; the individual responses to the same dosage level vary considerably. My experience indicates that the degree of sensitivity or resistance to LSD depends on complicated psychological factors rather than on variables of a constitutional, biological, or metabolic nature. Subjects who in everyday life have the need to maintain full self-control and have difficulties in relaxing and "letting go" can sometimes resist relatively high dosages of LSD (300 to 500 micrograms) and show no detectable changes. Occasionally, a person can resist a considerable dose of LSD if he has set this as a personal task for himself for any reason. He may decide to do this to defy the therapist and compete with him, to demonstrate his "strength" to himself and to others, to endure more than his fellow patients, or for many other reasons. Usually, however, more relevant unconscious motives can be found underlying such superficial rationalizations. Another cause for a high resistance to the effect of the drug may be insufficient preparation, instruction, and reassurance of the subject, a lack of his full agreement and cooperation, or absence of basic trust in the therapeutic relationship. In this case, the LSD reaction sometimes does not take its full course until the motives of resistance are analyzed and understood. Occasional sudden sobering, which can occur at any period of the session and on any dosage level, can be understood as a sudden mobilization of

This picture reflects the sudden mobilization of psychological defenses against the emergence of traumatic unconscious material in an LSD session. The subject feels absolutely sober, and the environment appears "more real" than usual. The objects in the room are sharply demarcated from each other and have fortified contours.

defenses against the emergence of unpleasant traumatic material. Among psychiatric patients, severe obsessive-compulsive neurotics are particularly resistant to the effect of LSD. It has been a common observation in my research that such patients can resist dosages of more than 500 micrograms of LSD and show only slight signs of physical or psychological distress. In extreme cases, it can take several dozen high-dose LSD sessions before the psychological resistances of these individuals are reduced to the point that they start having episodes of regression to childhood and become aware of the unconscious material that has to be worked through. The excessive resistance of obsessive-compulsive patients can be illustrated by the following clinical example.

Erwin, a twenty-two-year-old student, was referred to the LSD treatment program after four years of unsuccessful therapy for a severe obsessive-compulsive neurosis. Over the years, he had developed a very complicated system of obsessive thoughts and became so preoccupied with it that it paralyzed all his other activities. He was compelled to imagine in his mind's eye a geometrical structure with two coordinate axes and locate within this system all the problems and duties he encountered in his everyday life. At times he spent many hours desperately trying to find the proper location for some aspect of his existence, but always without success. Before admission, he felt that the center of gravity of his imaginary coordinate system was shifting to the left; this upset him enormously and resulted in feelings of tension, apprehension, anxiety, insecurity, and depression. In addition, Erwin suffered from various psychosomatic symptoms and tended to interpret them in a hypochondriacal way. He was referred for psycholytic therapy after several hospitalizations and unsuccessful treatment with tranquillizers, antidepressants, and drug-free psychotherapy. Erwin manifested a rather spectacular resistance to the effect of LSD. After psychological preparation of two weeks' duration, he started having regular LSD sessions in weekly intervals. The initial dose of 100 micrograms was increased by fifty to one hundred micrograms every week, since he barely showed any response. Finally, he was given 1500 micrograms intramuscularly, with the hope that this would overcome his resistance. Between the second and third hour of the session, when the effect of LSD usually culminates, Erwin felt bored and a little hungry; according to his description as well as external manifestations, nothing unusual was happening. He seemed to be so well composed and in such full control that he was allowed to go with the therapist to a kitchenette on the ward, cut a piece of bread with a knife, open a can of liver paste, and have a snack. After he was finished, he wanted to go to the social room in the ward and play chess, because he felt he needed some distraction from the uneventful and monotonous therapeutic experiment.

It took thirty-eight high-dose sessions before Erwin's defense system was reduced to the point that he started regressing into childhood and reliving traumatic experiences.

It became obvious after this and similar observations that high psychological resistance to LSD cannot be broken merely by an increase in dosage and that it has to be gradually alleviated by a series of sessions. It seems that there exists a saturation point for LSD somewhere between 400 and 500 micrograms; if the subject does not respond adequately to this dosage, additional LSD will not change anything in the situation.

After demonstrating that LSD does not have any clear, invariant drug effects on the dosage level commonly used in experimental and clinical work with human subjects, we can ask what the effects of LSD actually are. According to my experience, they are rather unspecific and can be described only in very general terms. In a great majority of sessions, there is an over-all tendency toward perceptual changes in various sensory modalities. Consciousness is usually qualitatively altered and has a dreamlike quality. Emotional reactivity is almost always greatly enhanced, and affective factors play an important role as determinants of the LSD reaction. A rather striking aspect of the LSD effect is a marked intensification of all mental processes and neural processes in general; this involves phenomena of a different nature and origin. Pre-existing and recent psychogenic symptoms as well as those that the individual had suffered from in childhood or at some later period of his life can be exteriorized, amplified, and experienced in the LSD sessions. Traumatic or positive experiences from the past connected with a strong emotional charge are activated, brought forth from the unconscious, and relived in a complex way. Various dynamic matrices from different levels of the individual and collective unconscious can be brought to the surface and consciously experienced. Occasionally, phenomena of a neurological nature can be amplified and manifested in the sessions; frequently these are pains associated with arthritis, dislocation of vertebral disks, inflammatory processes, or postoperative and post-traumatic changes. Particularly common is reliving of sensations related to past injuries and operations; it is interesting from the theoretical point of view that LSD subjects seem to be able to relive even pains and other sensations related to past operations that were conducted under deep general anaesthesia. The propensity of LSD to amplify various neurological processes is so striking that it has been used with success by several Czech neurologists as a diagnostic tool for the exteriorization of latent paralyses and other subtle organic damage of the central nervous system. The negative aspect of this interesting property of LSD is the fact that it can activate seizures in patients suffering from manifest epilepsy or those who have a latent disposition to this disease.

By and large, I have not been able to discover during the analyses of my data any distinct pharmacological effects of LSD in humans that would be constant and invariant and could therefore be considered drug specific. At the present time, I consider LSD to be a powerful unspecific amplifier or catalyst of biochemical and physiological processes in the brain. It seems to create a situation of undifferentiated activation that facilitates the emergence of unconscious material from different levels of the personality. The richness as well as the unusual inter- and intraindividual variability of the LSD experience can thus be explained by the decisive participation of extrapharmacological factors, such as the personality of the subject and the structure of his unconscious, the personality of the therapist or sitter, and the set and the setting in all their complexity. The capacity of LSD and some other psychedelic drugs to exteriorize otherwise invisible phenomena and processes and make them the subject of scientific investigation gives these substances a unique potential as diagnostic instruments and as research tools for the exploration of the human mind. It does not seem inappropriate and exaggerated to compare their potential significance for psychiatry and psychology to that of the microscope for medicine or the telescope for astronomy.

In the following chapters, I have attempted to outline the cartography of the human unconscious as it has been manifested in LSD sessions of my patients and subjects. I have been quite encouraged by the fact that in various areas of human culture there are numerous indications that the maps of consciousness emerging from my LSD work are fully compatible and sometimes parallel with other existing systems. Examples of this can be found in C. G. Jung's analytical psychology, Roberto Assagioli's psychosynthesis, and Abraham Maslow's studies of peak experiences, as well as religious and mystical schools of various cultures and ages. Many of these frameworks are based not on the use of psychedelic drugs but on various powerful nondrug techniques of altering consciousness. This parallel between the LSD experiences and a variety of phenomena manifested without chemical facilitation provides additional supportive evidence for the unspecific and catalyzing effect of LSD.

The description of the new model of the unconscious based on LSD research presents considerable difficulties. This model reflects a multidimensional and multilevel continuum of mutually overlapping and interacting phenomena. For didactic purposes, the object of discussion has to be dissected and its elements isolated from their broader contexts. Each attempt to communicate this model in a linear form necessarily results in a certain degree of oversimplification and artificiality. With full awareness of the disadvantages and limitations involved in such an undertaking, we can delineate for the purpose of our discussion the following four major levels, or types, of LSD experiences and the corresponding areas of the human unconscious: (1) abstract and aesthetic experiences, (2) psychodynamic experiences, (3) perinatal experiences, and (4) transpersonal experiences.

2 Abstract and Aesthetic Experiences in LSD Sessions

The phenomena described in this chapter usually occur in the initial stages of the LSD procedure when lower and medium dosages are used or at the beginning and end of the initial high-dose sessions. The incidence and importance of these experiences seems to diminish with an increasing number of LSD exposures, and they are seldom observed in more advanced sessions of the LSD series. Because of certain specific differences between the abstract phenomena experienced with the eyes closed and those occurring with the eyes open, it seems useful to describe these two groups separately.

If the subject keeps his eyes closed, the first change heralding the onset of the LSD reaction is usually a distinct animation of the visual field and enhancement of the entoptic (intraocular) phenomena. These involve visions of unusually colorful spots that change their shapes and make periodic transitions into complementary colors. A rather typical aspect of the abstract LSD experience are the afterimages. When the individual observes a certain object in the environment for a long time and then closes his eyes, the light contrasts and sometimes even a distinct image of this object can persist for several minutes. Such afterimages usually are very dynamic; they periodically appear and disappear and change into complementary colors. These phenomena are particularly vivid if the original percepts are rich in contrast, such as the sun, a chandelier with bright light bulbs, or a window frame against the sky. Occasionally, the colorful and dynamic mosaic of the entoptic field can be perceived as indistinct and fleeting images of fantastic and exotic scenery, such as visions of mysterious jungles, luscious bamboo thickets, tropical islands, Siberian taigas, or undersea kelp forests and coral reefs.

Quite frequently, the visual field is dominated by abstract geometric designs or architectural patterns that underlie all the dynamic color changes. The persons experiencing these elements often describe them as interiors of gigantic temples, naves of incredibly beautiful Gothic cathedrals, cupolas of monumental mosques, or decorations in Moorish palaces ("arabesques"). Sometimes these visions are compared with paintings of various abstract artists such as Piet Mondrian and Wassily Kandinski. On other occasions, the experiencers talk about phenomenal kaleidoscopic displays, magic sparkling fountains, and *jeux d'eau* or majestic fireworks. As a rule, subjects are fascinated and completely absorbed by these experiences; frequently, they spontaneously discover maneuvers that enhance them, such as increasing the intraocular pressure by spastic squeezing of the eyes, pressing the eyeballs, hyperventilation, and/or withholding of the breath.

With the eyes open, colors are typically very bright, penetrating, and explosive; the light and color contrasts are enhanced and deepened. Eye fixation is rather difficult, and the contours of perceived objects are blurred. Everything seems to be in undulating movement, and inanimate objects are frequently described as coming to life. A very characteristic perceptual change is ornamentalization and geometrization of human faces, animals, and objects. Many individuals experiencing such changes report that their perception changed in the direction of Seurat's or Van Gogh's paintings and that the LSD session helped them gain deep insight into the world of these painters, empathize with them, and understand their art. Equally frequent are allusions to the painters of the Fauvist school, such as Henri Matisse, and their use of ornamental designs in portraits and still lifes. Also, Gustav Klimt* and other

*Gustav Klimt (1862–1917) was an Austrian painter and founder and president of the Vienna "Secession." He is best known for his monumental murals in which human figures are depicted in silhouette form and flat surface without shadow alternates with decorative ornament.

Illusive transformation of the corner of the treatment room from an LSD session of the aesthetic type. The air appears to be full of strange vibrations and magical currents; the folds of a towel hanging on the wall are perceived as an elf.

artists of the Viennese "Secession," who combined in their paintings figurative motifs with mosaics and ornamental elements, are
mentioned in this connection. Occasionally, subjects liken the
increasing geometrization of reality to the progressive disintegration of color and form in the famous series of cat paintings by
Louis Wain.* All these changes are much more dramatic when
the experiencer focuses and fixates the eyes on a particular
segment of the environment. The visual field then becomes
more and more clouded and progressively narrows. The perceived area loses its fixed spatial and logical relations with the
surrounding world and becomes an autonomic experiential
microcosmos. The occurrence of afterimages is not necessarily
limited to the situation in which the eyes are closed. The persis-
tence of previous perceptions can also contribute to the richness
of the aesthetic experience with the eyes open. This is most
obvious when the individual observes his hand with stretched
fingers slowly moving in front of his eyes. As a result of persist-
ing afterimages, he can see different stages of this movement
simultaneously. The over-all effect is similar to that of time-lapse
or strobe-light photography.

Probably the most interesting perceptual changes in this
group are optical illusions. Various objects in the surroundings
can lose their usual forms; they seem to pulsate and be in a state
of strange instability and flux. During this process, they frequently appear grossly disproportional, distorted, and transformed. The subject's own body and the bodies of the persons
present in the session room show grotesque changes; some
anatomical parts can appear miniaturized, others magnified or
elongated. Similar bizarre distortions also involve the perception
of inanimate objects. As a result of this process, the perception of
the environment can be changed in a way that bears a striking
resemblance to the pictures of famous Cubist painters, such as
Pablo Picasso, Georges Braque, Fernand Léger, or Marcel

---

*Louis Wain (1860–1939) was an English painter who experienced a psychotic episode
in his mid-twenties. The dramatic changes of perception associated with this process are
clearly illustrated by a series of cat paintings showing all transitions from realistic
representations of these animals to geometrical and abstract pictures that have little
bearing on reality.

a

A series of drawings made by the author during an early LSD session. It shows the successive illusive transformation of a clock tower observed during the termination period of this session. The first picture is a sketch of the tower as perceived in a usual state of consciousness; the following pictures reflect optical distortions of the same object under the influence of 100 micrograms of LSD.

b

c

d

e

f

g

Duchamp. The fantasy process is usually considerably enhanced and contributes an important creative element to these perceptual changes. Amorphous surfaces, textures of objects, and spots on the floor or walls can be seen as fantastic animals, grotesque faces, or exotic scenery. The optical side of aesthetic LSD sessions can be so overwhelming and rich that it has been described as "orgies of vision."

The visual aspect of the aesthetic LSD experience is frequently complemented by comparable changes in the acoustical area. Typical is hypersensitivity to sounds; subjects perceive noises from the environment that are subliminal and that they would not notice under normal circumstances. Simultaneously, the ability clearly to differentiate sounds is impaired, which results in acoustic illusions; monotonous acoustic stimuli, such as running water or the buzzing of electric appliances, can be illusively transformed into beautiful music. Occasionally, sensory stimuli elicit responses in inappropriate receptors. A person under the influence of LSD can, for example, "see music" or "taste colors." The impulses coming through one sensory area evoke in this case very clear and distinct responses of the other senses. This is usually referred to as synaesthesia.

Sometimes there is very little actual perceptual distortion of the environment, but the latter is emotionally interpreted in an unusual way. It can appear incredibly beautiful, sensual, and inviting; or comical; very frequently, it is described as having a magical or a fairy-tale quality. Similarly, the emotional impact of sound can be modified. Not infrequently, LSD subjects discover dimensions in music that they were unable to perceive before. In the sessions, it appears to be possible to listen to music with one's whole being and with a completely new approach. Frequently, music seems to resonate in different parts of the body and to trigger powerful emotions. One of the most common statements one reads in subjects' reports about LSD sessions refers to the feeling that on the session day they *really* heard music for the first time in their life.

The aesthetic experiences seem to represent the most superficial level of the LSD experience. They do not reveal the unconscious of the subject and do not have any psychodynamic signifi-

An interesting optical illusion from a session with rich sexual symbolism. The subject, observing his own palm, saw it transformed into changing groups of nude female bodies. This phenomenon could be traced to problems related to excessive masturbation.

cance. The most important aspects of these experiences can be explained in physiological terms as a result of chemical stimulation of the sensory organs reflecting their inner structure and functional characteristics. It is interesting to mention in this connection that some of the phenomena from this group can be produced by various physical means. So, for example, geometrical and other elementary visions can be triggered by electrical stimulation of the optical pathways, mechanical pressure on the eyeball, or exposure to intense stroboscopic light. Some LSD subjects have also emphasized the similarity of such experiences to changes of signals resulting from technical disturbances of electronic gadgets, such as television or radio.

Occasionally, the geometrical and ornamental visions or elementary acoustic illusions in an LSD session appear to have some specific emotional connotation. The subject can, for example, feel that the abstract configurations are suggestive of the soft, warm, and sensuous world of the satisfied infant. They might also be experienced as disgusting and repulsive, dangerous and aggressive, sensuous and seductive, or lascivious and obscene. Such a situation represents a transition from the abstract to the psychodynamic level of the LSD experience. The emotions modifying and coloring the abstract imagery belong, in such cases, to relevant biographical material of the experiencer. Sometimes, abstract and figurative elements are combined into complex images; the transitional character of this phenomenon is particularly obvious. The following example from an LSD session of a psychiatrist participating in the LSD training program can be used as an illustration:

I was deeply enmeshed in an abstract world of whirling geometrical forms and exuberant colors that were brighter and more radiant than anything I have ever seen in my life. I was fascinated and mesmerized by this incredible kaleidoscopic show.

At one point, the geometrical structures became stabilized and got organized into the shape of a rather complicated ornate frame of a large Baroque mirror. It represented a maze of branches with rich foliage carved in wood. The mirror was divided into five or six compartments of irregular size separated by ramified offshoots of the frame.

To my great surprise, when I looked into these compartments, various interesting scenes started unfolding in front of my eyes. The persons participating in these scenes were highly stylized and slightly puppet-like. The general atmosphere was rather amusing and comical, but with a definite undertone of secrecy, mystery, and hypocrisy. I suddenly realized that I was watching a symbolic satire on my childhood, which was spent in a little provincial town in the world of *la petite bourgeoisie.* It was populated by characteristic figures representing the "cream" of the local society. The adults meeting in various combinations were highly inconsistent in their behavior and judgments about other people; they were indulging in petty gossip, playing endless ridiculous hypocritical social games, and exchanging little "secrets" of a sexual nature ("so that the children would not hear and know"). I experienced myself as a participant-observer of these grotesque shows, rather curious and excited, but frequently confused. To my surprise, all my emotions from that period of my life emerged from the deep unconscious and became real and vivid once again.

3 Psychodynamic Experiences in LSD Sessions

The experiences belonging to this category originate in the realm of the individual unconscious and in the areas of the personality accessible in usual states of consciousness. They are related to important memories, emotional problems, unresolved conflicts, and repressed material from various life periods of the individual. Most of the phenomena occurring on this level can be interpreted and understood in psychodynamic terms. The deciphering of these experiences requires knowledge of the basic principles of the unconscious dynamics as described by Freud, especially the mechanisms of dreamwork, and also familiarity with certain specific characteristics of the LSD state and its symbolic language. The least complicated psychodynamic experiences have the form of actual relivings of emotionally highly relevant events and vivid re-enactments of traumatic or unusually pleasant memories from infancy, childhood, or later periods of life. More complicated phenomena in this group represent pictorial concretization of fantasies, dramatization of wishful daydreams, screen memories, and complex mixtures of fantasy and reality. In addition to these, the psychodynamic level involves a variety of experiences that contain important unconscious material appearing in the cryptic form of a symbolic disguise, defensive distortions, and metaphorical allusions.

Psychodynamic experiences are particularly common in psycholytic therapy of psychiatric patients and in unsupervised LSD sessions of individuals who have considerable emotional problems. They are much less important in the sessions of persons who are emotionally stable and whose childhood was relatively uneventful. In the initial stages of psycholytic treatment, psychodynamic experiences can dominate many consecutive sessions before the underlying unconscious material is resolved and integrated and the patient can move to the next level. In psychedelic therapy, such biographical material usually occurs at the beginning and in the termination period of the session. Occasionally, psychodynamic experiences can dominate the entire course of a high-dose psychedelic session; generally, however, the special preparation, use of large doses of LSD, and the set and setting of this form of LSD therapy facilitate experiences from deeper levels of the unconscious that will be described later (i.e., perinatal and transpersonal phenomena).

The phenomenology of psychodynamic experiences in LSD sessions is to a large extent in agreement with the basic concepts of classical psychoanalysis. If psychodynamic sessions were the only type of LSD experience, the observations from LSD psychotherapy could be considered to be laboratory proof of the basic Freudian premises. The psychosexual dynamics and the fundamental conflicts of the human psyche as described by Freud are manifested with unusual clarity and vividness even in sessions of naïve subjects who have never been analyzed, have not read psychoanalytic books, and have not been exposed to other forms of implicit or explicit indoctrination.* Under the influence of LSD, such subjects experience regression to childhood and even early infancy, relive various psychosexual traumas and complex

*This statement might not appear convincing to the American reader, who is literally flooded by psychoanalytic information. It has to be emphasized, therefore, that because of special circumstances, the exposure of Czech subjects to psychoanalytic ideas has been minimal. At the time of the German occupation of Czechoslovakia in 1939 psychoanalytic books were taken from the libraries and burned by the Nazis, since Freud's work was considered a dangerous tool of the "Jewish–Bolshevik–Free Masonic indoctrination." After the Communist putsch and takeover in 1948, psychoanalytic literature, which had been reintroduced to libraries in the early postwar years, was displaced to special compartments of *libri prohibiti*, where they were accessible only to those Marxist philosophers with special permits who were writing critiques of the psychoanalytic doctrine. Soviet ideologists considered psychoanalysis a particularly dangerous product of the "capitalist, bourgeois and reactionary propaganda" aimed at subjugation of the working class. During these stormy years, the memorial tablet on the house in Příbor (Freiberg), Moravia, where Freud was born, was twice removed and returned to its original place. Only one psychoanalyst survived World War II in Czechoslovakia to provide the continuity of psychoanalytic training and education.

sensations related to infantile sexuality, and are confronted with conflicts involving activities in various libidinal zones. They have to face and work through some of the basic psychological problems described by psychoanalysis, such as the Oedipus and Electra complexes, castration anxiety, and penis envy.

In spite of this far-reaching correspondence and congruence, Freudian concepts cannot explain some of the phenomena related to psychodynamic LSD sessions. For a more complete understanding of these sessions and of the consequences they have for the clinical condition of the patient, as well as for the personality structure, a new principle has to be introduced into psychoanalytical thinking. LSD phenomena on this level can be comprehended, and at times predicted, if we think in terms of specific memory constellations, for which I use the name "COEX systems" (systems of condensed experience).* This concept has emerged from the analyses of the phenomenology of serial LSD sessions in the early phase of my research in Prague. It proved unusually helpful for understanding the drug-induced psychodynamic experiences during the initial stages of psycholytic therapy with psychiatric patients.

COEX Systems
(Systems of Condensed Experience)

A *COEX system* can be defined as a specific constellation of memories consisting of condensed experiences (and related fantasies) from different life periods of the individual. The memories belonging to a particular COEX system have a similar basic theme or contain similar elements and are associated with a strong emotional charge of the same quality. The deepest layers of this system are represented by vivid and colorful memories of experiences from infancy and early childhood. More superficial

---

*The existence of governing systems as important principles for understanding the dynamics of psycholytic therapy with LSD was independently discovered and described by H. Leuner.[11] He coined for them the term "transphenomenal dynamic governing systems" (*transphenomenale dynamische Steurungs-systeme-tdysts*). Although there are many similarities between the concept of the COEX system and that of *tdyst*, the terminological differentiation should be retained because of all the implications and ramifications attached to the concept "COEX system" within the framework presented here.

layers of such a system involve memories of similar experiences from later periods, up to the present life situation. Each COEX system has a basic theme that permeates all its layers and represents their common denominator; the nature of these themes varies considerably from one COEX constellation to another. Various layers of a particular system can, for example, contain all memories of the past exposures of an individual to humiliating and degrading situations that have damaged his self-esteem. In other instances, the common element can be anxiety experienced in regard to shocking and frightening events, claustrophobic and suffocating feelings evoked by various oppressive and restricting circumstances where there was no possibility of fighting back and defending oneself or escaping, as well as an intense sense of guilt and moral failure triggered by a number of specific situations. The experience of emotional deprivation and rejection in various periods of one's development is another common motif of many COEX constellations. Equally frequent are basic themes that depict sex as dangerous or disgusting, and those that involve aggression and violence. Particularly important are COEX systems that epitomize and condense the individual's encounters with situations endangering survival, health, and integrity of the body. The excessive emotional charge which is attached to COEX systems (as indicated by the often powerful abreaction accompanying the unfolding of these systems in LSD sessions) seems to be a summation of the emotions belonging to all the constituent memories of a particular kind.

Individual COEX systems have fixed relations to certain defense mechanisms and are connected with specific clinical symptoms. The detailed interrelations between the individual parts and aspects of COEX systems are in most instances in basic agreement with Freudian thinking; the new element from the theoretical point of view is the concept of the organizing dynamic system integrating the components into a distinct functional unit. The personality structure usually contains a greater number of COEX systems. Their character, total number, extent, and intensity varies considerably from one individual to another.

According to the basic quality of the emotional charge, we can

a

b

Two drawings made by an obsessive-compulsive patient in a psychodynamic LSD session in which he explored his lack of assertiveness, his submissiveness, and his role as a hen-pecked husband.

Picture (a) is a symbolic representation of his concept of the male role. The condensed image has the horns of an ox and the ears of a donkey; these two animals are often used as symbols of stupidity. The beard is stylized into a fish, suggesting the male's inability to assert himself verbally when confronted with a female. The over-all composition, however, has the form of a devil and reveals the patient's repressed aggression.

Picture (b) reflects this patient's concept of the female role. Beauty as an essential characteristic of femininity is symbolized by a rose. Sharp thorns, with dripping blood and various dangerous animals—such as scorpion, snake, and centipede—in the perianth, reveal the danger hidden in this beauty.

differentiate *negative COEX systems* (condensing unpleasant emotional experiences) and *positive COEX systems* (condensing pleasant emotional experiences and positive aspects of an individual's past life). Although there are certain interdependencies and overlappings, separate COEX systems can function relatively autonomously. In a complicated interaction with the environment, they influence selectively the subject's perception of himself and of the world, his feelings and ideation, and even many somatic processes.

In the following text, the concept of COEX systems will be illustrated by several clinical examples from psycholytic therapy. All these examples involve negative COEX systems, which are more frequent in psycholytic treatment and show a greater variety than the positive ones.

Peter, a thirty-seven-year-old tutor, was intermittently hospitalized and treated in our department during two years preceding the start of psycholytic therapy. Intensive psychotherapy and pharmacotherapy brought only superficial and temporary relief of his serious psychopathology. His major problems at that time were symptoms combining obsessive-compulsive and masochistic elements. He felt almost continuously compelled to find a man with certain physiognomic features and preferably clad in black. His basic intention was to make contact with this man, tell him his life story, and finally reveal to him his deep desire to be locked in a dark cellar, bound with a rope, and exposed to various diabolic physical and mental tortures. Unable to concentrate on anything else, he wandered through the streets and visited public parks, lavatories, railroad stations, and inns trying to find the proper person. He succeeded several times in persuading or bribing the individuals he selected to carry out what he requested. When this happened, he failed to experience masochistic pleasure and was instead extremely frightened and disliked the tortures. Having a special gift for finding persons with marked sadistic personality traits, he was twice almost killed, several times seriously hurt, and, on another occasion, his partner bound him and stole his money. Besides these problems, the patient suffered from suicidal depressions, tensions and anxieties, impotence, and very infrequent epileptiform seizures.

Retrospective analysis showed that his major symptoms started during compulsory employment in Germany* during World War II, when two Nazi officers forced him, at gunpoint, to engage in their homosexual practices. When the war was over, he discovered that these experiences had established in him a preference for the passive homosexual role in sexual intercourse. Several years later, he developed a typical fetishism for black male clothes. This gradually changed into the masochistic craving described above that brought him into therapy.

In a series of fifteen psycholytic sessions, a very interesting and important COEX system was sequentially manifested. Its most superficial layers were constituted by Peter's memories of traumatic encounters with his sadistic partners. On several occasions, the men he had contacted actually bound him with ropes, locked him in cellars without food and water, and tortured him by strangulation and flagellation. One of his sadistic complices bound him in a forest, hit him on the head with a large stone, and ran away with his wallet. Another of these individuals promised to lock Peter in a cellar that he supposedly had in his cabin in the woods. When they were traveling together to this weekend house, Peter was struck by the strange-looking, bulky knapsack of his companion. When the latter left the train compartment and went to the bathroom, Peter stepped on the bench and checked the contents of this suspicious baggage. He discovered a complete set of murderous weapons, including a gun, a large butcher knife, a surgical saw used for amputations, and a freshly sharpened hatchet. Panic-stricken, he jumped out of the moving train and suffered considerable injury; he was, however, convinced that this maneuver saved his life. These and similar dramatic episodes were relived in the early LSD sessions. In addition, the sadistic themes were also represented in a variety of symbolic forms.

A deeper layer of the same system was represented by Peter's experiences from the Third Reich. In the LSD sessions influenced by this part of the COEX constellation, he relived in detail his experiences with homosexual Nazi officers, including all the complicated feelings that these episodes evoked in him. In addition, he relived a variety of other war memories reflecting the atmosphere of Nazi tyranny. He had visions of banners with swastikas, pompous SS

---

*During World War II, the Nazis imported large numbers of young people from occupied territories to Germany and used them for slave labor in risky work situations, such as quarries, foundries, coal mines, and ammunition factories. This was referred to by the Germans as *Totaleinsetzung*.

military parades, gigantic halls in the Reichstag, and ominous eagle emblems, as well as emaciated prisoners in the concentration camps, raids of the Gestapo in private homes, and victims lined up in front of gas chambers.

The core experiences of the same system were related to Peter's childhood. In later sessions he regressed into experiences involving punishments used by his parents. It turned out that his mother used to lock him in a dark cellar for long periods of time without food, and his despotic father's method of punishing him was to whip him in a very cruel way with a leather strap. The patient at this point realized that his masochistic desires were a replica of the combined parental punishments.

During the reliving of these memories a striking oscillation of the patient's major problem was observed but not its long-term total disappearance. Finally, Peter relived the agonizing experience of his birth trauma in its full biological brutality. According to his later comment, it involved exactly those elements which he expected from the sadistic treatment he was so desperately trying to get: dark closed space, restriction of all body movements, and exposure to extreme physical and mental tortures. Reliving of the biological birth finally resolved his difficult symptoms.

Reliving of the birth trauma lies beyond the realm of psychodynamics as usually understood in traditional psychotherapy. It was included in the above case history for the sake of its logical completion; this phenomenon belongs to the next level of the LSD experience, which will be discussed in the following chapter.

A comparison of the preceding clinical example with the one that follows will demonstrate that, in spite of the far-reaching differences in content, various COEX systems show deep parallels in their formal dynamic structures. In each individual case, similar traumatic events from various life periods seem to be recorded in the memory banks in close connection with the oldest experience of such a series, which thus constitutes the primary trauma. The oldest event that forges the prototypical pattern forms the nucleus of the COEX constellation—the "core experience" of the system. The cluster of later memories is organized around this core; the whole constellation is then usually related to a particular facet of the biological birth (see the discussion of the perinatal matrices on page 95).

Renata, a thirty-two-year-old housewife, was repeatedly hospitalized in mental institutions for severe cancerophobia, obsessive-compulsive ideation and behavior, deep suicidal depressions, a tendency toward self-mutilation, and borderline psychotic symptoms. Although she had suffered from a variety of neurotic problems since her early childhood, her major symptoms started several years before her LSD therapy after her gynecologist told her that she had an ulceration of the uterine cervix. Since that time, she had been tormented by an excessive fear of cancer, alternating with hypochondriac suspicions or even delusions that she indeed already had cancer. She visited various out-patient clinics and hospitals insisting on every imaginable clinical investigation and laboratory test with such urgency and consistency that she began to be regarded as a menace by the health-care personnel. During several years, the suspicion of cancer remained unchanged, but the suspected site of the pathological processes shifted among the sexual organs, the brain, the oral and pharyngeal cavity, the bronchi and lungs, the stomach, and the vertebral column. Her fears frequently led her to seek out painful and dangerous interventions and manipulations. Thus, when she suspected tumors might be originating in her oral mucous membrane, she would take scissors and cut out pieces of her tongue and gums to eliminate the "growths." Several times this resulted in uncontrollable bleeding that brought her to the emergency room. On other occasions, she managed by constant anxious insistence to manipulate physicians into unnecessary self-prescribed interventions and diagnostic procedures. At a period when the lungs were the organ suspected of cancer, she forced the phthiseologists to perform four successive unindicated bronchoscopies (a rather painful procedure during which a long metal tube with a built-in optical system is inserted into the tracheobronchial pathways).

Renata also had considerable problems in her sexual life. It was extremely difficult for her to form intimate relationships and her experiences with men were rather traumatic and confusing. Instances of brutal sexual approaches and attempted rapes were the prevailing pattern. She had never experienced an orgasm during sexual intercourse. Sexual excitement regularly precipitated feelings of panic, intense fear of death, and, later, accentuation of her cancerophobia. Conversely, extreme anxiety, such as would occur during air raids in World War II, risky driving situations, and terrifying scenes in horror movies, would be sexually stimulating.

During her psycholytic therapy, a very strong and important COEX system intimately related to her major psychopathological problems was uncovered, relived, and integrated in a number of consecutive LSD sessions. The basic theme was an identification of the male element as brutal, sadistic, and extremely dangerous. In this context, there was a deep unconscious connection between sex and vital threat, insidious illnesses (such as cancer, venereal diseases, and leprosy) and death.

The most superficial layers of this COEX system involved memories of relatively recent traumatic experiences that occurred in her marital and professional life. She was married to a rather weak man who was very shy, inhibited, and sexually inexperienced, and toward whom she felt intellectually superior. Under these circumstances, she did not find the relationship threatening and felt that she had full control over the situation. The sexual life of the couple was very erratic and full of conflicts. It was several months before their marriage was sexually consummated, and following this the sexual contact between Renata and her husband was infrequent and irregular. After a few years of marriage, she refused sexual intercourse altogether; this coincided with the mentioned finding of the cervical ulceration. The husband, unable to find an outlet for his frustrated sexuality, grew increasingly impatient with this abnormal situation. He started molesting Renata, and, confronted with her decisive resistance, started abusing her physically and finally made several attempts at violent rape. Simultaneously, quite similar things were happening to Renata at her job. Several of her coworkers, independently of each other, became involved in a peculiar flirtation game with her. The resultant series of open sexual attacks frightened, puzzled, and irritated her. Memories of the above sexual assaults by her husband and coworkers formed the most accessible layers of this COEX system.

The deeper layers of the same system were related to her experiences in adolescence and postadolescence. In that period, she had several erotic relationships that all followed the same rigid and repetitive pattern. In each of them, there was a strong emotional attachment to her partner; she tended to regard her partners in an idealistic way, liked to go for long walks, have discussions about matters unrelated to their relationship, or exchange superficial and noncommittal manifestations of sympathy. However, whenever a

Picture of a symbolic vision showing the close relationship between sex and death in Renata's unconscious. It depicts a famous pestilence column in Prague that was built as a magic protection against plague epidemics. Here it is entwined by streaming spermatozoids. The patient interpreted pestilence, as well as leprosy, cancer, and venereal disease, as a punishment for sexual activities.

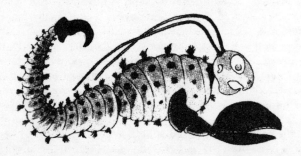

The vision of a fantastic animal that Renata saw in one of her LSD sessions as a symbolic representation of her cancerophobia. Analysis showed that it was a composite image with an interesting structure; all its pictorial details were actually overdetermined symbolic allusions to Renata's traumatic experiences with her stepfather, which had contributed to the psychogenesis of this symptom.

boy friend initiated even the most innocent sexual approach, such as touching, embracing, or kissing, she was overwhelmed with terror. It seemed to her that when such a situation occurred, her lover was actually changing physically and assuming animal features. Repeatedly, she fled from these situations in a state of panic anxiety and never wanted to see her partner again. Episodes of this kind were repeatedly relived in her LSD sessions with details of the physical setting, as well as the physical sensations and emotions involved.

After much struggle and emotional agony, Renata finally overcame the enormous resistances and defenses involved and was able to face the core experience of this system. This happened in many consecutive sessions and in a mosaic fashion; various fragments and facets of a complicated story were relived separately and then put together into a meaningful whole. According to the final reconstruction, the core experience consisted of the following events. When Renata was about seven or eight years old, her mother left the house on a Saturday afternoon and went to the theater with a relative. Renata stayed at home with her stepfather; at that time, she was very fond of him, and the two of them had frequent playful interactions with much physical contact. The stepfather had married Renata's mother at a late age (fifty-five) after leading the rather risky and adventurous life of a globetrotter; there was a considerable age difference between the partners. According to the relivings in the LSD sessions, on the critical day, the stepfather was in the bathroom killing a goose that was to be eaten for Sunday's lunch. During this bloody activity, he became sadistically aroused and sexually excited. He invited Renata to join him in the bathroom and started behaving in a strange way. He undressed her, touched and sucked different parts of her body, stimulated her genitals manually, and deflowered her digitally. Finally, he unbuttoned his pants and put his penis into her mouth. He asked her to suck and lick it, promising her that it would grow and get hard as a result of this activity. Renata supposedly finally witnessed ejaculation, which completely bewildered her. A rather important aspect of this scene was the change in the stepfather's appearance. He did not look the way she had known him; his eyes had a strange hectic gleam, and his face seemed to assume animal features. Some of the elements of this core experience could be traced back to an earlier episode that occurred when she was four years old. As she and her stepfather were playing in bed, he manipulated her down to his pelvic area, where she discovered his erect penis.

According to the relivings, this traumatic event had a complicated continuation afterward. The stepfather supposedly took Renata into the cellar, beat her, and used threats to make her keep the bathroom scene a secret. He forced her to swear that she would not relate to her mother what had happened. The punishments suggested for breaking the oath were her being locked forever in the dark cellar with her tongue cut off, or being killed.

When the described COEX system was being reduced and relived in a series of LSD sessions, Renata first had to work through the more recent traumatic experiences with her husband and male coworkers, then through the episodes with several of her lovers, and finally through various aspects of the core experience itself. The basic themes of the system were also represented in the LSD sessions in a variety of symbolic metaphors and allusions to books, movies, paintings, and mythological stories dealing with violence, rape, sex and death, sexual murders, abuse of children, pregnancy, and venereal disease. Once the traumatic experience was relived and integrated, Renata realized how deeply her neurotic symptoms and irrational behavior were related to the core experience. She found parallels between her cancerophobia and her childhood concept of pregnancy, which she expected and feared after the bathroom scene. The hypochondriac sensations in various organs that she interpreted as cancer could be traced to sensations related to her stepfather's manipulations. She identified her compulsion to visit various doctors as an unconsciously motivated drive to re-enact the scene with her stepfather. Undressing and touching during physical examinations, digital manipulations in the genital area during gynecological check-ups, dark and closed rooms during the X-ray investigations, and forceful insertion of a phallic instrument during the bronchoscopy, all these involved elements of the scene in the bathroom and cellar in a more or less disguised form. Renata also recognized to what extent she herself played a key role in the later repetitions of her traumatic encounters with men. It was an unusual combination of flirtation and seductive behavior with resistance and rejection that had a powerful sexually stimulating effect on her husband and her coworkers, and finally drove them to molest and assault her.

Renata's symptoms, although considerably modified and mitigated by these relivings and accompanying insights, did not disappear after the reliving of the COEX system and its core experience. Like Peter in the preceding example, Renata found a deeper source for her psychopathology in the profound and destructive energies associated with the trauma of birth. The basic aspects of her symptoms— panic anxiety, an experience of physical threat and damage, aggression directed inward and outward, respiratory difficulties (which she experienced in relation to her "lung cancer" and during bronchoscopies), various bizarre somatic sensations, as well as a peculiar mixture of sexual and aggressive feelings and confusion of sex and death— form an integral part of the birth experience. After Renata gained insight into this level, she discovered that the detailed content and dynamics of her cancerophobia that had appeared earlier as direct derivatives of her experience with her stepfather were also related in a very logical and meaningful way to the events occurring on the perinatal level.

The last clinical example shows that the COEX systems do not have to consist solely of memories of traumatization experienced in interpersonal relationships and human situations. Occasionally, traumatic events involving animals and other nonhuman elements, self-inflicted accidents, and injuries, as well as diseases and other situations endangering survival and body integrity, can be incorporated into the COEX constellation and play a very important role.

Richard was a twenty-six-year-old student who had suffered for several years from severe, unrelenting depression that resulted in six serious suicidal attempts. In one of these, he ingested rat poison, which, according to his words, reflected his feelings about himself and his critically low self-image. In addition, he had frequent attacks of intense, free-floating anxiety, excruciating headaches, agonizing cardiac pains and palpitations, and severe insomnia. The patient himself related most of his complaints to disturbances in his sexual life. Although he had many friendly relationships with women, he was not able to approach them sexually and create a situation conducive to intercourse. He tried to reduce his excessive sexual tension by intensive masturbation, but this was regularly followed by tormenting guilt feelings. At irregular intervals, he got involved in homosexual activities in which he always played a passive role. Here he was able to achieve momentary sexual satisfaction, but subsequent feelings of guilt and qualms of conscience were even stronger than those associated with masturbation. In a state of utter despair precipitated by his inability to handle his sexual drives, he attempted to castrate himself by ingesting large doses of estrogen hormones. He started psycholytic therapy after long, unsuccessful treatment with a number of conventional methods.

One of the most important COEX systems uncovered during Richard's LSD therapy was related to his passivity, helplessness, and the role of victim that he had tended to assume in a variety of life situations. The basic theme of this system was the encounter with an overwhelming external force that was encroaching on him and endangering him without giving him the least chance to defend himself or escape. The most superficial layers of this COEX constellation were related to fairly recent traumatic material from his life. Richard was expelled from the university after having had considerable trouble of a political nature during the so-called "Stalin personality cult." In the early LSD sessions, he relived these events and experienced desperate feelings of injustice and helplessness of the individual confronted with the powerful and destructive forces of a social and political nature operating in a totalitarian regime.

A deeper layer of the same system contained condensed memory material related to Richard's experiences with his brutal, despotic, and autocratic father, a chronic alcoholic who used physically to maltreat the patient as well as his mother in the most cruel way. In the course of LSD sessions, Richard relived many such episodes of abuse in a rather complex and realistic fashion. The most extreme of these incidents resulted in serious physical injuries; in one of his alcoholic intoxications, his father struck him so violently that he was propelled through a large window. Richard suffered multiple deep cuts and bled severely; he had to be taken to the emergency room of the local hospital, where the surgeon on duty sutured his wounds. This particular episode, as well as many others, was relived in the sessions with unusual vividness and powerful emotion.

In addition to these relivings, Richard experienced many symbolic scenes related to his father-conflict. In one of these sequences, he was autosymbolically transformed into a carp swimming around in a pond, and his father appeared as a fisherman with a large fishing rod; Richard—as the carp—was caught, scooped out of the water, and killed by a powerful blow of the fist.

The next layer of this COEX system consisted of several traumatic memories from childhood. The first of these supposedly happened when Richard was about seven years old; one day he tried to explore the inside of the family radio and got a strong electric shock. The second of these recollections was related to a serious childhood disease; reliving this incident, he experienced himself all wrapped in blankets and choking on diphtheric pseudomembranes clogging his throat. Another of these memories involved a situation in which he was drowning for a short time in his bathinette when his mother, who was bathing him, left for a short time to take care of food that was cooking on the stove.

The core experience of this system was most unusual and interesting. In spite of the genuine terror that Richard experienced while reliving it, this episode did not lack a certain situational humor. For some time preceding the full reliving of this memory, various rustic and agricultural elements kept appearing in Richard's LSD sessions in different sensory modalities. He saw scythes, sickles, and rakes, ripened grain gently moving with the wind, grazing cows and horses, field flowers against the blue sky, and loaves of bread and jugs with milk—a typical snack of farmers working in the fields. This was accompanied by sounds of farm tools and domestic animals (whinnying and neighing, mooing, barking, and cackling). He felt the breeze flowing over the fields and smelled the fragrance of ripe kernels of grain, freshly baked bread, field grass, and wild flowers. The emotional concomitants of these seemingly idyllic experiences were rather inappropriate; they involved feelings of anxiety, depression, and helplessness. In one of these sessions, Richard suddenly regressed deeply into infancy and experienced himself as a one-year-old baby swaddled in a blanket and lying on the grass by a field, while the adults were harvesting grain. He saw a cow approach him, graze in the immediate proximity of his head, and then lick his face several times with her huge, rough tongue. During the reliving of this episode, the head of the cow seemed gigantic and almost filled the session room. Richard found himself gazing helplessly into the monstrous salivating mouth of the cow and felt her saliva flowing all over his face. After having relived the happy ending of this situation, in which the adults discovered what was happening and rescued the baby, Richard felt enormous relief and a surge of vitality and activity. He laughed for a solid five minutes and was able to joke about his shocking encounter with the cow.

In a later session, Richard found a deep functional relationship between the basic theme of this COEX system and the experience of biological birth. He came to the conclusion that the birth trauma was the fundamental prototype of all the situations in which he felt absolutely helpless and at the mercy of a destructive external force.

After the experiences of rebirth, positive ecstatic feelings of long duration occurred in Richard's sessions. They brought about a far-reaching improvement of the clinical condition. His depressions, anxieties, and psychosomatic symptoms completely disappeared, and he felt full of activity and optimism. His self-image improved considerably, and he was able to form an erotic relationship with a woman and have the first heterosexual intercourse in his life.

COEX systems similar to the three above examples can be found in many psychiatric patients undergoing psycholytic treatment. Since these systems appear to be very important for the understanding of psychodynamic experiences in LSD sessions, it seems appropriate to discuss in greater detail the problems of their origin, dynamics, and their manifestation during the LSD procedure.

Origin and Dynamics of COEX Systems

Reliving of experiences constituting different levels of the COEX systems is one of the most frequent and constantly observed phenomena in LSD psychotherapy of psychiatric patients. This reliving is rather realistic, vivid, and complex; it is characterized by various convincing indications of regression of the subject to the age when he originally experienced the event in question. One of the most important aspects of this regression is that the body image always corresponds with the age into which the subject has regressed. Thus, the reliving of memories from early infancy typically involves feelings of disproportion between the size of the head and the rest of the body. Reliving memories from childhood with a sexual undertone, subjects state with surprise that their penis appears to be ridiculously small, or they might experience themselves without pubic hair and with undeveloped breasts. Quite common is a naïve perception of the world, lack of conceptual frameworks, and primitive emotions typical for the age to which a subject has regressed. Even more objective indicators can be mentioned in this connection, such as certain aspects of drawings made in the periods of regression or the presence of neurological reflexes typical for early developmental stages (i.e., the Babinski reflex, sucking reflex, or the so-called axial reflexes). Important emotional experiences from the past are relived with all the physiological, sensory, emotional, and ideational characteristics of the original reaction and frequently with a detailed realistic representation of the setting.

Some patients in psycholytic therapy are able to undergo a deep age regression of this kind during the first LSD session and with a relatively low dose. Such easy access to childhood memories seems to be particularly characteristic of hysterical patients. More typically, it requires several LSD sessions with medium dosages before a deeper regression to childhood can be observed. In exceptional cases, it takes a great number of exposures before an effective regression and reliving of childhood memories can occur. Such a resistance to the regressive effect of LSD is especially typical of patients with severe obsessive-compulsive neurosis.

The list of characteristic traumatic experiences that occur as core elements of negative COEX systems covers a wide range of situations that interfere with the security and satisfaction of the child. The oldest core experiences are related to the earliest stage of infancy, the suckling period. Quite frequent is the reliving of oral frustrations related to a rigid feeding schedule, to lack of milk, or to tension, anxiety, nervousness, and lack of love on the part of the nursing mother and her inability to create an emotionally warm, peaceful, and protective atmosphere. Equally frequent seem to be other traumatic experiences from infancy, such as exposure to cold and other unpleasant sensations, painful medical interventions, physical suffering during childhood diseases, forced ingestion or administration of repulsive liquids (cod-liver oil, various medicines, strong disinfectants), threatening sounds, bombardment by an overwhelming influx of impulses that the child is not able to integrate, careless treatment, and emotional deprivation. Occasionally, patients have reported experiences of being dropped by adults or older children, or falling out of a carriage or off a table, bed, or staircase. A typical group of unpleasant experiences is related to the trauma associated with weaning and unpleasant feelings during

A deep regression into early infancy, with reliving of distress and unpleasant experiences connected with nursing. A symbolic image of the "bad mother."

A drawing representing the ambivalent feelings experienced by a patient who regressed in his LSD session to an early oral level. Incorporation is perceived both as destruction of the object (symbolized here by large teeth) and loving union (symbolized by the heart).

artificial feeding, such as the hardness and coldness of the spoon, the bad taste of the meal, the excessive temperature of the food, or the impatience of the nursing person. Several patients relived problems connected with teething, when attempts to bite and chew caused self-inflicted pain.

Of special importance are events endangering the child's life by restriction of his respiration. The most frequent of these situations are suffocation after aspiration of liquids or solid objects, episodes of near drowning in the tub during bathing, diphtheria, whooping cough, pneumonia, adenoids restricting breathing, and the threat of being smothered by the breast or body of the sleeping mother.

Experiences from later infancy and childhood that are often found as important parts of negative COEX systems are problems connected with urination and defecation and conflicts with parental authority related to toilet training. Other important and frequently reported traumatic memories include observations of sexual activities in adults (particularly the primal scene in the Freudian sense, when the persons involved are the subject's own parents), the discovery of anatomical differences between sexes associated with castration fears or penis envy, sexual activities with peers, sexual seduction by adults resulting in premature sexual awakening, and the observation of delivery in humans or animals. Rather important experiences from this category are masturbatory manipulations associated with unrealistic fears and guilt feelings or discovered and punished by adults.

Traumatic memories from later periods of life, which are relived in close association with the core experiences, are unusually numerous and cover a rather wide range; in this context, we will mention only the most common of them. Emotional rejection of various sorts, as well as shocking and frightening events and cruel treatment resulting in psychological and physical suffering, are typical of this group. Equally common is marked parental preference for other children in the family and feelings of sibling rivalry, excessive use of negative techniques in childrearing, such as criticism, evoking of guilt feelings, reproaches, degrading or unfavorable comparison with others, and humiliation, derision, and devaluation experienced from parents, siblings, peers, teachers, and schoolmates. Other frequent situations are those characterized by complicated patterns of family interaction (especially the double-bind element in Gregory Bateson's sense), unreliable behavior of relevant adults involving neglect, betrayal, lying, and breaking of promises, and the observation of scenes that shatter parental authority and produce insecurity.

Events from later periods of life, such as prepuberty, very rarely appear as typical core experiences. If they do, they usually have the form of a repressed shocking situation in the sexual area, such as rape, seduction by stepparents or even parents, and observation of violent or disgusting sexual scenes. Usually the memories from later periods of life can be found in the more superficial layers of COEX systems that have core experiences from earlier childhood.

The list of pleasant childhood memories that constitute core experiences of positive COEX systems is much simpler than that of the traumatic ones. It includes episodes of security and satisfaction, such as "good breast" experiences and other types of libidinal and sensual pleasure, experiences of being loved, accepted, and appreciated, and feelings of excitement and adventure in relation to the natural environment, interesting animals, and play with peers.

The authenticity and objectivity of childhood memories as relived in LSD sessions is an open question. Ever since the first observations of this kind, I have considered it a rather interesting theoretical problem and have tried in each individual case to use all available means to achieve objective verification. It is easy to understand that the circumstances were not always favorable for such an undertaking. Sometimes I encountered poor recollection on the part of the living witnesses (parents, older siblings, acquaintances, family doctors, teachers, servants, maid, etcetera) and lack of objective records. On other occasions, the pertinent witnesses were dead or not available. It was not uncommon that the problems that made verification impossible were of an emotional nature. This was especially true of situations in which the witness supposedly participated in the relived event, and, to verify the recollection, would have had to admit personally or socially objectionable or unacceptable behavior. Occasionally, however, the unusual nature of the memory and specific circumstances made it possible to obtain valid data and to gain some insight into the problem of authenticity of some of the relivings and recollections in LSD sessions.

In such special instances, interviewing the living witnesses, as well as other types of investigations, often revealed the striking accuracy of some of these memories. It became obvious that events from early childhood and even infancy can be re-enacted in LSD sessions with incredible fidelity concerning even the tiniest detail. This could be questioned in cases where the patient took the initiative and collected the necessary evidence himself; one can imagine numerous ways in which the data could be contaminated under these circumstances. Much of the most striking supportive evidence came, however, from situations in which the examination was done by professionals who were systematically and meticulously avoiding any possible suggestive influence on the part of the subjects or witnesses in order to prevent such contamination. The problems and controversies encountered by researchers exploring this area can best be demonstrated by several clinical examples; they were selected from many dozens of similar records accumulated during a decade of psycholytic work done in Prague.

Dana, a patient with rather severe and complicated neurotic symptomatology, relived in one of her LSD sessions a traumatic episode from infancy that she tentatively located at the end of her first year of life. She described in great detail the interior of the room where this event happened to the point of being able to draw the elaborate pattern of embroidery on the bedspread and tablecloth. Dana's mother was independently asked to give her description of the room in question. When confronted with the material from the patient, she was absolutely astonished by the accuracy of the account concerning the traumatic event as well as its physical setting. Like many other parents confronted with such relivings, she found the idea of her daughter's having such reliable access to the circumstances of her early childhood rather startling and embarrassing. It activated in her strong guilt feelings and a tendency to apologetic explanations. She could not understand the mechanism by which this early memory was recovered. The description of the room was photographically accurate, even in the most minute detail, and its authenticity was unquestionable because of the very unusual character of the furniture and some of the objects involved. The room had a mirror of quite extraordinary design, the crucifix on the wall was an unusual piece of work, and the embroidery and furniture had very specific features. In this case, there did not seem to exist a possibility that this information could have been transmitted by some other means. Before the patient was two years old, the family left this house; shortly afterward, it was condemned and torn down. The interior decoration of the room was not part of their new life; Dana's mother gave away many of the things that formed the setting of the relived incident. There were no photographs of the room or of any of the described pieces, and the mother did not remember ever having mentioned any of the objects in front of the patient.

The second example involves a much more controversial memory; in this case, it was not the timing that was so surprising, but rather its content. The nature of the relived material was so improbable that the therapist considered this experience to be an obvious fantasy until additional observations made the issue more complicated.

Eva, a patient undergoing psycholytic therapy because of her numerous neurotic symptoms of a predominantly hysterical nature, relived in one of her LSD sessions a very unusual and dramatic event from her childhood. She related it to a period when she was nine years old. The reconstruction of the original sequence was as follows: She and her brother, who was one year younger, were at that time deeply interested in sexual matters and spent much time discussing the issues of conception, pregnancy, and delivery, as well as the puzzling problem of how a male and female participate in the reproductive process. Since their private inquiries did not seem to lead to any satisfactory conclusions, they decided one day to ask their father for information and an explanation. On hearing the children's request, the father decided that the best way to educate them would be through a practical demonstration. He called his wife into the room and forced her to undress; in spite of her objections and anxious resistance, he performed a demonstration of sexual intercourse in front of the children. During this act, he used a prophylactic; he explained to Eva and her brother its function and advantages. *Post coitum,* he opened the little door of the stove and disposed of the used condom by throwing it into the flames.

Reliving of this event was followed by considerable emotional relief. After integrating this experience, Eva realized that this memory seemed to explain many of her psychopathological symptoms and threw new light on her irrational behavior, in particular in sexual situations. It also clarified her hitherto obscure obsessive-compulsive preoccupation with the stove; on many occasions, she felt a strong urge to sit by it, gaze into the flames, and pick among the coals with a stick as if looking for something.

This event appeared to be highly improbable in spite of the fact that Eva's father was obviously an emotionally disturbed individual. He was a chronic alcoholic with many psychopathic and sadomasochistic features in his behavior. Occasionally, his wife and children had to run away from home or barricade themselves in the attic, because he was chasing them with a knife or hatchet threatening to kill them. These scenes did not remain a family secret; they were so dramatic and noisy that the neighbors became quite involved and irritated by what was happening. They were also appalled by his sadistic treatment of animals, particularly cats; he designed special cat traps, and when he caught a cat, he would nail it to the barn door and let it die in the sun. Even if this was unquestionable evidence of serious psychopathology on the part of the father, the idea of parental intercourse as a means of sexual education appeared too far-fetched to be considered seriously. Also, the knowledge that wild sexual fantasies are common in hysterical patients contributed to the doubts about the authenticity of this experience.

About two years later, Eva's father committed suicide in one of his alcoholic binges. Her younger brother was the first one to discover the corpse, and, with the help of a neighbor, had to carry his father's body out of the house. He reacted to this situation with an acute psychotic breakdown; he felt overwhelmed by panic anxiety and started seeing and hearing the ghost of his dead father. As had been the case in real-life situations, his father was chasing him and threatening to kill him. Driven by inhuman fear, Eva's brother ran away from home and spent many days in the southern part of the country roaming around the lake area and sleeping in the forests. There he was discovered, identified, and admitted to the hospital; he was finally assigned to our experimental LSD program and underwent psycholytic therapy. In one of his sessions, he relived, to the therapist's great surprise, exactly the same incident that his sister had recovered two years earlier. Both accounts were strikingly similar in all details and the timing was exactly the same. All the available information suggested that the incident was repressed in both siblings and that they never discussed this issue before their treatment. Eva had not shared her reliving with her brother, and there was no other exchange of information about her therapy.

Most of the experiences that an LSD subject accepts as actual relivings and not mere symbolic or fantasy products usually appear plausible, or at least possible, to an external observer. Once they are known, such experiences help to clarify the patient's symptoms and explain certain seemingly irrational elements in his or her behavior. The reliving of these events is also accompanied by dramatic changes in the clinical condition. Each of the relived episodes seems to contribute a certain missing link in the psychodynamic understanding of the patient's psychopathological symptoms. The totality of the emerged unconscious material then forms a rather complete gestalt, a more or less satisfying mosaic with a very logical and comprehensive structure. This is not dissimilar to the phenomenon that Sigmund Freud once described as the "jigsaw-puzzle principle" when discussing the logical cohesion of the material obtained in the psychoanalysis of neurotic patients.[6]

In exceptional cases, the relived experiences seem so unusual and have so many improbable features that it is hard to believe that they are authentic memories. According to my experience, the subject usually shares the doubts of the authenticity of such events with the therapist.

One of the most striking examples of this kind were the observations made in the psycholytic treatment of George, a patient with a severe character neurosis who was addicted to a number of analgesics, psychostimulants, and hypnotics. The deviations in his behavior almost bordered on psychosis, and he was repeatedly brought to the hospital in a comatose condition after having overdosed on various drugs. In many consecutive LSD sessions, George reported having relived six different scenes from his childhood in which he witnessed sadistic murders performed by his father on little girls. These

involved in each individual case various complicated modes of ingenious sexual abuse culminating in rape and then in a subsequent
bestial murder. He was able to describe the details of all the settings
in which their murders took place and all the details of the criminal
activities involved. In addition, he relived many scenes depicting all
imaginable kinds of incestuous and perverted sexual activities
between members of his family, nearest relatives, acquaintances, and
servants. In some of these, he was a mere observer, and in others, the
victim of abuse. Although it was highly improbable that these experiences actually took place, the formal aspects and mechanics of these
relivings, as well as the accompanying emotional and motor abreaction, appeared to be indistinguishable from those that were plausible
and had been verified as being authentic in the case of other subjects.
Also the consequences of these relivings for George's clinical condition were similar to those of real memories.

George's attitude toward these experiences oscillated for a long
time between accepting the possibility that his father was a sadistic
murderer and seeing the "relivings" as products of his own fantasy.
When he finally encountered in his sessions the brutality of the
biological birth, he assumed a very critical attitude in regard to the
veracity of these events and offered an alternative psychodynamic
interpretation. His final conclusion was that the "relivings" were
probably products of his desperate resistance against confronting the
birth experiences and a kind of reaction formation delaying their
emergence. In the violent scenes of murder, an adult male (his father)
was killing little girls; in the birth experience that he was reluctant to
face, an adult female (his mother) was killing a little boy (George).
The brutal and bloody character of the birth was maintained and
replicated in the fantasies of murder. As a result of effective defenses
against experiencing the vital threat of the birth trauma, the sex of
the protagonists was reversed, and George's role changed from the
victim to the observer. At this point, George realized that the content
of the "relivings" also satisfied his need for revenge on the female
element for the agony inflicted during the delivery. He felt that
similar psychodynamic mechanisms and motivating forces might
operate in cases of actual sadistic murders.

Having been repeatedly confronted with observations of this
sort, I realized that I was facing a modern replica of the old
problem of the objective reality of memories recovered during

psychoanalysis. Freud, in his early studies, found that each of his hysterical patients had a history of sexual seduction in childhood; he postulated that such a trauma represents the major etiological factor in the development of hysterical neurosis.[5] When he later collected sufficient evidence indicating that some of the alleged seductions or rapes obviously happened only in the fantasy of his patients, he was at first so discouraged that he almost gave up further psychoanalytic investigations. He transcended this problem when he realized that these phenomena represent a psychic reality for the patient without regard to their objective historical reality. We can follow Freud's example in regard to the relivings in LSD sessions; whether they are real memories or vivid fantasies derived from sources and created by mechanisms not sufficiently understood at present, they seem to be very relevant from the point of view of the patient's psychopathology, as well as the psychodynamics of LSD psychotherapy.

The reliving of childhood experiences accompanied by powerful emotional abreaction is a frequent and regular occurrence in LSD psychotherapy. This phenomenon has been reported by many therapists in various parts of the world. Even though the final reliving usually has the form of a single traumatic event that the subject locates in childhood or infancy, systematic observations of a number of consecutive sessions show that the situation is much more complicated. There are several clinical facts that seem to support the concept of the COEX systems as described above, according to which these childhood experiences represent the cores or deepest layers of complex memory constellations that function as governing dynamic systems.

First, it is the intensity of the emotional charge that has to be abreacted before the individual childhood memories can be fully relived. The amount of released emotions seems to be out of proportion to the severity and relevance of the traumatic events involved. There appears to be a considerable discrepancy between the "cause and effect" even if we take into consideration the biological, physiological, and psychological specificity of the early developmental stages and high vulnerability of the child's psyche. It makes more sense to see the emotional charge involved as a summation product that resulted from a number of similar traumatic situations from different periods of life.

Second, the reliving of traumatic childhood experiences is often followed by far-reaching changes in the clinical symptomatology, behavior patterns, values, and attitudes. The powerful transforming effect of the reliving and integration of such memories suggests that a more general dynamic principle is involved.

The third and most important reason for thinking in terms of memory constellations rather than individual memories is based on the content analysis of consecutive sessions of a psycholytic series. Before the subject can approach and relive a traumatic memory from early childhood (core experience), he usually has to face and work through many situations from later life that have a similar theme and involve the same basic elements. All these traumatic situations from different life periods are associated with emotions of the same quality and with identical defense mechanisms. Their reliving is accompanied by the same typical cluster of somatic symptoms, such as headache, nausea and vomiting, pains in various parts of the body, suffocation, muscular spasms, shaking, and tremors. One or several of these physical manifestations can occur as constant and repetitive concomitants of the content of various layers of a particular COEX system. An interesting observation from psycholytic therapy should be mentioned in this connection. In some subjects, certain organs of the body assume a very special role during the LSD procedure. For insufficiently understood reasons, these organs seem to have attracted and accumulated tensions originating in the organism in response to a number of traumatic situations during various stages of individual development. In the course of psycholytic therapy, the reverse process seems to occur, namely, the consecutive discharge of tensions of different origin from these target organs. The parts of the body most frequently involved in this process are the muscles, cardiovascular system, bowels, and the urogenital apparatus.

As mentioned above, COEX systems appear to be of fundamental significance for the understanding of LSD sessions with psychodynamic content. In addition, because of the nonspecific action of LSD, the knowledge of these systems derived from LSD research is directly applicable to the dynamics of the unconscious under nondrug conditions and to the functioning of the human personality in health and illness. It seems, therefore, appropriate to use the material from LSD psychotherapy and make an attempt to speculate about the origin of these systems and to reconstruct their dynamics.

The most important part of the COEX systems seems to be the core experience. It was the first experience of a particular kind that was registered in the brain and laid the foundations for a specific COEX system. The core experience, thus, represents a prototype, a matrix pattern, for the recording of subsequent events of a similar kind in the memory banks. It is not easy to explain why certain kinds of events have such a powerful traumatic effect on the child that they influence his psychodynamic development for many years or decades. Psychoanalysts have usually thought in this connection about constitutional and hereditary factors of an unknown nature. LSD research seems to indicate that this specific sensitivity can have important determinants in deeper levels of the unconscious, in functional dynamic matrices that are inborn and transpersonal in nature. Some of these factors, when brought to consciousness in LSD psychotherapy, have the form of ancestral, racial, or phylogenetic memories, archetypal structures, or even past-incarnation experiences. Another important fact might be the dynamic similarity between a particular traumatic incident in childhood and a certain facet of the birth trauma (or perinatal traumatization). In this case, the traumatic impact of a later situation would actually be due to the reactivation of a certain aspect of the psychobiological memory of the birth. The discussions of the transpersonal and perinatal factors would be premature before the corresponding levels of the unconscious have been described in the context of LSD psychotherapy. We will return to some of these questions in the following sections of this book.

In this context, we will limit our discussion to factors operating on the psychodynamic level. From this point of view, a variable of possible importance might be the existence of certain critical periods in the development of the child, comparable to those revealed in animals by ethological observations and experiments. In a specific critical period, the child could be especially vulnerable to experiences of a particular kind that would have little or no influence in a later or earlier developmental stage.

A factor that seems to be of paramount importance is the emotional atmosphere in the family and the interpersonal relations between its members. A single traumatic event can be of great pathogenic significance when it occurs against the background of a specific dysfunctional family structure. It also seems, however, that everyday pathogenic interaction with other members of the family, lasting for many months and years, can be continuously registered in the memory banks, summed up in a condensed way, and finally constitute a pathological focus which is comparable to that resulting from a macrotrauma. The core experience relived in LSD sessions represents in the latter case a sort of *pars pro toto* experience (one single experience representing the totality of similar events). It is interesting that patients themselves can usually identify the generalizing quality of such experiences even when they emerge during LSD sessions in the form of an allegedly single traumatic event.

Through a combination of the above factors (and possibly other variables that are unknown at the present time), a certain event in the child's life becomes the core of a COEX system. Once the core experience is imprinted, it serves as a memory matrix, and later similar experiences are recorded in close connection with the original event. This repeated apposition of additional layers can finally result in the specific dynamic memory constellation that I refer to as the COEX system. The formation of the peripheral layers can evidently involve two different dynamic mechanisms. Sometimes the addition of new memories occurs in a rather mechanical way. Life can bring forth important emotional experiences that, in one way or another, resemble the core experience. Because of the analytic and synthetic work of the memory, these experiences are included into COEX systems on the basis of identical components or general similarity. Detailed analysis of the records from psycholytic therapy suggests, however, that a much more important dynamic mechanism is involved. In the earliest stages of development, the child is a more or less passive victim of the environment and usually has no active role in the core experiences that would be worth consideration. Later on, this situation changes, and the individual gradually becomes more and more instrumental in structuring his interpersonal relations and his general life experiences. Once the foundations of a COEX system are laid, they seem to influence the subject in regard to his perception of the environment, his experiencing of the world, his attitudes, and his behavior. Under the influence of the core experience, he develops strong specific expectations and generalized anticipations toward certain categories of people and certain situations. These follow the general pattern of the core experience and can be logically derived from its particular content. As a result of an early traumatic event or repetitive experience, the child can, for example, develop a strong feeling that people generally cannot be trusted; in such a situation, one is constantly on guard, and each new person is considered to be a potential enemy or aggressor. Another type of traumatic experience can create a conviction that emotional involvement brings about a great risk of disappointment and emotional injury, and that it is a weakness that should be avoided at all costs. Similarly, a specific childhood experience may make the individual feel that sexual experiences are dangerous, revolting, or humiliating. Sometimes such convictions reach a high degree of generalization; because of certain negative childhood experiences, a man may consider all women weak and unreliable; capricious, irrational, and erratic; or lascivious and seductive. Similarly, a woman may see all men as basically brutal and sadistic; dominated by low instinctual drives in their sexual life; or essentially promiscuous and unfaithful. Such *a priori* attitudes and expectations result in specific maladjustive behavior of the subject toward all new persons of a certain category encountered later in life. These persons will be treated in the modality dictated by the nature of the pertinent core experience (or COEX system). The subject perceives such individuals as symbolic representatives of the group to which his unconscious has assigned them, and he approaches and treats them accordingly. As a result of this, he is not able to form new interpersonal relationships in an effective and adaptive way conducive to realistic and satisfactory interaction. A healthy assimilation of new figures into one's interpersonal world requires the ability to assume a relatively neutral, tentative, and expectant attitude until mutual contact and interpersonal interaction with them provides enough feedback information to allow for a realistic assessment. With increasing amounts of concrete information, the nature of a developing relationship then gradually tips to the positive or negative side depending on the actual experience with a particular interpersonal partner. The individual capable of approaching new human situations in this way has a reasonable chance of treating other people not only in terms of whom and what they represent to him but also in terms of who they really are. A person whose new human encounters are contaminated by the influence of strong negative COEX systems enters new relationships heavily biased. Because of the reciprocal nature of human relationships, the behavior patterns based on strong *a priori* attitudes evoke in the interpersonal and social environment specific complementary counterreactions. The resulting constellation then represents an approximate replica of the original situation of the core experience.

This can be demonstrated in the examples previously described. Under the influence of his strong COEX system, Peter actively searched for sadistic persons of a certain kind and initiated interaction with them. He was thus instrumental in creating situations that represented repetitions of the original traumatic events from his childhood constituting the core experience of the same system. Renata was obviously a predominantly passive victim in the nuclear traumatic situation; although she might have contributed to it by her childish coquetry and seductiveness, it was her stepfather who played a major role in setting the pattern. In her later life, however, she unconsciously structured her relationships with men according to the old pattern and played a very active and important role in its many subsequent traumatic repetitions. The unusual accumulation of sexual assaults and attempts at rape is certainly far beyond any statistical probability and strongly indicates that her contribution to these scenes of sexual traumatization was essential. In Richard's case, the powerful COEX system described above not only blocked his activity and ability to assert and defend himself in an effective way but also resulted in specific behavior that drew the hostility of the outside world. During his university studies, for example, he attracted the attention of the authorities by his attitudes and became a scapegoat in a situation in which many of his colleagues, who basically shared his political opinion, managed to survive without joining the system, collaborating, or compromising themselves.

A core experience can thus be followed in later life by many accidental or self-inflicted situations of a similar kind. This continuous activation and reinforcement of the original pathogenic constellation by many interactions in later life can perhaps explain the intensity of the emotional charge attached to individual COEX systems. This mechanism could also account for the strong effect that these systems have in terms of influencing a person's behavior and for the frequently dramatic therapeutic effects following their reduction, abreaction, and integration.

The principle of summation of emotional charges attached to various layers of the COEX system is only one explanation for the enormous amount of affective energy that usually has to be discharged before the core experience is recovered and the system extinguished and integrated. Another powerful source of energy can be found in the underlying perinatal matrices. The similarity between the birth experience and certain traumatic events in later life could perhaps allow for a discharge of deep emotional and instinctual energies bound to this most fundamental trauma in human life at a time when a COEX system emerges in the LSD session (see the chapter "Perinatal Experiences in LSD Sessions").

The gradual successive growth of COEX systems by the mechanism of positive feedback* described could account for the latency or "incubation" period between the original traumatic events and future neurotic or even psychotic breakdowns. Manifest psychopathological symptoms seem to occur at a time when the COEX system reaches a certain critical extension, and traumatic repetitions contaminate important areas of the patient's life and interfere with the satisfaction of his basic needs. This

---

*The term "positive feedback" is used here in the cybernetic sense, not in the way it is frequently used in individual or group psychotherapy. The interpersonal feedback that the individual receives in human situations that are influenced by a strong COEX system tends to increase the original error and deviation from the norm rather than correct it.

concept is in full agreement with numerous observations from psycholytic therapy of psychiatric patients. Detailed analysis of the dynamics of their symptoms reveals deep parallels between the content of the core experiences of their COEX systems and patterns of their interpersonal interaction at the time of the onset of clinical symptomatology. In many instances, multiple repetitions of the basic themes of one or more COEX systems in important segments of the interpersonal field seem to precede immediately the first manifestation of the emotional or psychosomatic disorder. In addition, the symptoms themselves can frequently be understood as a symbolic enactment of the core experience. This can best be illustrated in the case of Renata. The beginning of her cancerophobia coincided with the attempts at rape by her husband and several of her coworkers and with a gynecological examination that indicated that her genital organs were impaired (cervical ulceration). As previously described, her cancerophobia and the symptomatic behavior involved were symbolically related to the core experience.

Manifestation of COEX Systems in LSD Sessions

The activation of a strong negative COEX system in an LSD session and its emergence into the experiential field has typical consequences for the content and course of this session. The previously continuous flow of images, emotions, ideas, and body sensations is suddenly disturbed, and their inner consistency and mutual congruence are disrupted. This is accompanied by certain typical phenomena that can be considered heralds of an emerging COEX system.

The visions experienced in this state become confused, disconnected, and fragmented. Subjects frequently liken them to a flood or whirlpool; they refer to such experiences as "sensory goulash," "merry-go-round," or simply chaos. However, it is possible to differentiate in this amorphous mixture fragments of human or animal bodies, portions of a landscape, pieces of furniture, children's toys, or various other objects from everyday life. This condition is often compared to a delirium or to a wild,

Two pictures representing the visions that accompany the emerging of a child-hood memory in an LSD session of the psychodynamic type. The chaotic mosaic consists of elements of the original traumatic event and of various symbolic variations on its basic theme.

feverish nightmare. Later, when the core experience is relived and its content clearly recognized, some of the sensory fragments can be retrospectively identified as elements of the original traumatic memory from childhood and others as symbolic and metaphorical variations on its basic theme.

Another typical indicator of an emerging COEX system is dissociation between affect and content. Many aspects of LSD experiences of this kind appear at first completely absurd and incomprehensible and can be understood only retrospectively after the whole system is known. Thus, for example, the vision of a trivial object, such as a water tap, a jug, a chair, an innocent doll, or a nice piece of embroidery, can be associated with panic anxiety, aggressive outbursts, sexual excitement, suicidal depression, or disgust accompanied by severe nausea and vomiting. Later reconstruction usually shows that this seemingly absurd and paradoxical connection has its intrinsic logic after all. Once the core experience is fully available, it becomes clear that the quality of the emotional reaction is consistent with the nature of the original trauma. The association between the affect and various trivial objects reflects the fact that the latter formed an integral part of the setting in which the traumatic event took place.

Unmotivated and unexplainable mood qualities of great intensity are also indicative of surfacing COEX systems. Panic anxiety; severe depression, often occurring with suicidal ideation; feelings of isolation and loneliness; intense disgust; irrational guilt or inferiority feelings; childlike helplessness; feelings of moral and physical depravity; strong sexual excitement; caustic self-hatred, or general aggressive tension; all such initially incomprehensible emotions can be later identified as logical and integral parts of the pertinent COEX systems.

Dramatic physical and motor manifestations frequently anticipate an emerging COEX system. Some of these somatic symptoms suggest a strong activation of the autonomic nervous system; these involve nausea and vomiting, breathing difficulties, various cardiovascular complaints, profuse salivation or sweating, and sudden diarrhea. Very common are sensations of intense pain in different parts of the body, such as the head, neck muscles, stomach, bowels, urinary bladder, uterus, and testicles. Typical motor manifestations that belong to this category include generalized or localized muscular tension, tremors, jerks, shaking and twitches, complicated twisting movements, and catatoniform excitement or stupor. It seems that repetitive and stereotypical movements and particularly verbal manifestations (verbigerations) have a very high indicative value. Before the elements of a strong COEX system start emerging into consciousness, the patient may incessantly repeat the same words or sentences. This repetition usually has a very mechanical quality suggestive of a loop on a tape-recorder. The above description includes all the somatic symptoms that have been observed on various occasions to be concomitants of emerging traumatic experiences. In practical therapeutic situations, all of these are never simultaneously present in relation to one particular COEX system. In some instances, one of them will occur as an indicator; more commonly, they appear in typical clusters.

It seems to be more than coincidence that all the phenomena that function as heralds of emerging COEX systems are experienced with extreme intensity in the sessions in which subjects are reliving the birth trauma. It is likely that the complex of sensations and innervations associated with the birth process is the deepest matrix for these manifestations.

For the time period during which elements of a COEX system are emerging into consciousness and dominate the experiential field, this system assumes a governing function and determines the nature and content of the LSD session. The subject's perception of himself and of the environment is distorted and transformed in the direction of the basic motif and the specific components of the emerging COEX constellation. The illusive transformations of the persons present in the sessions frequently reflect the protagonists in the relived experiences, and specific changes of the treatment room or physical environment are related to the setting in which the incident took place. They can also represent symbolic variations on the general theme, persons, and scenery involved. The governing function of the unfolding COEX system is not, however, limited to perceptual changes. The general emotional atmosphere and specific mood qualities, the nature and context of the thought processes, the reaction to the environment, and the individual's behavior are also characteristically influenced. The determining function of activated COEX systems for the content of LSD sessions can be shown in the case material discussed earlier.

When Peter was working through the most superficial layers of the described COEX system, he saw the therapist transformed into his past sadistic partners or into figures symbolizing aggression, such as a butcher, murderer, medieval executioner, Inquisitor, or cowboy with a lasso. He perceived the therapist's fountain pen as an Oriental dagger and expected to be attacked with it. When he saw on the table a knife with a staghorn handle used for opening envelopes, he immediately saw the therapist changing into a violent-looking forester. On several occasions he asked to be tortured and wanted to suffer "for the doctor" by withholding urination. In this period the treatment room and view from the window were illusively transformed into various settings where the patient's adventures with his sadistic partners took place. When the older layer from World War II was dealt with, the therapist was seen as Hitler and other Nazi leaders, concentration-camp commanders, SS members, and Gestapo officers. Instead of ordinary noises, Peter heard the ominous sounds of soldiers' boots in the corridor, music of the fascist parades by the Brandenburg Gate, and the national anthems of Nazi Germany. The treatment room was successively transformed into a room in the Reichstag with eagle emblems and swastikas, a barrack in a concentration camp, a jail with heavy bars in the window, and even a death cell. When the core experiences from childhood were emerging in these sessions, the therapist was perceived as punishing parental figures; Peter tended to display toward him various anachronistic behavior patterns characteristic of his relationship with his father and mother. The treatment room was frequently turning into various parts of his home setting in childhood, particularly into the dark cellar in which he was repeatedly locked up by his mother.

Similar dynamics were observed in the LSD sessions of Renata. When she was working on the most superficial layers of the described COEX system, the face of the therapist on several occasions was transformed into that of her husband. She suspected that he, like her husband, harbored aggressive feelings toward her and that he was seriously tempted to use physical violence against her. Occasionally, she hallucinated a lecherous expression on the therapist's face and expected to be sexually attacked by him. In the transference relationship, she displayed attitudes typical of her matrimonial situation. When she was reliving the layer related to her postadolescence, the therapist was successively transformed into various boy friends from that time. The environment was perceived as the locations where she dated these individuals, such as public parks, a school dormitory, and specific places in the countryside. At a time when the core experience of her COEX system was being uncovered in the sessions, the therapist assumed the characteristics of her stepfather—his facial expression and gigantic hairy hands covered with pigmented spots. He appeared to be clad in the suit, shirt, and tie that her stepfather used to wear. On another occasion, the therapist appeared transformed into a famous Czech sadistic murderer of children. The elements of the core experience also strongly influenced the transference relationship. Renata alternately experienced panic anxiety with expectations of an aggressive sexual assault from the therapist, and an excessive sexual drive with a tendency to attack him. There was a very strong oral emphasis in her sexual urges, and she was preoccupied with the idea of carrying out fellatio. Most of the other phenomena in these sessions could be explained as symbolic representations of or allusions to the core experience. On occasions, the stepfather appeared in the form of a dangerous animal, such as a python or terrifying giant lizard. There were also many scenes depicting abuse of children and sexual violence, as well as allusions to movies, plays, and books with these themes, such as John Knittel's *Via Mala* or Friedrich Dürrenmatt's *Pledge*. Another interesting phenomenon in these sessions was a recurrent vision of a tower in various stages of collapse and destruction. According to Renata's descriptions, these functioned as an indicator or barometer of the therapeutic progress. In addition to having a complex multilevel and overdetermined symbolic meaning, they also reflected the gradual changes in the patient's defense system and the degree of her resistance to facing the core experience. Because of their highly illustrative nature, these drawings are reproduced in full in this book.

When Richard was working through the most recent layers of his COEX system, related to his political persecution, the red chair in the room was transformed into an insatiable terrifying monster with an open mouth threatening to devour him; it symbolized for him the "red terror" he had been exposed to in his life. A picture on the wall changed into a poster the Nazi propagandists had disseminated in Czechoslovakia during World War II as a warning against the perils of Soviet expansion. It showed a giant red hand with ominous claws descending on the Prague castle. It bore the inscription "If it grabs you, you will perish." The chief transference problem at this time was Richard's suspicion that the therapist might be a member of the Communist party, and he had doubts whether the therapist could be trusted. Before reliving the experience of being shocked by electric current, Richard saw the therapist as a large science-fiction robot made up of a complicated system of condensers, transformers, solenoids, relays, and cables. Electrical sparks indicating high voltage scintillated on this robot's surface, and a flashing red light on his head signaled immediate danger. Richard was afraid an electrical discharge would emanate from the therapist's body and strike him; he also manifested an intense fear of light bulbs, electrical sockets, plugs, and electrical appliances in the room. In the sessions in which Richard was working through his traumatic experiences with his father, he suspected that the therapist was drunk; he also saw him transformed into various characters, including chronic alcoholics, a tramp, or a bum, and eventually into the image of his own alcoholic father. He expected rejection, neglect, cruelty, and maltreatment from the therapist. While approaching the core experience, Richard perceived the therapist as a farmer; the setting looked rustic, and sounds and smells reminded him of a hot summer day in the fields.

Another interesting observation concerning the manifestation of COEX systems in LSD sessions should be mentioned in this connection. Whenever the traumatic event involves an interpersonal situation, it seems that the subject, while reliving it under LSD, has to experience and work through the roles of all the persons involved. Thus, if the basic theme represents an aggressive assault against him, he must relive both the role of the victim, with all the emotional and physical feelings involved, and that of the aggressor.* If the subject happened to be the observer of such a scene, he would eventually experience all

---

*This situation is a psychodramatic pictorial analogue of what Anna Freud described in her *The Ego and the Mechanisms of Defense* as identification with the aggressor.[4]

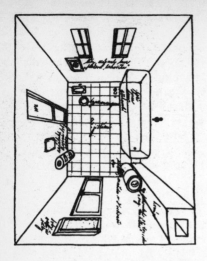

Renata's drawing showing a bird's-eye view of the bathroom where the traumatic event took place.

A series of drawings illustrating the progress of Renata's LSD therapy and various stages of her working through the traumatic material from childhood.

(a) The vision of a tower that Renata had in one of her LSD sessions when she approached the event in the bathroom for the first time. The walls of the tower represent her defenses, which prevent her from identifying the traumatic event. As the inscriptions indicate, the tower is made of anxiety, the event in the bathroom is situated inside the tower; and the arrows represent the attacks of LSD.

(b) Vision of the same tower in a later LSD session. The attacks have already damaged the walls considerably, but the tower has been repaired with iron plates. One spot where an arrow penetrated inside the tower has been covered with crossed strips of adhesive bandage. (This is an ambiguous symbol, since it simultaneously depicts a part of the original traumatic scene— the red cross on the little first-aid box hanging on the wall of the bathroom.)

(c) The vision that Renata had immediately after a deep immersion into the reliving of the traumatic memory. The tower is collapsing; the blood flowing from the cracks between the stones is related to the killing of the goose and to bleeding associated with the digital defloration of Renata by her step-father.

(d) This vision immediately followed the experience described in (c). On the left side is the family house with the bathroom in the attic. The high stack of the factory bends over the street and touches the small chimney of the house. In the same visual field there is a target with the bull's-eye hit. ("That's it, here we are.") Renata discovered by herself the sexual symbolism of this vision.

(e) In one of the following LSD sessions the tower appeared as a ruin of a monument. Grass and trees growing in the ruins represent the prospect of new life. The memorial tablet on the monument functions also as a television screen, on which the event from the bathroom can be seen with great accuracy.

(f) Full reliving of the traumatic event resulting in a temporary ego disintegration. This was symbolized by the vision of a gigantic explosion in which both the tower and Renata were torn to pieces.

(g) This picture represents the scene that immediately followed the total destruction. The therapist appeared, gently assembled the pieces of Renata's body, and put them together. While he was holding her in his arms, a large rainbow appeared as a symbol of hope and optimism for the future.

(h) In a picture from one of the following LSD sessions, only a few stones of the original tower are left. They are arranged in a circle and surround a fireplace. A new, much smaller tower appeared, symbolizing the reinstitution of defenses on a lower level.

(i) An experience immediately following that shown in the preceding picture. Renata is sitting by the fireplace as a savage woman broiling and devouring the therapist. The licking of his femur has a symbolic meaning and points to the fellatio of the original scene. Surprised by her own brazenness, Renata drew for comparison a scene symbolizing her attitude to the therapist a year before this session.

(j) A picture showing further development and modification of the small tower; it has acquired a spiral staircase and has changed into an observation tower. From the top Renata can now see accurately what happened in the bathroom. At the same time she can perceive things from a much broader perspective, since her horizon has widened considerably.

(k) During one of the following sessions, a burrow in the ground appeared on the site of the original tower. Its appearance coincided with the process of transformation of anxiety into libidinal feelings and with Renata's discovery of her femininity.

(l) In a later vision, the burrow appeared deepened and broadened; the soldier's helmet inside it symbolized Renata's marriage and some past traumatic experiences.

(m) A picture showing further development of the burrow; it has now changed into a rotating spiral formation ("screw") penetrating deeper into the earth. Renata recognized by herself the sexual meaning of this vision.

(n) This is the last vision of the "tower series." The originally solid structure reappears as a fata morgana, a mirage on a hot desert. The scorching heat symbolizes Renata's liberated libido; the bottom of the tower (Tour Eiffel in Paris) suggests oral-genital contact (French love), which at this point dominated Renata's fantasies and daydreams.

three roles involved. So, for example, full reliving of the typical Freudian "primal scene"—that is, the situation of a child witnessing sexual intercourse between his parents—involves successive identification with the role of the aggressive male, the victimized female, and the observer.

Dynamic Interaction between the COEX Systems and Environmental Stimuli

Detailed study of the content and dynamics of individual LSD sessions within a psycholytic series, as well as long-term analysis of the changes in the patient's clinical symptomatology and life situation in the free intervals between the sessions, reveal very intricate interrelations between the COEX systems and environmental factors. These observations seem to be of such basic relevance that they deserve special notice. The preceding section described how a COEX system activated in an LSD session determines the nature of the patient's experience and the way in which he perceives the environment. This is quite regularly associated with a strong tendency to exteriorize the content of a particular layer of the COEX constellation, act it out in the treatment situation, and shape the actual circumstances of the session according to the basic theme involved. If we analyze the dynamics of this phenomenon, we find a very interesting underlying mechanism. It is apparently very difficult and disturbing to perceive a deep incongruence between one's inner feelings and sensations and events in the external world. It seems much more acceptable to experience various unpleasant emotions as being an appropriate reaction to actual circumstances existing at present in objective reality than to perceive them as incomprehensible and unexplainable elements coming from within. An LSD subject tortured in the session by otherwise irrational guilt feelings can thus tend to attack the therapist, offend him, behave in a way that he himself considers utterly inappropriate, or break some basic rules of therapy. The guilt feelings can then be attached to the actual happenings in the here and now and appear adequate and congruent with the situation. Similarly, feelings of anxiety and awareness of a serious threat originating in the unconscious can result in maneuvers aimed at provoking hostility in the therapist. Incomprehensible feelings of anxiety then assume the form of concrete and familiar fears, such as that of losing the therapist's support and endangering the continuation of therapy. Since these artificially created situations are usually less relevant than the original traumatic events, the tendency to exteriorize the COEX systems can represent a very effective defense mechanism against the emerging unconscious material. This tendency can be exemplified by an incident from the psycholytic therapy of Renata, whose case history was presented earlier.

In several consecutive LSD sessions, Renata insisted on leaving the treatment room whenever she felt nauseated and was afraid she would vomit, in spite of the fact that several emetic basins were available by the couch. The therapist soon became aware that this behavior involved some unusual defense mechanisms, and the issue was openly discussed. Renata explained that she was doing this to protect the therapeutic relationship, which was essential for the continuation of her treatment. She felt that the therapist would be utterly disgusted with her if he had to witness such a "repulsive" act as vomiting, and he might even consider termination of LSD therapy. She was reassured that vomiting was a rather common occurrence in the sessions and that the therapist had assisted many patients in such situations without feeling uncomfortable. It was emphasized that it was important for her to confront this situation and that abreactive vomiting under LSD frequently has very therapeutic consequences. Her previous approach was then clearly labeled as resistance and unconscious "sabotage" of the treatment progress. In the first LSD session following this discussion, Renata was able to vomit into the emetic vessel with help, encouragement, and positive emotional feedback from the therapist. This was accompanied by full reliving of a humiliating scene from childhood in which she was violently sick while riding in a bus with her mother; she vomited profusely and soiled the clothes of a passenger in the adjacent seat. Her mother was terribly embarrassed and upset, made a big drama out of this incident, and later frequently reminded Renata of this "shameful and shocking" event and of her "impossible" behavior.

The tendency to exteriorize unconscious material can be unusually strong and may create difficult and demanding situations for the therapist. Since the patient often exerts an enormous effort to drive him into various roles corresponding to the theme of the COEX system, these situations can represent a real challenge from the point of view of transference-countertransference dynamics. It is absolutely essential for successful continuation of therapy that the therapist not allow himself to be manipulated into roles that replicate the traumatic elements of the original situations. He has to meet a difficult task of being deeply involved in the process and providing genuine human support and yet maintaining the therapeutic role that allows him to be sufficiently detached to recognize these exteriorizing maneuvers, interpret them, and approach the patient in a way conducive to a corrective emotional experience.

The mechanism described above has its dynamic counterpart; it is the tendency of external stimuli to activate corresponding COEX systems and facilitate their manifestation in the sessions. This happens in those instances where specific external influences, such as elements of the physical setting, interpersonal environment, or therapeutic situation, bear a resemblance to the original traumatic scenes or contain identical components. This seems to be the cue for understanding the extraordinary significance of various extrapharmacological factors for the dynamics of LSD sessions. The physical and interpersonal milieu, the behavior of the therapist or other persons present in the session, and even various accidental events during the session can have a far-reaching influence on its content, course, and outcome. The activation of a COEX system by specific external stimuli accidentally introduced into the therapeutic situation can be illustrated by a sequence from an LSD session of Peter, whose condensed case history was given earlier.

One of the important core experiences that Peter uncovered in his LSD therapy was a memory of being locked by his mother in a dark cellar and denied food while the other members of the family were feasting. The reliving of this memory was triggered quite unexpectedly by the angry barking of a dog that ran by the open window of the treatment room. The analysis of this event showed an interesting relationship between the external stimulus and the activated memory. Peter recalled that the cellar his mother used for punishment had a small window overlooking the neighbor's courtyard; the neighbor's German shepherd, chained to his doghouse, barked almost incessantly on the occasions when Peter was confined in the cellar.

People in LSD psychotherapy often manifest seemingly inappropriate and highly exaggerated reactions to various environmental stimuli; such overreacting is specific and selective and can be usually understood in terms of the dynamics of the governing COEX systems. Thus, patients are particularly sensitive to what they consider uninterested, cold, and "professional" treatment when they are under the influence of memory constellations that involve emotional deprivation, rejection, or neglect by their parents or other relevant figures in their childhood. When they are working through the problems of rivalry with their siblings, patients attempt to monopolize the therapist and want to be the only or at least the favorite patient. They find it difficult to accept that the therapist has other patients, and they can be extremely irritated by any sign of interest paid to somebody else. Patients who on other occasions do not mind or even wish to be left alone during a session cannot bear the therapist to leave the room for any reason when they are tapping the memories related to childhood loneliness.

Another important dynamic mechanism must be mentioned in this connection; it is of crucial significance for the understanding of various complications of LSD treatment, especially prolonged reactions and so-called "flashbacks." When a strong COEX system is activated in an LSD session but not resolved by the reliving of the core experience, the subject can stay under its influence for an indefinite period of time following the session. In this case, the two-sided dynamic interaction that was described earlier can also be observed outside the session context. Such a subject experiences intensification of the clinical symptoms related to this system and perceives the environment as distorted in a specific way. In addition, he may manifest a tendency to exteriorize the general theme of the system or its elements in various sectors of his everyday life. He may overreact to certain situations and be selectively oversensitive to certain circumstances. His behavior can involve complicated psychological maneuvers that tend to provoke specific reciprocal attitudes in his interpersonal partners. The resulting situation can then be an approximate replica of the traumatic event that remained repressed and unresolved in the previous session. The observation of such dynamic interrelations led to the formulation of the hypothesis concerning the origin and dynamics of COEX systems described earlier. They were important for the recognition of the self-reinforcing nature of these systems and the concept of the apposition of new layers in different periods of the individual's life through the mechanism of "self-fulfilling prophecy."

The foregoing discussion has focused specifically on negative COEX systems; however, similar dynamics can be demonstrated to exist in the case of positive ones. This has important implications for the technique of LSD psychotherapy and for the integration of therapeutic changes. The introduction of positive elements into the set and setting of LSD sessions tends to facilitate the emergence of positive COEX systems. This can be a theoretical explanation and justification of the importance of such variables as the factor of trust in the relationship with the therapist; an aesthetically pleasing, safe, and comfortable setting; the playing of peaceful music toward the end of the session; the use of physical contact; and exposure to a beautiful natural environment. These elements are frequent components of spontaneously emerging positive COEX constellations; conversely, when they are introduced into LSD sessions, they tend to facilitate the occurrence of positive experiences. A person who is under the influence of a positive COEX system during the terminating period of an LSD session usually radiates on the following days a sense of optimism about life and perceives the world and other people as predominantly good and friendly. This new, more open and sincere approach to people in the individual's social network usually evokes reciprocal responses of a similar nature and creates a basis for a gradual positive reformulation of interpersonal relationships.

Serial psychodynamic LSD sessions can be viewed as a process of gradual unfolding, abreaction, and integration of various levels of negative COEX systems and opening the pathways for the influence of positive ones. An emerging COEX system assumes a governing influence on all the aspects of the experience. Elements of a particular COEX constellation keep appearing in the sessions until the oldest memory, the core experience, is relived and integrated. Following this, such a system permanently loses its governing function and its derivatives never reappear in subsequent LSD sessions. Afterward, another system takes over and dominates the experiential field. Frequently, various levels of two or more COEX systems alternate in their governing function in a particular session or sequence of sessions.

LSD sessions seem to cause profound changes in the dynamics and mutual interrelations of COEX systems and to initiate dramatic shifts in their selective influence on the subject's ego. Understanding of this process is essential for psychotherapeutic work with LSD on the psychodynamic level. The applications of this concept in the clinical use of LSD will be discussed in a forthcoming book focusing predominantly on the practice of LSD psychotherapy; in this context, the clinical implications will be only briefly outlined.

It has already been mentioned that an individual LSD session can result in the activation of a particular COEX system. If the unconscious material is not worked through, the subject may remain under the influence of this system after the session in spite of the fact that the effect of the drug has already worn off. On other occasions, the resolution may be incomplete and result in a precarious emotional balance; in such cases, various factors that weaken the defense system, such as sleep deprivation, exhaustion, fasting, alcohol, marijuana, or physical disease, may at a later time disturb this equilibrium and cause a temporary reemergence of the unresolved unconscious material. This balance can also be disturbed by emotional stress, especially when the problems involved are of a similar nature to those that remained unresolved in the last session. This constitutes the mechanism of belated reoccurrences of LSD-like experiences, popularly referred to as "flashbacks." If, on the contrary, the reliving of an important COEX system is completed toward the end of the session and no other negative system takes over, the termination period has the form of a highly positive, tension-free experience. When this happens earlier in the session, a positive COEX system may dominate the experiential field, and the individual will relive sequences of positive memories from his life. In the latter two instances, the postsession interval is usually characterized by a striking clinical improvement. In some of the sessions, a "COEX transmodulation" can be observed, namely, a shift from the hegemony of one negative system to that of another. This can result in a remarkable qualitative change of the clinical symptomatology; occasionally, this transformation can be so dramatic that the patient moves into a completely different diagnostic category.

The time period necessary for the resolution of different COEX systems shows enormous inter- and intraindividual variability. Sometimes a less important and rather circumscribed COEX system can be reduced, relived, and integrated in a single session. Usually, this process takes a greater number of sessions, especially in severely disturbed psychiatric patients. In exceptional cases, a very strong, extensive, and ramified system can govern the experiential field in as many as fifteen or twenty consecutive LSD sessions. Comparable variability exists in regard to the total amount of psychodynamic material that has to be experienced and integrated in serial LSD sessions. In some of the subjects, the Freudian problems prevail in many consecutive sessions; others move relatively quickly to deeper levels of the unconscious. However, whatever the time or number of sessions required for this development, sooner or later the elements of the individual unconscious tend to disappear from the LSD experience and each individual undergoing psycholytic therapy enters the realms of the perinatal and transpersonal phenomena that will be described in the following chapters.

4 Perinatal Experiences in LSD Sessions

The basic characteristics of perinatal experiences and their central focus are the problems of biological birth, physical pain and agony, aging, disease and decrepitude, and dying and death. Inevitably, the shattering encounter with these critical aspects of human existence and the deep realization of the frailty and impermanence of man as a biological creature is accompanied by an agonizing existentialist crisis. The individual comes to realize, through these experiences, that no matter what he does in his life, he cannot escape the inevitable: he will have to leave this world bereft of everything that he has accumulated and achieved and to which he has been emotionally attached. The similarity between birth and death—the startling realization that the beginning of life is the same as its end—is the major philosophical issue that accompanies the perinatal experiences. The other important consequence of the shocking emotional and physical encounter with the phenomenon of death is the opening up of areas of spiritual and religious experiences that appear to be an intrinsic part of the human personality and are independent of the individual's cultural and religious background and programing. In my experience, everyone who has reached these levels develops convincing insights into the utmost relevance of the spiritual and religious dimensions in the universal scheme of things. Even hard-core materialists, positivistically oriented scientists, skeptics and cynics, and uncompromising atheists and antireligious crusaders such as the Marxist philosophers suddenly became interested in a spiritual search after they confronted these levels in themselves.

To prevent misunderstanding, it is necessary to emphasize that the encounter with death on the perinatal level takes the form of a profound firsthand experience of the terminal agony that is rather complex and has emotional, philosophical, and spiritual as well as distinctly physiological facets. The awareness of dying and death in this situation is not mediated by symbolic means alone. Specific eschatological content of the thought processes and visions of dying individuals, decaying cadavers, coffins, cemeteries, hearses, and funeral corteges occur as characteristic concomitants and illustrations of this death experience; its very basis, however, is the actual feeling of the ultimate biological crisis, which subjects frequently confuse with real dying. It is not uncommon that the individual involved in such an experience loses the critical insight that he is in a psychedelic session and becomes convinced that he is facing imminent death.

The indications of a serious crisis are not, however, of a purely subjective nature. The sequences of dying and being born (or reborn) are frequently extremely dramatic and have many biological manifestations apparent even to the outside observer. The subject may spend hours in agonizing pain, with facial contortions, gasping for breath and discharging enormous amounts of muscular tension in various tremors, twitching, violent shaking, and complex twisting movements. The color of the face may be dark purple or deathly pale, the pulse excessively accelerated and thready, and the respiration rate oscillating in a wide range; sweating can be profuse, and nausea with projectile vomiting is a frequent occurrence.

In a way that is not quite clear at the present stage of research, the above experiences seem to be related to the circumstances of the biological birth. LSD subjects frequently refer to them quite explicitly as reliving of their own birth trauma. Those who do not make this link and conceptualize their encounter with death and the death-rebirth experience in a purely philosophical and spiritual framework quite regularly show the cluster of physical symptoms described earlier that can best be interpreted as a derivative of the biological birth. They also assume postures and

The experience of suffocation and dyspnea in an LSD session in which the patient was reliving the birth trauma.

A picture representing the horrors of the birth trauma experienced in a symbolic form in the LSD session. The helpless and fragile fetus is hanging from the top of a large cupola by its umbilical cord; the destructive uterine forces are symbolized by the gigantic claws and beaks of birdlike monsters.

move in complex sequences that bear a striking similarity to those of a child during the various stages of delivery. In addition, these subjects frequently report visions of or identification with embryos, fetuses, and newborn children. Equally common are various authentic neonatal feelings as well as behavior, and visions of female genitals and breasts.

Because of these observations and other clinical evidence, I have labeled the above phenomena *perinatal experiences*. A causal nexus between the actual biological birth and the unconscious matrices for these experiences still remains to be established. It appears appropriate, however, to refer to this level of the unconscious as Rankian; with some modification, Otto Rank's conceptual framework is useful for the understanding of the phenomena in question.*

Perinatal experiences are a manifestation of a deep level of the unconscious that is clearly beyond the reach of classical Freudian techniques. The phenomena belonging to this category have been neither described in psychoanalytic literature nor taken into consideration in the theoretical speculations of Freudian analysts. Moreover, classical Freudian analysis does not allow for explanation of such experiences and does not offer an adequate conceptual framework for their interpretation.

In psycholytic treatment utilizing LSD with psychiatric patients, these levels are usually reached after a greater number of sessions of a psychodynamic nature. In subjects without serious emotional problems, the perinatal phenomenology usually occurs earlier in the procedure. In psychedelic therapy, which uses high dosages of LSD and where the sessions are much more internalized, perinatal elements are frequently observed in the first or second session. This appears to be the case whether the subjects are normal volunteers, individuals dying of cancer, or psychiatric patients. For reasons that are, at the present time, not quite clear, alcoholics and drug addicts seem to have easier access to the perinatal realm of the unconscious than individuals with psychoneurotic problems, especially those with a considera-

---

*The Viennese psychiatrist Otto Rank, a renegade from the mainstream of orthodox psychoanalysis, emphasized in his book *The Trauma of Birth* (1927) the paramount significance of perinatal experiences.[16]

ble obsessive-compulsive component in their clinical symptomatology.

LSD-assisted psychotherapy is not the only situation that can facilitate the manifestation of perinatal experiences. Occasionally, this level of the unconscious can be activated by forces from within the organism or from without. The processes involved are as yet insufficiently understood by contemporary psychiatry. Clinicians can thus see perinatal elements in a variety of psychotic conditions, especially manic-depressive psychoses and schizophrenia. However, examples of perinatal experiences can also be found outside the psychopathological framework. Similar experiences have been observed and described by psychotherapists of various orientations utilizing experiential techniques with normal and neurotic individuals.* Numerous additional examples can be found in anthropological and ethnographic literature. Since time immemorial, powerful procedures have existed in many ancient and so-called primitive cultures that appear to facilitate such experiences in individuals as well as groups. Here, these experiences were and are produced almost exclusively in a sacred context, either on special occasions, such as rites of passage and initiation rites, or as a matter of everyday practice in ecstatic religions. The techniques employed by these cultures cover a wide range of methods, from the use of psychoactive substances of plant and animal origin, trance dancing, fasting, sleep deprivation, shock, and physical torture, to elaborate spiritual practices such as those developed within the Hindu and Buddhist traditions.

Perinatal experiences represent a very important intersection between individual psychology and transpersonal psychology or, for that matter, between psychology and psychopathology, on one hand, and religion, on the other. If we think about them as related to the individual birth, they would seem to belong to the framework of individual psychology. Some other aspects, however, give them a very definite transpersonal flavor. The intensity of these experiences transcends anything usually considered

---

*These techniques include bioenergetics and other approaches based on the Reichian tradition, Gestalt therapy, encounter groups, marathon sessions, and Paul Bindrim's nude marathon.

to be the experiential limit of the individual. They are frequently accompanied by identification with other persons or with struggling and suffering mankind. Moreover, other types of clearly transpersonal experiences, such as evolutionary memories, elements of the collective unconscious, and certain Jungian archetypes, frequently form an integral part of the perinatal matrices. LSD sessions on this level usually have a rather complex character, combining very subjective experiences with clearly transpersonal elements.

It seems appropriate to mention in this connection a category of experiences that represents a transitional form between the Freudian psychodynamic level and the Rankian level. It is the reliving of traumatic memories from the life of the individual that are of a physical rather than a purely psychological nature. Typically, such memories involve a threat to survival or body integrity, such as serious operations or painful and dangerous injuries, severe diseases, particularly those connected with breathing difficulties (diphtheria, whooping cough, pneumonia), instances of near drowning, and episodes of cruel physical abuse (incarceration in a concentration camp, exposure to the brainwashing and interrogation techniques of the Nazis or Communists, and maltreatment in childhood). These memories are clearly individual in nature, yet, thematically, they are closely related to perinatal experiences. Occasionally, the reliving of physical traumas occurs simultaneously with perinatal phenomena as a more superficial facet of the birth agony. Observations from LSD psychotherapy seem to suggest that memories of somatic traumatization have a significant role in the psychogenesis of various emotional disorders, particularly depression and sadomasochism; this concept is as yet unrecognized and unacknowledged in present-day schools of dynamic psychotherapy.

Elements of the rich and complex content of LSD sessions reflecting this level of the unconscious seem to appear in four typical clusters, matrices, or experiential patterns. Searching for a simple, logical, and natural conceptulization of this fact, I was struck by the deep parallels between these patterns and the clinical stages of delivery. It proved to be a very useful principle for both theoretical considerations and the practice of LSD psychotherapy to relate the above four categories of phenomena to consecutive stages of the biological birth process and to the experiences of the child in the perinatal period. Therefore, for the sake of brevity, I usually refer to the four major experiential matrices of the Rankian level as *Basic Perinatal Matrices (BPM I–IV)*. It must be re-emphasized that this should be considered at the present stage of knowledge only as a very useful model, not necessarily implying a causal nexus.

The Basic Perinatal Matrices are hypothetical dynamic governing systems that have a function on the Rankian level of the unconscious similar to that of the COEX systems on the Freudian psychodynamic level. They have a specific content of their own, namely, the perinatal phenomena. The latter have two important facets or components: biological and spiritual. The biological aspect of perinatal experiences consists of concrete and rather realistic experiences related to the individual stages of the biological delivery. Each stage of biological birth appears to have a specific spiritual counterpart: for the undisturbed intrauterine existence it is the experience of cosmic unity; the onset of the delivery is paralleled by feelings of universal engulfment; the first clinical stage of delivery, the contractions in a closed uterine system, corresponds with the experience of "no exit" or hell; the propulsion through the birth canal in the second clinical stage of the delivery has its spiritual analogue in the death-rebirth struggle; and the metaphysical equivalent of the termination of the birth process and of the events in the third clinical stage of the delivery is the experience of ego death and rebirth. In addition to this specific content, the basic perinatal matrices function also as organizing principles for the material from other levels of the unconscious, namely for the COEX systems, as well as for some types of transpersonal experiences that occasionally occur simultaneously with perinatal phenomena, such as the archetype of the Terrible Mother or the Great Mother, identification with other individuals or groups of people, animal identification, or phylogenetic experiences.*

*The definition and detailed description of transpersonal experiences will be given in the following chapter.

BASIC PERINATAL MATRICES

BPM I	BPM II	BPM III	BPM IV
RELATED PSYCHOPATHOLOGICAL SYNDROMES			
schizophrenic psychoses (paranoid symptomatology, feelings of mystical union, encounter with metaphysical evil forces, karmic experiences); hypochondriasis (based on strange and bizarre physical sensations); hysterical hallucinosis and confusing daydreams with reality	schizophrenic psychoses (elements of hellish tortures, experience of meaningless "cardboard" world); severe inhibited "endogenous" depressions; irrational inferiority and guilt feelings; hypochondriasis (based on painful physical sensations); alcoholism and drug addiction	schizophrenic psychoses (sadomasochistic and scatological elements, automutilation, abnormal sexual behavior); agitated depression, sexual deviations (sadomasochism, male homosexuality, drinking of urine and eating of feces); obsessive-compulsive neurosis; psychogenic asthma, tics, and stammering; conversion and anxiety hysteria; frigidity and impotence; neurasthenia; traumatic neuroses; organ neuroses; migraine headache; enuresis and encopressis; psoriasis; peptic ulcer	schizophrenic psychoses (death-rebirth experiences, messianic delusions, elements of destruction and recreation of the world, salvation and redemption, identification with Christ); manic symptomatology; female homosexuality; exhibitionism
CORRESPONDING ACTIVITIES IN FREUDIAN EROGENIC ZONES			
libidinal satisfaction in all erogenic zones; libidinal feelings during rocking and bathing; partial approximation to this condition after oral, anal, urethral, or genital satisfaction and after delivery of a child	oral frustration (thirst, hunger, painful stimuli); retention of feces and/or urine; sexual frustration; experiences of cold, pain, and other unpleasant sensations	chewing and swallowing of food; oral aggression and destruction of an object; process of defecation and urination; anal and urethral aggression; sexual orgasm; phallic aggression; delivering of a child, statoacoustic eroticism (jolting, gymnastics, fancy diving, parachuting)	satiation of thirst and hunger; pleasure of sucking; libidinal feelings after defecation, urination, sexual orgasm, or delivery of a child
ASSOCIATED MEMORIES FROM POSTNATAL LIFE			
situations from later life where important needs are satisfied, such as happy moments from infancy and childhood (good mothering, play with peers, harmonious periods in the family, etc.), fulfilling love, romances, trips or vacations in beautiful natural settings; exposure to artistic creations of high aesthetic value; swimming in the ocean and clear lakes, etc.	situations endangering survival and body integrity (war experiences, accidents, injuries, operations, painful diseases, near drowning, episodes of suffocation, imprisonment, brainwashing and illegal interrogation, physical abuse, etc.); severe psychological traumatizations (emotional deprivation, rejection, threatening situations, oppressing family atmosphere, ridicule and humiliation, etc.)	struggles, fights, and adventurous activities (active attacks in battles and revolutions, experiences in military service, rough ocean, rough airplane flights, cruises on stormy ocean, hazardous car driving, boxing); highly sensual memories (carnivals, amusement parks and nightclubs, wild parties, sexual orgies, etc.); childhood observations of adult sexual activities; experiences of seduction and rape; in females, delivery of their own children	fortuitous escape from dangerous situations (end of war or revolution, survival of an accident or operation); overcoming of severe obstacles by active effort; episodes of strain and hard struggle resulting in a marked success; natural scenes (beginning of spring, end of an ocean storm, sunrise, etc.)

PHENOMENOLOGY IN LSD SESSIONS

undisturbed intrauterine life: realistic recollections of "good womb" experiences; "oceanic" type of ecstasy; experience of cosmic unity; visions of Paradise; *disturbances of intrauterine life:* realistic recollections of "bad womb" experiences (fetal crises, diseases and emotional upheavals of the mother, twin situation, attempted abortions), cosmic engulfment; paranoid ideation; unpleasant physical sensations ("hangover," chills and fine spasms, unpleasant tastes, disgust, feelings of being poisoned); association with various transpersonal experiences (archetypal elements, racial and evolutionary memories, encounter with metaphysical forces, past incarnation experiences, etc.)

immense physical and psychological suffering; unbearable and inescapable situation that will never end; various images of hell; feelings of entrapment and encagement (no exit); agonizing guilt and inferiority feelings; apocalyptic view of the world (horrors of wars and concentration camps, terror of the Inquisition; dangerous epidemics; diseases; decrepitude and death, etc.); meaninglessness and absurdity of human existence; "cardboard world" or the atmosphere of artificiality and gadgets; ominous dark colors and unpleasant physical symptoms (feelings of oppression and compression, cardiac distress, flushes and chills, sweating, difficult breathing)

intensification of suffering to cosmic dimensions; borderline between pain and pleasure; "volcanic" type of ecstasy; brilliant colors; explosions and fireworks; sadomasochistic orgies; murders and bloody sacrifice; active engagement in fierce battles; atmosphere of wild adventure and dangerous explorations; intense sexual orgiastic feelings and scenes of harems and carnivals; experiences of dying and being reborn; religions involving bloody sacrifice (Aztecs, Christ's suffering and death on the cross, Dionysos, etc.); intense physical manifestations (pressures and pains, suffocation, muscular tension and discharge in tremors and twitches, nausea and vomiting, hot flushes and chills, sweating, cardiac distress, problems of sphincter control, ringing in the ears)

enormous decompression, expansion of space, visions of gigantic halls; radiant light and beautiful colors (heavenly blue, golden, rainbow, peacock feathers); feelings of rebirth and redemption; appreciation of simple way of life; sensory enhancement; brotherly feelings; humanitarian and charitable tendencies; occasionally manic activity and grandiose feelings; transition to elements of BPM I; pleasant feelings can be interrupted by *umbilical crisis:* sharp pain in the navel, loss of breath, fear of death and castration, shifts in the body, but no external pressures

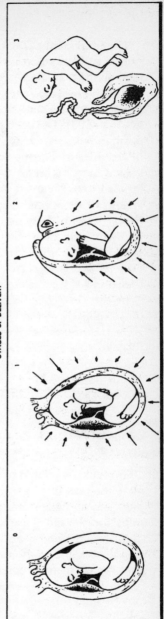

STAGES OF DELIVERY

0   1   2   3

The individual perinatal matrices have fixed associations with certain typical categories of memories from the lives of subjects; they are also related to specific aspects of the activities in the Freudian erogenic zones, and to specific psychopathological syndromes and psychiatric disorders (see the synoptic paradigm on pp. 102–103). The deep parallel between the physiological activities in the consecutive stages of biological delivery and the pattern of activities in various erogenic zones, in particular that of the genital orgasm, seems to be of great theoretical significance. It makes it possible to shift the etiological emphasis in the psychogenesis of emotional disorders from sexuality to perinatal matrices, without denying or negating the validity of many basic Freudian principles. Even within such an extended framework, psychoanalytic observations and concepts remain useful for the understanding of occurrences on the psychodynamic level and their mutual interrelations.

In the text that follows we will discuss the biological and obstetric basis of the individual perinatal matrices, their experiential content, their function as organizing principles for other types of experiences, and their specific relation to physiological activities in the Freudian erogenic zones. The perinatal matrices will be discussed in the order in which the corresponding stages of biological birth follow each other during delivery.

Perinatal Matrix I. Primal Union with the Mother (Intrauterine Experience before the Onset of Delivery)

This matrix is related to the original condition of the intrauterine existence, during which the child and mother form a symbiotic unity. Unless some noxious stimuli interfere, the conditions for the child are optimal, involving security, protection, appropriate milieu, and satisfaction of all needs. This is, of course, not always the case. There exists a broad continuum of transitions, from pregnancies where these optimal conditions are disturbed only occasionally and for a short time (for example, by mild intercurrent diseases, dietary trespasses, occasional use of cigarettes and alcohol, a temporary stay in a very noisy environment, gynecological examinations, sexual intercourse in the later months of pregnancy) to pregnancies where they are hardly ever met (for example, in cases of serious infections and endocrinal or metabolic diseases of the mother; severe toxicosis; chronic anxiety, tension, and emotional stress; work in an inappropriate milieu with excessive noise and vibrations; drug addiction and chronic intoxications; cruel treatment of the mother, with repeated concussions; attempts at artificial abortion by various means). Though these disturbances of pregnancy are usually considered in regard to the future development of the child only as a source of possible somatic damage, observations from LSD psychotherapy seem to suggest that the child might also experience these noxious influences on a primitive subjective level. If this is the case, we could then differentiate between the "good" and the "bad" womb along the lines hypothesized by psychoanalysts in the case of the "good" and the "bad" breast. The sum of undisturbed intrauterine experiences during pregnancy might, in regard to the future stability of the personality, play an important role comparable to that of positive nursing experiences.

Undisturbed intrauterine experiences are only exceptionally described in the early LSD sessions of an individual but are a frequent occurrence later on. Some subjects describe rather realistic complex recollections of the original embryonal situation. They experience themselves as extremely small, with a typical disproportion in size between head and body, and can feel the surrounding liquid and sometimes even the umbilical cord. These experiences are associated with a blissful, undifferentiated, oceanic state of consciousness. Frequently, the concrete biological elements are missing and the activation of this matrix manifests itself as an *experience of cosmic unity*. Its basic characteristics are transcendence of the subject-object dichotomy, exceptionally strong positive affect (peace, tranquillity, joy, serenity, and bliss), a special feeling of sacredness, transcendence of time and space, an experience of pure being, and a richness of insights of cosmic relevance. Subjects frequently talk about timelessness of the present moment and say that they are in touch with infinity. They refer to this experience as ineffable and emphasize the failure of linguistic symbols and the structure of our language to convey the nature of this event and its significance. Descriptions of cosmic unity are usually full of paradoxes violating the basic laws and the very essence of Aristotelian logic. An individual can, for example, talk about this experience as being contentless and yet all-containing; everything that he can possibly conceive of seems to be included. He refers to a complete loss of his ego and yet states that this consciousness has expanded to encompass the whole universe. He feels awed, humbled, and utterly insignificant but, at the same time, has the feeling of an enormous achievement and experiences himself in cosmic proportions, sometimes to the extent of feeling identified with God. He can perceive himself and the rest of the phenomenal world as existing and not existing at the same time; and the forms of material objects as being empty and emptiness as having a form. The subject in this state feels that he has access to direct insightful knowledge and wisdom about matters of fundamental and universal significance. Usually this does not involve concrete information about specific technical details that could be pragmatically utilized. Rather, it is a complex revelatory insight into the essence of being and existence.* This insight is typically accompanied by feelings of certainty that such knowledge is ultimately more real and relevant than our concepts and perceptions regarding the world that we share in a usual state of consciousness.

The type of tension-free, melted ecstasy exemplified by the feeling of cosmic unity can be referred to as "oceanic ecstasy" (in contrast to "volcanic ecstasy," to be described later in relation to BPM III). In a subject whose eyes are closed, it occurs as an independent complex experience. With the eyes open, the same individual has a sense of merging with the environment and feelings of unity with perceived objects. The world is seen as a place of indescribable radiance and beauty. The element of reasoning and the need for rational analysis is considerably reduced, and the universe becomes "a mystery to be experienced, not a riddle to be solved." In this state, the subject finds it

---

*Several sophisticated subjects referred in this context to the Upanishads and the famous quotation, "Knowing That, the knowledge of which gives knowledge of everything."

difficult to see any negative aspects in the world and in the very structure of the cosmic design; everything appears perfect, everything is as it should be.* At this point, the world appears to be a friendly place where a childlike, passive-dependent attitude can be assumed with full confidence and with feelings of complete security. For an individual in this state of mind, evil seems to be unimportant, ephemeral, or nonexistent; as we will see later, this selective perception of the universe is in sharp contrast with that typical for a subject experiencing the elements of BPM II.

The feelings of cosmic unity described by LSD subjects seem to be closely related to, if not identical with, the transcendental experiences characterized by Walter Pahnke's mystical categories[15] and those for which Abraham Maslow[13] coined the term "peak experiences." In psychedelic sessions, this phenomenon functions as an important gateway to a variety of transpersonal experiences that will be discussed in detail in the next chapter. In the further transpersonal unfolding of the experiential pattern of cosmic unity, the transcendence of time and space can assume a rather concretized form and be illustrated by a number of specific images. An individual may experience a sequence of visions that allows for interpretation in terms of regression in historical time. This involves a variety of embryonal sensations, ancestral memories, elements of the collective unconscious, and evolutionary experiences accompanied by phylogenetic flashbacks and Darwinian insights. A corresponding transcendence of the usual space limitations can be illustrated by identification with other persons and groups of persons and with animals, plants, and even inorganic matter. An important variation of this development is the subjective identification with the physical universe as we know it, with its galaxies, solar systems, and myriads of individual stars. Visions of various deities and of

---

*This attitude toward the universe does not have to result in inactivity and passive acceptance of the status quo. It is compatible with a creative life style, striving for self-actualization, and various reformatory tendencies. This can be illustrated by a quotation from one of Baba Ram Dass's lectures: "The world is absolutely perfect, including your dissatisfaction with it and your efforts to change it." This statement in the lecture was related to the Hindu tradition and not to Ram Dass's drug experiences.

Jungian archetypes are another characteristic sequence in the experience of cosmic unity.

Disturbances of intrauterine life seem to have a specific phenomenology in LSD sessions. As in the case of undisturbed experiences, individuals occasionally report quite realistic recollections of their fetal existance. They can feel like an embryo in the womb, have specific embryonal sensations, and experience various degrees and forms of intrauterine distress. The type of interference can sometimes be identified, through the use of adult cues, as being due to the mechanical competition with a twin, a physical disease of the mother, her emotional upheaval—such as intense anxiety or aggression—an attempted abortion, or various other noxious stimuli. These episodes of distress usually alternate with the positive experiences described earlier.

Besides such realistic experiences, there are other manifestations of intrauterine discomfort. The vision of a star-filled sky, typical of ecstatic episodes, can suddenly become blurred with an ugly film. There appear visual disturbances similar to those on a television screen, accompanied by various unpleasant somatic symptoms. The most frequent of these are physical signs resembling an attack of influenza, such as feelings of weakness, headache, chills, trembling, and localized tremors of small muscles. Equally frequent are symptoms of an alimentary intoxication or "hangover," namely, nausea, disgust, dyspepsia, increased peristaltic movements, and gas in the intestines. A typical concomitant of these episodes is a specific, unpleasant taste in the mouth which is usually described as having a certain biological quality (old bouillon, decomposed blood, ammonia), combined with an inorganic admixture (metallic taste, iodine, iron, or simply "poison").

These somatic symptoms differ diametrically from those accompanying the birth experience. There are usually no objective signs of suffocation and no dramatic behavior manifestations, such as bizarre postures, twisting movements, violent shaking, or spastic contractions of large groups of muscles. The individual does not experience external pressures on the head and the body, or feelings of constriction and oppression. All symptoms are much more subtle, and they are experienced with clear consciousness, whereas in the birth sessions the subject is absorbed in the life-death struggle. During the episodes of experiencing intrauterine distress, the effect of LSD can occasionally be limited to this physical symptomatology, and perceptual changes might be completely absent. The individual might complain that the dose of LSD is too small or that the drug is ineffective. However, when the episode of distress is worked through and integrated, the nature of the session changes and an intense experience of cosmic unity ensues.

There exists some evidence that the visions of *various demons and wrathful deities* that appear in these sessions and seem to separate the subject from the blissful universe are also closely related to intrauterine disturbances and embryonic crises. Like the deities related to positive intrauterine experiences, they can take the form of demons known from different cultures or can be identified as archetypal figures. In addition to demonic encounters and episodes of physical distress, some individuals also experience various sequences that they label as reliving of memories from previous incarnations. The nature of the experiences from this category can be illustrated by an advanced session from a psycholytic series of a professional who participated in the LSD training program.

During a session in which he alternately experienced episodes of "good" and "bad" womb, he felt that he developed new insight into the understanding of demons from several cultures—in particular, India and Tibet. He suddenly saw a striking relationship between the state of mind of the Buddha sitting on the lotus in deep meditation and that of an embryo in a good womb. The demons surrounding the peaceful Buddha figure on many Indian and Tibetan religious paintings appeared to him to be representatives of various forms of disturbances of the intrauterine existence. The subject could distinguish among them the bloody, openly aggressive, and ferocious ones, symbolizing the dangers of biological birth; the others, more insidious and lurking, represented the noxious influences in the intrauterine life. On another level, he was simultaneously experiencing episodes that appeared to be past-incarnation memories. It seemed as if elements of bad karma entered his present life in the form of disturbances of his embryonal existence and as negative experiences during the period when he was nursed. He saw the experiences of the "bad womb" and "bad breast" as transformation points between the realm of the karmic law and the phenomenal world governed by natural laws as we know them.

Subjects experiencing in their LSD sessions episodes of intrauterine distress often describe perceptual and conceptual distortions that bear an unusual resemblance to the world of the schizophrenic. Those LSD subjects who have relatives or acquaintances actually suffering from schizophrenia or paranoid conditions can feel at this point fully identified with these persons and develop a deep psychological understanding of their problems. Numerous psychiatrists and psychologists undergoing the LSD training program also reported that they kept remembering or actually visualizing their psychotic patients and were able to tune in to their world and understand them. Observations from such sessions suggest that undisturbed intrauterine experiences are closely related to religious and mystical enlightenment. Conversely, the subjective concomitants of disturbances of the intrauterine life appear to be the source of schizophrenic experiences and paranoid conditions. The closeness between these two situations and the easy change from one to another might explain the sometimes precarious boundary between schizophrenia and spiritual enlightenment, as well as the spontaneous occurrences of religious and mystical experiences in some severely disturbed psychotics.

As far as the relationship to memory mechanisms is concerned, the positive aspects of BPM I seem to represent the basis for the recording of all later life situations in which the individual is relaxed, relatively free from needs, and not disturbed by any painful and unpleasant stimuli. Reliving of memories characterized by feelings of satisfaction, security, and other highly positive emotions occurs in LSD sessions in close connection with the ecstatic feelings of BPM I, either simultaneously or alternating with them. The positive COEX systems associated with this matrix involve happy periods from infancy and childhood, such as full satisfaction of anaclitical needs, carefree and joyful games and playing with peers, or harmonious episodes from family life. Memories from later life that appear in this context include particularly satisfactory love relationships, with intense emotional and sexual gratification. Similarly important are memories of encounters with natural beauty, exemplified by sunrises and sunsets, peaceful oceans and lakes, the colorful flora and fauna of coral reefs and other aspects of the undersea world, blue or star-filled skies, tropical islands, luscious and flourishing jungles, high mountains, romantic rivers, forest landscapes, and illuminated stalagmite caverns. Man-made creations of unusual aesthetic value also have a rather significant role in this context. Images of various beautiful paintings, sculptures, artifacts, and jewels, as well as churches, temples, castles, and palaces that the subject has seen in the past, emerge quite regularly in close connection with the ecstatic feeling related to BPM I. Particularly significant seems to be the association of a special kind of music and dance with this perinatal matrix. The same is true about bathing and swimming in mountain streams, waterfalls, large clean rivers and lakes, or the ocean.

The associations with unpleasant aspects of BPM I represent the negative mirror image of the situation described. Memories belonging to this category involve distorted communication in the family of origin, childhood dysfunctions and diseases; highly industrialized cities and other unattractive scenery; polluted air, lakes, and rivers; and distasteful or distorted pieces of art.

In regard to the Freudian erogenic zones, the positive aspects of BPM I coincide, on one hand, with a biological and psychological condition in which there are no tensions in any of these zones and all the partial drives are satisfied. On the other hand, satisfaction of the needs in these zones (satiation of hunger, release of tension by urination, defecation, sexual orgasm, or delivery of a child) can result in a superficial and partial approximation to the tension-free ecstatic experience described above.

The following description of an LSD training session of a psychiatrist can be used as an illustration of a psychedelic experience governed by positive and negative aspects of BPM I.

In spite of a relatively high dose of LSD (300 micrograms), the latency period seemed to be excessively long. The first manifestations did not occur until more than an hour after ingestion of the drug, but even then, for at least another hour, they were negligible. I did not experience any major perceptual or emotional changes, only a complex of subtle physical symptoms resembling the onset of flu. They involved a feeling of general malaise, cold chills, a strange and unpleasant taste in my mouth, slight nausea, and intestinal discomfort. Waves of fine tremors and twitches were occurring in various muscles of my body, and my skin was covered with droplets of sweat.

About two hours after the administration of the drug, I became impatient; I could not believe that a high dose of LSD that in my previous sessions had produced dramatic changes—to the point that on occasions I was afraid that my sanity or even my life was at stake—could evoke such a minimal response. I decided to close my eyes and observe carefully what was happening. At this point the experience seemed to deepen, and I realized that what with my eyes open appeared to be an adult experience of a viral disease now changed into a realistic situation of a fetus suffering some strange toxic insults during its intrauterine existence. I was greatly reduced in size, and my head was considerably bigger than the rest of the body and extremities. I was suspended in a liquid milieu and some harmful chemicals were being channeled into my body through the umbilical area. Using some unknown receptors, I was detecting these influences as noxious and hostile to my organism. I could also perceive the offending quality of the intruding substances in my gustatory buds; the sensation seemed to combine the taste of iodine with that of decomposing blood or old bouillon.

While this was happening, I was aware that these toxic "attacks" had something to do with the condition and activity of the maternal organism. Occasionally, I could distinguish influences that appeared to be due to alimentary factors—ingestion of alcohol, inappropriate food, or smoking—and others that I perceived as chemical mediators of my mother's emotions—anxieties, nervousness, anger, conflicting feelings about pregnancy, and even sexual arousal. The idea of astute consciousness existing in the fetus and the possibility of subjective awareness of all the nuances of its interaction with the mother were certainly contrary to my preconceptions based on my medical training. The reality and concrete nature of these experiences, as well as their very convincing quality, presented for a while a very serious conflict for the "scientist" in me. Then all of a sudden the resolution of this dilemma emerged; it became clear to me that it was more appropriate to consider the necessity of revising present scientific beliefs—something that has happened many times in the course of the history of mankind—than to question the relevance of my own experience.

When I was able to give up my analytical thinking and accept the experience for what it was, the nature of the session changed dramatically. The feelings of sickness and indigestion disappeared, and I was experiencing an ever-increasing state of ecstasy. This was accompanied by a clearing and brightening of my visual field. It was as if multiple layers of thick, dirty cobwebs were being magically torn and dissolved, or a poor-quality movie projection or television broadcast were being focused and rectified by an invisible cosmic technician. The scenery opened up, and an incredible amount of light and energy was enveloping me and streaming in subtle vibrations through my whole being. On one level, I was still a fetus experiencing the ultimate perfection and bliss of a good womb or a newborn fusing with a nourishing and life-giving breast. On another level, I became the entire universe; I was witnessing the spectacle of the macrocosm with countless pulsating and vibrating galaxies and *was* it at the same time. These radiant and breathtaking cosmic vistas were intermingled with experiences of the equally miraculous microcosm—from the dance of atoms and molecules to the origins of life and the biochemical world of individual cells. For the first time, I was experiencing the universe for what it really is—an unfathomable mystery, a divine play of energy. Everything in this universe appeared to be conscious. After having had to accept the possibility of fetal consciousness, I was confronted with an even more startling discovery: consciousness might actually pervade all existence. My scientific mind was heavily tested by this possibility until I realized that although many of these experiences were incompatible with our common sense, they were not necessarily out of the realm of science. These revelations were certainly not more baffling than the implications of Einstein's theory of relativity, quantum mechanics, various astronomical concepts, and modern cosmogenetic theories. Pantheistic religions, Spinoza's philosophy, the teachings of the Buddha, the Hindu concepts of Atman-Brahman, *maya* and *lila*—all these suddenly came alive and were illuminated with new meaning.

This incredibly rich and complex experience lasted for what seemed to be eternity. I was oscillating between the state of a distressed, sickened fetus and a blissful and serene intrauterine existence. At times, the noxious influences took the form of archetypal demons or malevolent creatures from the world of fairy tales. I was getting insights as to why the child's psyche is so fascinated and captivated by various mythic stories and their characters. Some of these insights were, however, of a much broader relevance. The craving for the reinstitution of the state of total fulfillment that was once experienced in the womb appeared to be the ultimate motivating force of every human being. This principle seemed to underlie the inevitable course of the unfolding of fairy tales toward a happy ending, as well as the revolutionary's dream of a future Utopia; the artist's need for acceptance, acclamation, and ovation; or the ambitious race for possessions, status, and fame. It became clear to me that here was the answer to mankind's most fundamental dilemma: this insatiable craving and need cannot be satisfied by any degree of achievement and success in the external world. The only answer is to reconnect with this place in one's own mind, in one's own unconscious. I suddenly understood the message of so many spiritual teachers that *the only revolution* that can work is the inner transformation of every human being.

During what seemed to be episodes of reliving of positive memories of fetal existence, I experienced feelings of basic identity and oneness with the universe; it was the Tao, the Beyond that is Within, the *Tat tvam asi* (Thou art That) of the Upanishads. I lost my sense of individuality; my ego dissolved, and I became all of existence. Sometimes this experience was intangible and contentless, sometimes it was accompanied by many beautiful visions—archetypal images of Paradise, the ultimate cornucopia, golden age, or virginal nature. I became fish swimming in crystal-clear waters, butterflies floating in mountain meadows, and seagulls gliding by the ocean. I *was* the ocean, animals, plants, the clouds—sometimes all these at the same time.

On one occasion, the good-womb experience seemed to open into time instead of space. To my utter astonishment, I relived my own conception and various stages of my embryological development. While I was experiencing all the complexities of the embryogenesis, with details that surpassed the best medical handbooks, I was flashing back to an even more remote past, visualizing some phylogenetic vestiges from the life of my animal ancestors. The scientist in me was struck by another riddle: can the genetic code, under certain circumstances, be translated into a conscious experience? I decided to ponder this problem later and surrendered to the enticing display of the mysteries of nature.

Nothing concrete happened later in the afternoon, and, in the evening hours, I spent most of this time feeling one with nature and the universe, bathed in golden light that was slowly decreasing in intensity. Only reluctantly was I giving up this experience and returning to my usual consciousness. I felt, however, that something of utmost relevance had happened to me on this session day and that

I would never be the same. I reached a new feeling of harmony and self-acceptance, and a global understanding of existence that is difficult to define. For a long time I felt as though I was composed of pure energy and pure spiritual vibrations, totally unaware of my physical existence. Late in the evening, my consciousness gradually returned into what appeared to be a healed, wholesome, and perfectly functioning body.

Perinatal Matrix II. Antagonism with the Mother (Contractions in a Closed Uterine System)

The second perinatal matrix is related to the first clinical stage of delivery. The intrauterine existence that is under normal circumstances close to ideal has come to an end. The world of the fetus is disturbed, at first insidiously through chemical influences, later in a grossly mechanical way by periodic uterine contractions. This creates a situation of extreme emergency and vital threat, with various signs of intense physical discomfort. In this phase, the uterine contractions encroach on the fetus, but the cervix is closed and the way out is not yet open. The mother and the child are a source of pain for each other and are in a state of biological antagonism and conflict.

There exists a considerable variation in the duration of this stage (as well as in the duration of the entire process of the delivery). It can be surmised that this experience is more devastating in a pathological delivery with a prolonged course due to a narrow pelvis or pelvic obstructions, abnormal fetal position, ineffective uterine contractions, excessive size of the child, and other types of complications. It is, however, conceivable that the fear and confusion of an inexperienced mother or a distinctly negative or strongly ambivalent attitude of the mother toward the unborn child or toward the process of delivery itself can make this phase more difficult (for both mother and child). Such feelings could interfere with the physiological interplay between the uterine contractions and the opening of the cervix.*

Elements of BPM II may occur in LSD sessions in a purely biological form as realistic recollections of this particular stage of

---

*It is interesting to mention in this connection that many of my female subjects who relived in their LSD sessions the delivery of their children developed insights into how their negative feelings and attitudes interfered with the process of delivery.

the birth process. More frequently, however, the activation of this matrix results in a rather characteristic spiritual experience of "no exit" or "hell." The subject feels encaged in a claustrophobic world and experiences incredible physical and psychological tortures. This experience is characterized by a striking darkness of the visual field and by ominous colors. Typically, this situation is absolutely unbearable and, at the same time, appears to be endless and hopeless; no escape can be seen either in time or in space. Frequently, the subject feels that even suicide would not terminate it and bring relief.

The characteristic elements of this pattern can be experienced on several different levels; these levels can occur separately, simultaneously, or in an alternating fashion. The deepest levels are related to various concepts of hell, to situations of unbearable physical, psychological, and metaphysical suffering that will never end, as they have been depicted by various religions. In a more superficial version of the same experiential pattern, the subject is preoccupied with the situation in this world and perceives it with a very definite negative bias. He is selectively aware only of the ugly, evil, and hopeless aspects of existence. Our planet is perceived in this stage as an apocalyptic place full of terror, suffering, wars, epidemics, accidents, and natural catastrophes. The individual is unable to find or appreciate anything good in the universe, whether positive aspects of human nature, pleasant episodes in life, natural beauty, or the perfection of artistic creations. Typical for this experience is empathy and identification with the victimized, downtrodden, and oppressed. A subject can experience himself as thousands of soldiers who have died on the battlefields of the whole world from the beginning of time, as the tortured victims of the Spanish Inquisition, as prisoners of concentration camps, as patients dying of terminal diseases, as aging individuals who are decrepit and senile, as mothers and children dying during delivery, or as inmates maltreated in chronic wards of insane asylums. Another typical category of visions related to this perinatal matrix involves the dehumanized, grotesque, and bizarre world of automata, robots, and mechanical gadgets, the atmosphere of human monstrosities and anomalies in circus sideshows, or of a meaningless "honky-tonk" or "cardboard" world.

A drawing representing the experience of deep depression, hopelessness, and despair in an LSD session.

For a person experientially tuned in to elements of BPM II, human life seems bereft of any meaning. Existence appears not only nonsensical but monstrous and absurd, and the search for any meaning in life completely futile and, *a priori*, doomed to failure. People are seen as thrown into this world without any choice as to whether, where, when, and to whom they are to be born. The only certainty in life appears to be the fact that its duration is limited and that it will end. The fact of human mortality and the impermanence of all things is seen as Damocles' sword hanging over us during every minute of our lives and annihilating any hope that anything has meaning.

A subject experiencing the encounter with death within the framework of BPM II frequently makes the link between the agony of birth and that of death, which further reinforces his nihilism. In such a situation, he feels as though he is dying in the present moment and becomes deeply involved in eschatological ideation. At the same time, he can feel that his present agony is identical with the suffering that he experienced during his biological birth. He can also see himself in the future at the very end of his life and find that these same feelings are involved in the terminal agony. We suffer when we are born, and we die in suffering; the agony of birth is identical with the agony of death. Whatever we attempt to do in between cannot change the fact that in death we are all equal and find ourselves in the same situation that we faced during birth. We entered this world helpless, naked, and without personal possessions, and so we will leave it.

This existentialist crisis is usually illustrated by a variety of visions depicting the meaninglessness of life and the absurdity of putting forth any effort to change this fact. Such visions can show the life and death of powerful kings and dictators, persons who have achieved extraordinary fame and reputation, or those who have accumulated unbelievable riches. The implicit or explicit message here is that in death such persons are not any different from ordinary people, simpletons, beggars, and pan-handling monks. Subjects who have faced this profound existen-tialist crisis frequently comment that this experience has helped them to understand the deepest meaning of expressions such as *memento mori, vanitas vanitatum,* or "Thou art dust and to dust shalt thou return."

For sophisticated individuals, this experience usually results in a fresh understanding and appreciation of existentialist philoso-phy and the works of such individuals as Martin Heidegger, Søren Kierkegaard, Albert Camus, and Jean Paul Sartre. Sartre and other existentialist philosophers and writers seem to be especially tuned in to this experiential complex, without being able to find the only possible solution, which is transcendence. LSD subjects often refer to Sartre's play *Huit Clos (No Exit),* as a brilliant description of the feelings they experienced when they examined their lives and their interpersonal relationships under the influence of the "no exit" stencil of BPM II. Some also refer to Céline's *The Journey to the End of the Night* as an excellent example of the selective focus on the negative aspects of human existence.

Agonizing feelings of separation, alienation, metaphysical loneliness, helplessness, hopelessness, inferiority, and guilt are standard components of BPM II. Whether the individual looks at his present situation and behavior or explores his past, the circumstances and events of his life seem to confirm that he is a worthless, useless, and bad human being. Guilt feelings are usually quite out of proportion to the events to which the individual attaches them. They appear to have a primary quality intrinsic to human nature and can reach the metaphysical dimension of the Biblical primal sin. Another important dimension of the "no exit" situation is the feeling of pervading insanity; subjects typically feel that they have lost all mental control and become permanently psychotic, or that they have gained the ultimate insight into the absurdity of the universe and will never be able to return to the merciful self-deception that is a necessary prerequisite for sanity.

The symbolic images that accompany the experiences of BPM II cover a rather broad cultural range. Most common are visions of "hells" as described and depicted by various religions; these can involve traditional Christian representations of hell, the underworld of the ancient Greeks, and comparable elements from the Hindu and Buddhist traditions. Particularly frequent' are references to famous figures from Greek chthonic mythology: Sisyphus in his futile attempts to deliver a heavy boulder to the top of a mountain, Ixion fixed to a rolling wheel, Tantalus vexed by agonizing thirst and hunger with grapes and water seemingly within his reach, and Prometheus chained to a rock and tortured by an eagle who feeds on his liver. Greek tragedy, with its emphasis on an unrelenting and irreconcilable curse, on guilt transcending generations, and on inevitable fate seems to be closely related to this area and is an important source of symbolic illustrations. A common image from the same tradition is that of the Erinyes, symbolizing consuming guilt and qualms of conscience.

The Biblical themes occurring in this context involve the story of Adam and Eve's expulsion from Paradise, Christ's visions in the garden of Gethsemane, and, particularly, his ridicule and humiliation *(ecce homo)*, his suffering while carrying the cross to Calvary, and his biological and psychological agony during the crucifixion itself ("Father, why hast thou forsaken me?"). The concept of the Dark Night of the Soul, as described in the writings of Saint John of the Cross, was also occasionally mentioned in this context. Another interesting source of symbolic images is the Buddha's life, the significance of his Four Passing Sights,* and the emphasis on suffering as expressed in his Four Noble Truths.

Occasionally, situations and characters from world literature and specific creations of famous painters occur in LSD sessions within the framework of the second perinatal matrix. Most frequent of these are references to Dante's descriptions of inferno in his *Divine Comedy,* scenes from Émile Zola's books describing dark and repulsive aspects of human nature, and Fëdor Dostoevski's novels, with their emotional suffering, atmosphere of insanity, and scenes of senseless brutality. Especially pertinent seem to be Edgar Allan Poe's macabre stories of inhuman tortures and horror. The paintings appearing in this context include Hieronymus Bosch's pictures of nightmarish and bizarre creatures, James Ensor's gloomy world of skeletons and morbid masquerades, Francisco Goya's images of the horrors of the war, the apocalyptic visions of Salvador Dali and other surrealists, and numerous famous representations of hell and the Last Judgment.

The individual trapped in the "no exit" situation clearly sees that human existence is meaningless, yet feels a desperate need to find meaning in life. This struggle often coincides with what is experienced as the attempts of the fetus to escape from the closed uterine system and save its life. The impossible task of finding meaning in life might appear in this context as a necessary condition for being born into the world and terminating the unbearable "no exit" situation.

An interesting variety of the second perinatal matrix seems to be related to the very onset and the initial stages of the delivery. This situation is experienced in LSD sessions as an increasing

*The so-called Four Passing Sights precipitated the Buddha's decision to leave his family and his luxurious life in the palace, and stimulated his search for enlightenment. During his walks into the environs of the city, he saw successively four scenes that made an indelible impression on his mind: the first of them was an old man, decrepit, with broken teeth, gray hair, and a crooked and bent body; the second one was a person lying by the road, racked with disease; on the third occasion, he saw a corpse; and finally, during his fourth walk, he encountered a monk with a shaven head and clad in an ocher robe. It is certainly interesting to notice that it is the brutal encounter with the phenomena of the decrepitude of old age, disease, and death (BPM II) which seems to be instrumental in changing the emphasis of the LSD subjects from their worldly ambitions to a spiritual search.

awareness of an imminent and vital danger or as *cosmic engulf-ment*. There is intense anxiety, but its source cannot be identi-fied; the atmosphere of insidious threat may result in paranoid ideation. Not infrequently, the subject interprets these alarming feelings as evil influences coming from members of various secret organizations or inhabitants of other planets, as poisoning, noxious radiation, or toxic gases. Intensification of this experi-ence typically results in the vision of a gigantic and irresistible whirlpool, a cosmic maelstrom sucking the subject and his world relentlessly to its center. A frequent experiential variation of this dangerous engulfment is that of being swallowed and incorpo-rated by a terrifying monster, such as a giant dragon, python, octopus, whale, or spider. A less dramatic form of the same experience seems to be the theme of descent into the under-world and the encounter with various monstrous entities.

Typical physical symptoms associated with BPM II involve extreme pressures on the head and body, ringing in the ears (resembling the sensations experienced when diving in deep water), excruciating pains in various parts of the body, difficul-ties with breathing, massive cardiac distress, and hot flushes and chills.

As a memory matrix, BPM II represents the basis for the recording of all unpleasant life situations in which an over-whelming destructive force imposes itself on the passive and helpless subject. The most typical and frequent examples are situations endangering survival and body integrity. Thus, the recollection of sensations connected with various operations, such as appendectomy, tonsillectomy, setting of broken extremi-ties, and difficult tooth extractions, or even the complex reliving of the circumstances of such procedures, occurs quite regularly in this context. The same is true for physical diseases, injuries and accidents, excessive muscular exertion and exhaustion, experiences of imprisonment and brutal methods of interroga-tion, and those involving prolonged, extreme hunger and thirst. It has already been mentioned above that diseases and situations involving suffocation seem to be of special significance from this point of view. In subjects who experienced a dramatic war situation in a passive role (siege, air raid, captivity), or were trapped in a claustrophobic situation (coal mine, avalanche, debris of collapsed houses, an underwater passage), the memories of such events also occur in LSD sessions in close association with elements of BPM II. On a somewhat more subtle level, this category also involves memories of a helpless person's psychological frustrations, such as abandonment, emotional rejection or deprivation, threatening events, and constricting or oppressing situations in the nuclear family.

In regard to Freudian erogenic zones, this matrix seems to be related to a condition of unpleasant tension in all of them. On the oral level, it is hunger, thirst, and painful stimuli; on the anal level, retention of feces; and, on the urethral level, retention of urine. The corresponding phenomena on the genital level are sexual frustration and excessive tension, as well as pains experienced by the delivering mother in the first stage of labor. If we think of the whole surface of the skin as an erogenic area, we can also include physical pain and unpleasant sensations in different parts of the body.

The following training session of a young social scientist was dominated almost exclusively by elements of BPM II and can be used as an excellent example of the phenomenology of this matrix.

In this session the onset of the drug seemed to take a very long time. After a period of impatience that was covering anxiety, I began to experience a distinct feeling of malaise. The sickness enveloping me was at first very subtle. Mild feelings of nausea and tension were making themselves manifest. Soon the nausea and tension were intensified to a point where every cell seemed to be involved. It is difficult indeed to describe this experience: it was so all-encompassing. The slightly humorous description of every cell in my body being drilled by a dentist begins to convey the atmosphere of impending disaster, emergency, and excruciating pain that for me seemed to last for eternity. Although I saw no images, I began to think of Petronius, Seneca, Sartre, and other philosophers who deemed suicide the only meaningful death. I had the fantasy of lying in a bath of warm water and my life's blood flowing out from my veins. In fact, I am quite convinced that had I the means at that time, I would have killed myself. I was totally submerged in a situation from which there would be no escape except through death. And like life, the absurdity of it all, the exhaustion of carrying my pain-filled body through days, years, decades, a lifetime, seemed insane to me. Why did I have to be involved in something so utterly futile and painful as living, only to meet my death in agony? This state persisted for hours. I thought I would never leave that place, yet even though there was an element of strangeness about this state of consciousness, I recognized it as something familiar. It was a state that I had experienced before in various forms; in fact, it seemed to be the underlying matrix which has influenced my world view and my mode of existence. To live it so intensely, if only for a few hours, in the form of an amplified hell from which there was no escape was an important lesson. I knew during the latter part of this experience that I no longer wanted to dwell on the suffering aspects of mankind, but did I have any choice in this matter? I felt that I would do anything to escape, but was there any way of escaping? I suddenly realized that on some level, I did not have any choice in this situation. I was being propelled through intimate, cellular suffering, and it was being done to me; I could not turn it on or off. I thought about karma here and started trying to puzzle out what in my past was responsible for leading me to such a monstrous place. But no amount of analysis yielded up any answers. I felt trapped in a maze from which there was no egress. I was stuck and that was my fate, to be someplace that was not the creation of living but being caught on the wheel of suffering. I loathed my fixation on suffering, but the more I could not accept my fate, the more difficult it became for me. It was as though I was a prisoner in a concentration camp and the harder I tried to get out the more I would be beaten, the more I struggled to free myself the tighter the bonds would become. And yet, I knew somewhere deep inside that I had to fight, that I had to escape, and that I would, but how? This unrelenting anguish lasted for hours and persisted even into the latter portion of the session. In a nearly normal state of consciousness, I still felt myself torn with anguish. I recognized more clearly the feelings that leak out of my unconscious to influence my daily life; they had all manifested themselves like familiar enemies. And I wondered when the battle would be done. . . .

Perinatal Matrix III. Synergism with the Mother (Propulsion through the Birth Canal)

This matrix is related to the second clinical stage of delivery. The uterine contractions continue, but the cervix stands wide open, and the difficult and complicated process of propulsion through the birth canal gradually unfolds. For the fetus, this involves an enormous struggle for survival, with mechanical crushing pressures and frequently a high degree of suffocation. The system is no longer closed, however, and a perspective of termination of the unbearable situation has appeared. The efforts and interests of the mother and child coincide; their joint intense striving is aimed at ending this often painful condition. During the conclusion of this stage, the child can come into contact with various kinds of biological material, such as blood, mucus, urine, and feces.*

From the experiential point of view, this perinatal matrix is quite complex; it involves a variety of phenomena on different levels which can be arranged in a rather typical sequence. In LSD sessions, it is experienced either as the reliving of the elements of the actual biological situation or in a symbolic form of the death-rebirth struggle, or both. BPM III has four distinct experiential aspects—namely, titanic, sadomasochistic, sexual, and scatological. It is important to emphasize that, in spite of this phenomenological variety, the underlying theme of the experiences related to BPM III is the encounter with death. It takes, however, specific forms that are clearly distinguishable from those described under BPM II.

The most important characteristic of this pattern is the atmosphere of a *titanic struggle*, frequently attaining *catastrophic proportions*. The intensity of painful tension reaches a degree that appears to be far beyond what any human can bear. The individual experiences sequences of immense condensation of energy and its explosive release and describes feelings of powerful currents of energy streaming through his whole body. The visions typically accompanying these experiences involve scenes of natural disasters and the unleashing of elemental forces, such as exploding volcanoes, devastating earthquakes, raging hurricanes, cyclones and tornadoes, electric storms, gigantic comets and meteors, expanding novas, and various cosmic cataclysms.

---

*In deliveries conducted outside the medical setting and without the use of enema and catheterization, the involvement of feces and urine is quite common. Also, in many of the deliveries in the early decades of this century, the Latin saying *inter faeces et urinas nascimur* (we are born among feces and urine) reflected a clinical reality rather than a philosophical metaphor.

Equally frequent are images of similar events related to human activities, particularly to advanced technology—explosions of atomic bombs, thermonuclear reactions, giant power plants and hydroelectric stations, high voltage cables, electrical condensers and flash discharges, the launching of missiles or spaceships, firing of guns and rockets, massive air raids, and other dramatic aspects of war destruction. Some individuals describe complex catastrophic events and scenes of havoc, such as the destruction of Atlantis, the end of Pompeii or Herculeum, the annihilation of Sodom and Gomorrah, the Biblical Armageddon, or even an invasion from another planet, not dissimilar to H. G. Wells's *War of the Worlds*. Less frequently, the images involve destruction by water rather than by the element of fire; here the individual experiences the enormous power of flooding rivers, stormy oceans, and tidal waves or waterfalls, and, of course, frequently, the atmosphere of the Biblical deluge.

One aspect of such experiences related to BPM III deserves special emphasis—namely, the fact that the suffering and tension involved are intensified far beyond the level which the subject used to consider humanly possible. When it reaches the absolute experiential limit, the situation ceases to have the quality of suffering and agony; the experience then changes into a wild, ecstatic rapture of cosmic proportions that can be referred to as "volcanic ecstasy." In contrast to the peaceful and harmonious "oceanic ecstasy" typical of the first perinatal matrix, the volcanic type of ecstasy involves enormous explosive tension with many aggressive and destructive elements. Subjects usually alternate experientially between the anxiety and suffering of the victim or victims and the ability to identify with the fury of the elemental forces and to enjoy the destructive energy. In the state of "volcanic ecstasy," various polar sensations and emotions melt into one undifferentiated complex that seems to contain the extremes of all possible dimensions of human experience. Pain and intense suffering cannot be distinguished from utmost pleasure, caustic heat from freezing cold, murderous aggression from passionate love, vital anxiety from religious rapture, and the agony of dying from the ecstasy of being born.

The *sadomasochistic element* is a prominent and constant feature

A symbolic self-portrait drawn by a patient after one of his LSD sessions, which was characterized by aggression oriented both outward and inward. A stylized bird of prey is crushing with its right claw a helpless mouse. The left claw is transformed into a cannon and turned against the predator's own head. The antique car on top reflects a play on words (self-portrait = auto-portrait) but also suggests the relationship of this type of aggression to reckless driving.

Four pictures representing unbridled murderous aggression, which is a frequent experience in perinatal LSD sessions.

of experiences related to the third perinatal matrix. The sequences of scenes accompanied by enormous discharges of destructive and self-destructive impulses and energies can be so powerful that subjects refer to them as "sadomasochistic orgies." They involve tortures and cruelties of all kinds, bestial murders and mass executions, violent battles and revolutions, exterminating expeditions such as the crusades or the conquest of Mexico and Peru, mutilations and self-mutilations of religious fanatics as exemplified by various sects of flagellants or the Russian Skopzy,* bloody ritual sacrifice or self-sacrifice, the kamikaze phenomenon, various terrifying modes of bloody suicide, or the senseless slaughtering of animals. Individuals tend to identify with ruthless dictators, tyrants, and cruel military leaders responsible for the death of thousands or millions of people, such as Emperor Nero, Genghis Khan, Francisco Pizarro, Hernando Cortes, Hitler, or Stalin. Other personalities known for their sadistic perversions also occur occasionally in this context: Salome, Cesare Borgia, Vlad Tepes of Transylvania ("Count Dracula"),** Elizabeth Báthory,*** as well as famous contemporary mass murderers. LSD subjects tuned in to BPM III feel that they not only can understand the motivations of such deviants but that they themselves harbor in their unconscious forces of the same nature and intensity and could, under certain circumstances, commit similar crimes. They can assume quite readily all the roles involved in complex sadomasochistic scenes, such as the group sacrifice of Christians in ancient Rome by immolation on crosses or by predatory beasts in the arena, the Aztec hecatombs in which tens of thousands of victims were ritually slaughtered in a single day, the burning of heretics in mass auto-da-fés of the

---

*Skopzy (Russian word meaning literally "rams") was a Russian religious sect, the members of which mutilated themselves, in particular by self-castration.

**Vlad Tepes, or the Voivode Dracula, was a minor ruler who, in the fifteenth century, governed the small province of Walachia. His nickname, *tepes*, means literally "the impaler"; it refers to his habit of impaling executed victims on the ends of pointed sticks. According to some sources, he was responsible for the execution of over a hundred thousand victims. He was used by the Irish writer Bram Stoker as an inspiration for his novel *Dracula.*

***Elizabeth Báthory was a sixteenth-century Hungarian countess who tortured young girls and then murdered them so that she could bathe in their blood. She was also known for her excessive use of an ingenious torturing gadget, the iron maiden.

Holy Inquisition, or the cool and premeditated atrocities of the Nazis. The power struggle in the royal courts and political circles of all ages, with its "cloak and dagger" atmosphere, is another frequent symbolism of this type.

If the two above aspects of BPM III, namely the titanic and the sadomasochistic, are experienced in a mitigated form, visions and experiences of various wild adventures result. The most typical of these are hunts for large and dangerous animals, fights with monstrous constrictor snakes, encounters of scuba divers with sharks, octopi, and other treacherous sea creatures, ancient gladiator combats, discoveries of new continents and battles of the conquistadors with the original inhabitants, outer-space explorations and science fiction-type adventures, as well as acrobatic flying, parachuting, hazardous car races, boxing, and other dangerous sports.

Another important aspect of the third perinatal matrix is *excessive sexual excitement.** According to the descriptions of LSD subjects, the sensations involved resemble the first part of the sexual orgasm, characterized by a progressive increment of instinctual tension. Here, however, it is incomparably more intense and appears to be generalized to the entire organism, rather than limited to the genital area. Individuals sometimes spend hours in overwhelming sexual ecstasy, expressing their feelings in orgiastic movements. The accompanying images reflect endless varieties of wild orgies, with all the possible variations of sex. Subjects can identify with Oriental harem owners, with participants in phallic worship or in unbridled fertility rites, with male and female prostitutes and pimps, or with historical personalities and fictional characters who became famous as sexual sym-

---

*It is an interesting theoretical problem why excessive sexual tension and excitement is an important and standard component of the birth experience. Observations from LSD sessions as well as several other areas seem to indicate that this association has a physiological basis. That suffocation and ischemia result in intense sexual stimulation has been observed in criminals executed by hanging (frequent occurrence of erection and even ejaculation in males dying on the gallows) and also in persons who attempted suicide by hanging and were rescued. The intimate link between physical suffering and sexual excitement is also well known from psychopathology. In sadomasochism, inflicting or experiencing pain is a necessary prerequisite for sexual satisfaction. Observations from extreme war situations, where captives and prisoners were exposed to inhuman tortures, seem to suggest that the ability to transcend excessive suffering into pleasure and even ecstasy is intrinsic to human nature.

bols, such as Don Juan, Jacopo Casanova, Rasputin, Father Grandier, Mary Magdalene, Maria Theresa, and Poppaea. An individual can experience scenes from Soho, Pigalle, and other famous red-light and night-club districts of the world, participate in the most ingenious strip shows and group orgies, become part of Babylonian religious ceremonies involving indiscriminate promiscuous sex, or witness and partake of wild primitive rituals with sensual rhythmic dances and a strong sexual undertone.

A particularly common element occurring in these sessions is the atmosphere of colorful, dynamic, and lascivious carnivals, with the characteristic mixture of amusing, exhilarating, and joyful elements with the bizarre, grotesque, and macabre ones. The unleashing of the otherwise repressed sexual and aggressive impulses constitutes another similarity between LSD experiences of this type and the atmosphere of carnivals in Rio de Janeiro, Nice, and Trinidad or the Mardi Gras in New Orleans, to which the LSD subjects so frequently refer in this context.

The *scatological aspect* of BPM III seems to belong to the final stage of the death-rebirth struggle and often immediately precedes the experience of birth or rebirth. Its essential characteristic is an intimate encounter with various kinds of biological material, identified as mucus, sweat, products of putrefaction, menstrual blood, urine, and feces. In addition to visual and tactile elements, this experience also involves rather realistic olfactory and gustatory sensations. Subjects may have very authentic feelings of eating feces, drinking blood or urine, or sucking on putrefying wounds. Also quite frequent are fantasies or vivid experiences of cunnilingus performed under rather unhygienic conditions. Initially, the individual has a strong negative reaction toward the biological materials involved; he finds them disgusting and revolting. It is not exceptional, however, that this attitude later changes into passive acceptance or even strange primitive enjoyment.*

---

*These experiences seem to be closely related to some unusual sexual perversions, such as coprophilia (fascination by feces and other materials usually considered revolting), coprophagia (eating feces in or outside of a sexual framework), and urolagnia (drinking of urine). The observations from LSD sessions add a new dimension to the understanding of these abnormalities. The deepest motivational force for these deviations appears to be the association between the contact with such biological materials and the termination of the agonizing experience of birth.

Sometimes the scatological elements appear in a symbolic pictorial form, such as tons of garbage emanating disgusting odors, piles of decomposing offal or decaying fish, putrefying human corpses and animal cadavers, neglected pigsties with large dunghills and stagnating urine, giant overflowing cesspools, and the bowels of urban sewer systems. Mythological symbolism observed in this context involves such images as Hercules cleaning the stables of King Augeas, the Harpies contaminating the food of the helpless, blind Phineus, and the Aztec goddess of childbirth and carnal lust, Tlacoltentl, or Devourer of Filth, who was believed to take away the sins of mankind.

One important experience related to the third perinatal matrix deserves mentioning in this connection. It is the encounter with consuming fire, which is perceived as having a purifying quality. The individual who, in the preceding experiences, has discovered all the ugly, disgusting, degrading, and horrifying aspects of his personality finds himself thrown into this fire or deliberately plunges into it and passes through it. The fire appears to destroy everything that is rotten and corrupt in the individual and prepares him for the renewing and rejuvenating experience of rebirth. Sophisticated subjects referred in this context to the medieval practices of exorcizing evil forces by the immolation of heretics and persons accused of witchcraft, to the self-sacrifice by fire of the Buddhist monks, and to the test by fire that was part of the sequence of initiation into the hermetic tradition. Such subjects reported that they achieved interesting insights into these phenomena, as well as a new understanding of the symbolism of certain pieces of art, such as the rejuvenating fire that maintained the eternal youth of the high priestess in Rider Haggard's *She* and the immolation of Siegfried and Brünnhilde at the end of Richard Wagner's *Götterdämmerung* that heralds the twilight of the old gods. A very appropriate symbol associated with the idea of the purifying fire seems to be that of the phoenix, the legendary bird who sets his nest on fire and finds his death in the flames; the heat of the fire facilitates the hatching of a new phoenix from an egg in the burning nest.

The religious symbolism of BPM III is typically related to religions that use and glorify bloody sacrifice as an important part of their ceremonies. Quite frequent are allusions to the terrible punishing God, Yahweh, of the Old Testament and to the stories about Abraham and Isaac, the Biblical deluge, the ten Egyptian scourges, and the destruction of Sodom and Gomorrah. Similarly, a vision of Moses and the burning bush can appear in this context; the Ten Commandments seem to represent a specific safeguard against all the negative aspects and temptations of man that become so clearly manifested in BPM III. Elements from the New Testament particularly involve the symbolism of the Last Supper and the transcending aspects of the crucifixion and of Christ's suffering, as well as the positive aspects of the Last Judgment. The concept of purgatory in different cultural variations belongs to this category as well. Particularly frequent are images from various Pre-Columbian cultures focusing on human sacrifice and self-sacrifice, such as is found in the ceremonies of the Aztec, Mayan, or Olmec religions. Ritual cannibalism also seems to be rooted in this experiential matrix. Sometimes subjects report elaborate scenes of worship of bloodthirsty deities resembling Kali, Moloch, Hecate, Astarte, Huitzilopochtli, or Lilith. The ambiguous symbol of the sphinx, which seems to represent the destructive female element as well as the transcendence of the animal aspect in man, deserves special notice here. Visions of religious ceremonies involving sensuality, sexual arousal, and wild rhythmic dances, from the bacchanalia of the ancient Greeks to aboriginal tribal rituals, are quite common symbolic illustrations of the rebirth struggle. Some individuals describe experiences that strongly resemble those preceding the Buddha's enlightenment, particularly the effort of the "master magician of the world illusion," Kama-Mara (Desire-Death), to discourage the Buddha from his spiritual search by the use of sexual temptation and the threat of death.

One observation that deserves attention is the relevance of BPM III for the understanding of phenomena occurring as part of the Satanic Mass and the Black Sabbath rituals. In this context, sex, usually in the form of group orgies, is combined with extreme sadomasochistic elements including animal or human sacrifice, ritual defloration, and psychological or physical torture. Frequently there is an emphasis on biological material, such as blood, menstrual discharge, miscarried fetuses, and intestines. The setting is usually morbid and macabre, and the general atmosphere is that of blasphemy, horror, and death. A peculiar mixture of sex, death, and scatology appears to be quite common, as exemplified by instances of sexual intercourse performed among the entrails of a disemboweled animal or in the cemetery in an open grave. The combination of perverted sex, sadomasochism, scatology, and an emphasis on death, with elements of blasphemy, inverted religious symbolism, and a quasi-religious atmosphere, is characteristic of BPM III. Subjects tuned in to this matrix frequently report experiences of participating in Walpurgis Night, in a Black Mass, or in satanic sexual practices. This usually results in insights into the psychology of the Inquisitors and witch-hunters. These experiences seem to suggest a far-reaching similarity between the state of mind of the actual practitioners of the black art and their fanatic persecutors. The behavior of both these groups betrays the influence of the third perinatal matrix.

In LSD sessions, elements typical of BPM III are frequently intermingled with images related to famous paintings or works of specific writers and philosophers. Particularly common are references to thematically related pictures by the fantastic realists and surrealists, to Leonardo da Vinci's sketches of diabolic war machines and his bizarre human caricatures, and Peter Paul Rubens' world of obese and sensuous mythological figures indulging in opulent feasts and bacchanalian orgies. Many of Vincent van Gogh's paintings seem to contain mitigated elements of volcanic ecstasy, as exemplified by his canvases of high cypresses reaching toward the glowing sun, fields of undulant ripe corn, and an atmosphere full of dynamic vibrations. The Gothic spirit is especially relevant for the third perinatal matrix—both the courageous and challenging forms of its architecture, which seem to reflect intense spiritual striving, and El Greco's tall and slender ascetic figures, which appear to be straining toward the sky. Also frequent are illusions to *purgatorio*, exemplified in Dante Alighieri's *Divine Comedy*, to the esoteric symbolism in the second volume of Goethe's *Faust*, to some of the tales of Edgar Allan Poe, and to the basic themes in Richard Wagner's operas, particularly *Tannhäuser*, *Parsifal*, and the *Nibe-*

lungenring. In this regard, the experience of volcanic ecstasy seems to be closely related to Friedrich Nietzsche's concept of the Dionysian element in man. References to famous thrillers and gothic novels as well as to science-fiction literature are so numerous in this context that detailed treatment would transcend the framework of this discussion.

The experiences of BPM III are often accompanied by illuminating insights into human nature, society, and culture. They seem to throw a new light on the phenomena of violence, war, and revolution; the psychology of sex; and various aspects of the world's religions and artistic movements. In this connection, a subject will typically scrutinize the value system that has previously dominated his life. He has to reconsider the sensibleness of complicated power schemes as compared to a simple and quiet existence; the relevance of love and interpersonal relationships versus professional ambitions aimed at status, fame, and possessions; and the emotional value of pursuing shallow and promiscuous sexual adventures instead of cultivating one meaningful love relationship. It is in the context of this perinatal matrix that the hierarchy of values appears to undergo the most profound transformation and crystallization.

A typical cluster of physical manifestations regularly accompanying BPM III seems to confirm the relationship of this matrix to the biological birth trauma. These physical manifestations include enormous pressure on the head and body; choking, suffocation, and strangulation; torturing pains in various parts of the organism; serious cardiac distress; alternating chills and hot flushes; profuse sweating; nausea and projectile vomiting; increased bowel movements; urge to urinate, accompanied by problems of sphincter control; and generalized muscular tension discharged in various tremors, twitches, shaking, jerks, and complex twisting movements.

As a memory matrix, BPM III can be associated with recollections of active attacks in wars and revolutions, hunting for wild animals, dramatic experiences in the military service, hazardous driving, parachuting or acrobatic diving, and wrestling and boxing with a strong enemy. Another typical group of memories that are relived in this context involves experiences in amusement parks and night clubs; wild parties, with abuse of alcohol and promiscuous sex; colorful carnivals; and other highly sensual adventures. Primal scenes from childhood, including sadistic interpretation of sexual intercourse and experiences of seduction by adults, as well as sexual molestation and rape, also seem to belong to this category. It was frequently observed that female subjects reliving their own birth usually re-experienced, on a more superficial level, the delivery of their children. Both experiences were usually relived simultaneously, so that these women often could not tell whether they were giving birth or being born themselves.

In regard to the Freudian erogenic zones, BPM III seems to be related to those activities that lead to sudden relief and relaxation after a prolonged period of tension. On the oral level, it is the act of chewing and swallowing of food (but also termination of gastric discomfort by vomiting); on the anal and urethral level, it is the process of defecation and urination after prolonged retention. On the genital level, we can find striking parallels between this matrix and the first stage of sexual orgasm, as well as the process of delivering a child. Statoacoustic eroticism—such as intense rocking and jolting of children, gymnastics, and acrobatics—also seems to be related to BPM III.

At least a certain portion of aggression in all the erogenic zones seems to be derived from BPM III. Oral aggression with cramps of the chewing muscles can be traced back to the frustration the child experiences in the birth canal, where its jaws are locked together by external pressure. Shortcut connections can be demonstrated to exist between the elements of this matrix and anal, urethral, and phallic aggression. Reflex urination or even defecation by both mother and child during delivery seems to suggest a deep involvement of these functions. A combination of libidinal feelings and painful physical sensations with extreme aggression in this phase seems to be the basic root for later masochistic and sadistic tendencies.

Although the phenomenology of BPM III is too ramified and complex to be manifested in its entirety in any single LSD session, the following account of the training session of a clinical psychologist and psychotherapist has enough of the essential characteristics of this perinatal matrix to be used as a good example in this context.

The first thing I remember from this session was feeling a very important relationship with Joan (the co-therapist)—loving her in some strong and unfamiliar way. It then developed that a good part of the love that I was feeling for her was a sense of oneness with her and anticipation that some very large and terrifying thing was in store for me in this session in relation to this identification with Joan. It quickly became apparent that what this large and terrifying thing was was the birth experience and that Stan and Joan were my parents. Not that I thought they were my biological parents—I knew who they were—but that I thought they were my new parents taking me on this second birth experience and that Joan was giving birth to me. But the identity with her made it the case that I was giving birth to her as well and that we were, in fact, giving birth to each other.

I had a powerful sense that I was in touch with one of the most basic cosmic processes, but there was some strange problem about my being a man who could never give biological birth, that somehow I was breaking the cycle. Then that vanished and I experienced some ancient feminine archetype in myself, that of the delivering mother. The role of mother was somehow clearer to me than the role of baby for a long time. I felt filled with my baby who was both myself and Joan, and totally frustratingly unable to give birth, to open myself and let go. I was a mother without a vagina, a mother without the birth canal, a mother with no way to give birth to the life pounding inside of me. I struggled and struggled to find a way to let go, to let it out, to give birth. I never succeeded.

The experience of being born was very, very confused. I never really clearly saw the birth canal or the process of birth or the relief of birth. I only knew that I was being pushed and crushed and wildly confused. The clearest part of my role as baby was being immersed in what seemed to me like filth and slime that was all over me and in my mouth choking me. I tried and tried to spit it out, to get rid of it and finally managed to clear my mouth and throat with a huge scream, and I began to breathe. That was one of the major moments of release in the session. Another aspect of the birth experience was the confusion resulting from the fact that the genitals and thighs of the woman were the place of sex and love and also the place where this nightmare of birth and filth had happened.

There were many images of the torturer and the tortured as the same person, very much as the mother and the baby were the same person. At one point, I experienced the horrors of Buchenwald, and I saw Stan as a Nazi. I had no hatred for him, only a profound sense that he, the Nazi, and I, the Jew, were the same person, and that I was as much the torturer and the murderer as I was the victim; I could feel myself as Nazi as well as Jew.

At one point I felt dangerous and warned Joan to be careful of me. I felt my teeth becoming dangerous, poisonous fangs, and I knew I was turning into a vampire. I found myself aloft in a dark night on great bat wings with my ominous fangs bared and my claws venomous and extended. I felt I was one of a group of witches, a coven of witches, riding the night air ... death riding the night air filled with stars but no moon, dangerous evil filled with the power of the witch. Something ended that; I think it was the change in the music. The scene passed and I fell into an ecstatic, floating, shimmering radiance.

For a long time then the next section as I recall it was tremendously erotic. I went through a whole series of sexual orgies and fantasies in which I played all roles and in which Joan and Stan were sometimes involved and sometimes not. It became very clear to me that there was no difference between sex and the process of birth and that the slippery movements of sex were identical with the slippery movements of birth. I learned easily that every time the woman squeezed me I had to simply give way and slide wherever she pushed me. If I did not struggle and did not fight, the squeezing turned out to be intensely pleasurable. Sometimes I wondered if there would be an end and no exit and if I would suffocate, but each time I was pushed and my body was contorted out of shape, I let go and slid easily into wherever I was being sent. My body was covered with the same slime as it was earlier in the session, but it no longer was a bit disgusting. It was the divine lubricant which made it so easy to give way and be pushed and guided. Over and over again I had the experience that "this is all there is to it" and "it is so incredibly simple"—that all the years of struggle, of pain, of trying to understand, of trying to think it out were all absurd and that all the time it had been right here in front of me; that it was so very simple. You simply let go and life squeezes you and pushes you and gentles you and guides you through its journey. Amazing, fantastic, what an extraordinary joke that I had been so fooled by the complexities of life! Over and over again I had this experience and laughed with intense pleasure.

Perinatal Matrix IV. Separation from the Mother (Termination of the Symbiotic Union and Formation of a New Type of Relationship)

This matrix is related to the third clinical stage of delivery. The agonizing experiences culminate, the propulsion through the birth canal is coming to an end, and, finally, the ultimate intensification of tension and suffering is followed by a sudden relief and relaxation. The period of impeded and usually insufficient supply of oxygen is terminated as well. The child takes its first deep breath and its respiratory pathways open and unfold. The umbilical cord is cut and the blood that previously circulated in the umbilical vessels is redirected into the pulmonary area. The physical separation from the mother has been completed, and the child starts its existence as an anatomically independent individual. After full physiological balance is re-established, the new situation is incomparably better than the two preceding stages, but it is in several important aspects worse than the original undisturbed primal union with the mother. The biological needs of the child are not being satisfied on a continuous basis, nor is it automatically protected from extremes of temperature, disturbing noises, changing intensity of light, and unpleasant tactile sensations. To what extent the experiences in the postnatal period (BPM IV) approximate the prenatal experiences (BPM I) depends to a great degree on the quality of mothering.

Like the other matrices, BPM IV has a biological and a spiritual facet. Its activation in LSD sessions can result in a concrete, realistic reliving of the circumstances of the biological birth. This can sometimes involve surprising and quite specific details that can on occasion be verified by independent questioning of witnesses. Most frequent are references to the odors of the anaesthetics used, sounds of surgical instruments or other noises, type of illumination in the room or operation setting, and, particularly, certain aspects of the birth (breech position, umbilical cord twisted around the neck, use of forceps, resuscitation maneuvers).

The manifestation of BPM IV on a symbolic and spiritual level constitutes the *death-rebirth experience;* it represents the termination and resolution of the death-rebirth struggle. Suffering and agony culminate in an experience of total annihilation on all levels—physical, emotional, intellectual, ethical, and transcendental. The individual experiences final biological destruction, emotional defeat, intellectual debacle, and utmost moral humiliation. This is usually illustrated by a rapid sequence of images of events from his past as well as from his present life situation. He feels that he is an absolute failure in life from any imaginable point of view; his entire world seems to be collapsing, and he is losing all previously meaningful reference points. This experience is usually referred to as *ego death*.

After the subject has experienced the very depth of total annihilation and "hit the cosmic bottom," he is struck by visions of blinding white or golden light and has the feelings of enormous decompression and expansion of space. The general atmosphere is that of liberation, redemption, salvation, love, and forgiveness. The individual feels cleansed and purged, as if he has disposed of an incredible amount of "garbage," guilt, aggression, and anxiety. He experiences overwhelming love for his fellow men, appreciation of warm human relationships, solidarity, and friendship. Such feelings are accompanied by humility and a tendency to engage in service and charitable activities. Irrational and exaggerated ambition, craving for money, status, prestige, or power appear in this state to be absurd and childish desires; it is difficult to believe that these values were once considered important and were so assiduously pursued.

It should be obvious from this description that there are certain overlapping elements between BPM IV and BPM I. As a matter of fact, the experience of biological birth and spiritual rebirth is often followed by feelings of cosmic unity. In this context transcendental elements merge together with the "good womb" and "good breast" experiences and pleasant childhood memories into one single complex. The individual's appreciation of natural beauty is greatly enhanced, and a simple and uncomplicated way of life in close contact with nature appears to be the most desirable mode of existence. The depth and wisdom in systems of thought that advocate this orientation toward life— whether they be Rousseau's philosophy or the teachings of Taoism and Zen Buddhism—seem obvious and unquestionable.

In this state, all the sensory pathways are wide open and there is an increased sensitivity and enjoyment of the perceptual nuances discovered in the external world. The perception of the environment has a certain primary quality; every sensory stimulus, be it visual, acoustic, olfactory, gustatory, or tactile, appears to be completely fresh and new, and, at the same time, unusually exciting and stimulating. Subjects talk about *really* seeing the world for the first time in their lives, about discovering entirely new ways of listening to music, and finding endless pleasure in smells and tastes.

The individual tuned in to this experiential realm usually discovers within himself genuinely positive values, such as a sense of justice, appreciation of beauty, feelings of love, self-respect, and respect for others. These values, as well as motivations to pursue them and act in accordance with them, seem to be, on this level, an intrinsic part of the human personality. They cannot be interpreted in psychoanalytic terms as reaction formations to opposite tendencies or as sublimation of primitive instinctual drives. The individual experiences them without any conflict, as a natural, logical, and integral part of a higher universal order. It is interesting in this connection to point to the striking parallels with Abraham Maslow's concept of metavalues and metamotivations, derived from observations of persons who had spontaneous "peak experiences" in their everyday life.[14]

In an individual who has completed the death-rebirth sequence and stabilized under the influence of BPM IV, the feelings of joy and relief are accompanied by deep emotional and physical relaxation, serenity, and tranquillity. Occasionally, it can be observed that the feelings of liberation and personal triumph are accentuated and exaggerated to the point of becoming a caricature. The behavior of a person in this state has a driven and manic quality; he cannot sit or lie quietly, runs around advertising loudly the overwhelming beauty and significance of his experience, wants to arrange a big party to celebrate this event, and makes grandiose plans for changing the world. This situation indicates that the experience of rebirth has not been fully completed. Such an individual is already experientially tuned in to BPM IV but is still under the influence of unresolved elements of BPM III, particularly anxiety and aggression. After these residual negative underlying feelings are worked through and integrated, the experience of rebirth appears in a pure form.

The positive atmosphere of BPM IV can also be suddenly interrupted by a specific complex of unpleasant symptoms. It involves piercing and penetrating pains in the umbilical area, which usually radiate and are projected to the urinary bladder, penis, and testicles, or the uterus. They are accompanied by breathing difficulties, feelings of agony and emergency, sensations of dramatic shifts within the body, and intense fear of death and of castration. This fear can be associated with the reliving of memories of events that involved threat of castration or were interpreted as such. Most common of them is the procedure of circumcision; in uncircumcised persons, other surgical interventions on the penis (such as an operation for fimosis) or in its proximity (such as reposition of a scrotal or inguinal hernia, and painful inflammations of the foreskin). Female subjects can relive in this connection sensations associated with dilation of the cervix and curettage, artificial abortions complicated by infections, severe cystitis, and postpartum and other gynecological inflammations. This episode, usually of short duration, was identified by some subjects as reliving of the crisis connected with the cutting of the umbilical cord. It can be distinguished from similar experiences related to the previous stage (BPM III) by a complete absence of feelings of external pressure and by the fact that the pains are localized in the pelvic area. Observations from LSD sessions indicate that this experience represents a deep source of castration fears.

The religious and mythological symbolism of the fourth perinatal matrix is rich and multiform and, like the other matrices, can draw on different cultural traditions. The experience of ego death is frequently associated with images of various terrifying and destructive deities mentioned earlier. A subject can experience himself as being sacrificed to the goddess Kali; while suffering the terminal agony, he has to face her horrible image, listen to the chilling rattle of the skulls on her necklace, and kiss and lick her bloody vagina. He can also identify with a baby thrown by his mother into the devouring flames glowing inside a gigantic statue of Moloch and can share with many other infants the death in this immolation ritual. The final destruction has on several occasions been experienced as coming from a powerful crushing step of Shiva the Destroyer performing his awe-inspiring dance in the burning-ground. Another frequent symbol of the ego death is the experience of the victim sacrificed to the Aztec sun god Huitzilopochtli; here the individual feels that his body is being opened by an obsidian knife and his living heart torn out of his body by the high priest. The death-rebirth sequence is often symbolized by identification with specific deities, such as the Pre-Columbian god Quetzalcoatl appearing in the form of a plumed serpent, or the Egyptian god Osiris, killed and dismembered by his evil brother Set, and reassembled by his wife and sister Isis. Occasionally, other deities symbolizing death and resurrection—among them Dionysus, Orpheus, Persephone, and Adonis—appear in a similar context.

Probably the most common symbolic framework for this experience is Christ's death on the cross and his resurrection, the mystery of Good Friday, and the unveiling of the Holy Grail. These are typically associated with intuitive insights into the fundamental significance and relevance of this symbolism as the deepest core of the Christian faith. As a result of such experiences, even those subjects who were previously strongly opposed to Christianity genuinely appreciate the value of this spiritual message. The perinatal roots of Christianity are clearly revealed by its simultaneous emphasis on agony and death (Christ on the cross), the perils of the newborn child (Herod's killing of the children), and on maternal care and protection (the Virgin Mary with little Jesus).

An individual who has overcome all the enormous hardships and vicissitudes of the birth agony and is enjoying the experience of rebirth usually has triumphant and heroic feelings, typically accompanied by images of superhuman achievements or of a final victory over various mythological monsters: Hercules as a baby vanquishing the gigantic snakes that attacked him or as an adult accomplishing difficult labors, Saint George slaying the dragon, Theseus defeating the Minotaurs, Mithra killing the bull in the sacrificial cave, or Perseus outwitting and slaughtering Medusa. Other terrifying creatures emerging in this context resemble the Sphinx, Hydra, Chimaera, Echidna, Typhon, and similar representatives of the mythological bestiary. The experience of rebirth also involves the element of victory of the forces of good and light over those of evil and darkness. This aspect can be illustrated by images such as those of the Vedic god Indra's decimating with his thunderbolt hosts of demons of darkness, the Nordic god Thor's smashing dangerous giants with his magic hammer, or the victory of the armies of Ahura Mazda over those of Ahriman as described in the ancient Persian Zend Avesta.

The liberating aspect of rebirth and the affirmation of positive forces in the universe are frequently expressed in visions of radiant, blinding light that has a supernatural quality and seems to come from a divine source. Occasionally, translucent heavenly blue haze, beautiful rainbow spectrums, or displays of subtle and intricate patterns resembling peacock feathers can occur in lieu of clear light. Very characteristic of this stage are nonfigurative images of God perceived as pure spiritual energy, as a transcendental or cosmic sun. A special type of this experience appears to be the Atman-Brahman union as described in sacred Hindu texts. Here the individual feels that he is experiencing the innermost divine core of his being. His individual self (Atman) is losing its seemingly separate identity and is reuniting with what is perceived as its divine source, the Universal Self (Brahman). This results in feelings of immediate contact or identity with the Beyond Within, with God (*Tat tvam asi* or "Thou art That" of the Upanishads). Also quite common are personified images of God, exemplified by the traditional Christian representation of God as a benevolent wise old man, sitting on a richly decorated throne and surrounded by cherubim and seraphim in radiant splendor. Some subjects experience at this point union with the archetypal Great Mother or a more specific version thereof, such as the Divine Isis of the ancient Egyptians. Another representation of this same theme is the symbolism of entering Valhalla or being admitted to the feast of the Greek gods on Mount Olympus and enjoying the taste of nectar and ambrosia.

Secular symbolism related to BPM IV involves the overthrow of a tyrant or despotic ruler, the defeat of a totalitarian political regime, the end of a long and exhausting war, survival in natural catastrophes, or the termination of a dangerous and critical situation. Very typical for this perinatal matrix are visions of gigantic halls with richly decorated columns, huge statues of white marble, and crystal chandeliers.

The symbolism involving images related to nature deserves a special notice. Before the discussion of the elements occurring in the context of BPM IV, it seems appropriate to make a few general comments. There exist quite characteristic and fixed associations between individual perinatal matrices and cosmobiological cycles, seasons of the year, and certain aspects of natural phenomena. Thus, images related to BPM II typically involve barren winter landscapes; arid and inhospitable deserts; the moon's surface and other settings hostile to life; black and dangerous-looking caverns; treacherous swamps; the beginning of tempests and ocean storms, with increasing atmospheric tension and darkening of the sky; and the eclipsed and setting sun. BPM III is associated with images showing the raging of elemental forces in nature, such as volcanic eruptions, hurricanes, electric and ocean storms, earthquakes and cosmic catastrophes, as well as dangerous jungles and the undersea world teeming with predators. Symbolism characteristic of BPM IV selectively depicts situations following periods of elemental outbursts and crises, such as spring landscapes with melting snow or ice breaking on rivers;* luscious meadows and idyllic pastures in springtime, with shepherds playing flutes; trees covered with fresh buds and blossoms; the quiet and peaceful atmosphere after a tempest, with beautiful rainbows in the skies; crystalline sunrises after cold nights; and deep oceans calmed after wild storms. Particularly characteristic and appropriate symbols for BPM IV seem to be high, snow-capped mountain peaks touching the blue sky, with refreshingly cold air and streaming sunlight; the spiritual achievement of rebirth is frequently represented as the successful ascent of a steep, high peak. Also the innocent world of newborn animals, birds hatching from eggs, and parents feeding their young appear frequently in this context. To complete the series of parallels between perinatal matrices and phenomena of nature, it has to be added that images typical of BPM

---

*The explosive release of emotional and physical repressive and restricting forces (liberation from the "character armor") is often symbolically expressed as cracking icebergs or melting masses of snow and the free flow of water released from them.

I selectively depict scenes in which natural beauty is combined with safety, fertility, and generosity.

Physical manifestations typical of BPM IV are prolonged withholding of breath, suffocation, and increasing muscular tension, followed by sudden inspiration, relief, relaxation, and feelings of perfect physiological well-being.

In regard to memory, BPM IV represents the matrix for the recording of situations characterized by escape from danger. In this context, subjects can relive memories from periods immediately following wars and revolutions, with particular emphasis on joyful celebrations, as well as survival in air raids, accidents, operations, serious diseases, or situations of near drowning. Another typical group of recollections involves various difficult life situations which the subject resolved by his own active effort and skill. All marked successes of the entire life can occur in connection with this matrix as if in a rapid flashback.

As far as the Freudian erogenic zones are concerned, this matrix corresponds on all developmental levels with the condition of satisfaction following activity that discharges or reduces tension. On the oral level, it is satisfaction of thirst and hunger (or termination of severe nausea by vomiting) or the pleasure accompanying sucking or following oral destruction of an object; on the anal level, it is the satisfaction following defecation, and, on the urethral level, the relief evoked by emptying the urinary bladder. The corresponding phenomenon on the genital level is the relaxation immediately following sexual orgasm; in females, it is also the pleasure associated with the delivery of children.

The transition from BPM III to BPM IV and the phenomenology of the fourth perinatal matrix can be well illustrated by the following excerpt from a training LSD session of a clergyman.

The music began to sound distorted and it was moving very rapidly. The crescendos were like sharp thrusts of a spear upward. At this point I started to experience considerable confusion. I was still aware of my identity and that I was lying on the couch in the treatment room. Waves of heat began to pass over me and I was vaguely aware of perspiring. The trembling was still going on and I began to feel a little bit of nausea at this point. Then quite suddenly my wild symphony took over. It was as if I were first at the top of a roller coaster gradually being drawn over the precipice, losing control, and being quite unable to arrest the downward plunge that I could see was ahead of me. One analogy I thought of was that this was like swallowing a keg of dynamite with the fuse already lit. The fuse was inaccessible, the dynamite was going to explode, and there was nothing I could do about it. The last thing I can remember hearing before my roller coaster began going down was music that sounded as though it came from a million earphones. My head was enormous at this time, and I had a thousand ears, each one with a different headset on, each earphone bringing in a different music. This was the greatest confusion I have ever felt in my life. I was aware of being on the couch; I was dying right there and there was *nothing* I could do about it. Every time I would try to stop it, I became panicky and terror-ridden. The only thing to do was to go toward it. The words "trust and obey," "trust and obey," "trust and obey" came through to me and in what seemed like a flash, I was no longer lying on the couch and did not have my present identity. Several scenes began to take place; it seemed as though they happened all at once, but let me string them out to try to make some sense of them.

The first scene was plunging down into a swamp filled with hideous creatures. These creatures were moving toward me, but they were unable to reach me. All of a sudden the swamp was transformed into a canal in Venice just under the Bridge of Sighs. My family, my wife, and my children were standing on the bridge looking down at me in this swamp. There was no expression on their faces; they were simply standing there looking at me.

The best way of describing this roller coaster and this entrance into the loss of control would be to compare it to walking on a slippery, very slippery surface. There would be surfaces all over the place and finally all of them would become slippery and there would be nothing left to hold on to. One was slipping, slipping and going further and further down into oblivion. The scene that finally completed my death was a very horrible scene in a square of a medieval town. The square was surrounded by Gothic cathedral façades and from the statue niches in these façades and from the gargoyle downspouts in the eaves animals, persons, animal-human combinations, devils, spirits—all the figures that one observes in the paintings of Hieronymus Bosch—came down from the cathedrals into the square and moved in on me. While the animals, the humans, the demons pressed in upon me in the square before these Gothic cathedrals, I began to experience intense agony and pain, panic, terror, and horror. There was a line of pressure between the temples of my head, and I was dying. I was absolutely certain of this—I was dying, and I died. My death was completed when the pressures overwhelmed me, and I was expelled into another world.

It turned out that this outer world was to be a continuation of deaths at a very different level, however. Now the panic, the terror were all gone; all that was left was the anguish and the pain as I participated in the death of all men. I began to experience the passion of our Lord Jesus Christ. I was Christ, but I was also everyone as Christ and all men died as we made our way in the dirgelike procession toward Golgotha. At this time in my experience there was no longer any confusion; the visions were perfectly clear. The pain was intense, and the sorrow was just, just agonizing. It was at this point that a blood tear from the face of God began to flow. I did not see the face of God, but his tear began to flow, and it began to flow out over the world as God himself participated in the death of all men and in the suffering of all men. The sorrow of this moment is still so intense that it is difficult for me to speak of it. We moved toward Golgotha, and there in agony greater than any I have ever experienced, I was crucified with Christ and all men on the cross. I was Christ, and I was crucified, and I died.

When all men died on the cross, there began the most heavenly music I have ever heard in my entire life: it was incredibly beautiful. It was the voice of angels singing, and we began slowly to rise. This was again almost like birth; the death on the cross happened, and there was a swishing sound as the wind rushed from the cross into another world. The gradual rising of all men began to take place. These were great processions in enormous cathedrals—candles and light and gold and incense, all moving up. I had no sense of my personal existence at this time. I was in all the processions, and all the processions were in me; I was every man and every man began to rise. The awe and splendor of this rising was almost beyond description. We were rising toward light, higher and higher, through majestic white marble pillars. We left behind the blues, the greens, the reds, and the purples, the gold of the cathedrals, and the royal garbs of some of the people. We rose into whiteness; the columns we were rising between were white and pure. The music was soaring, everyone was singing, and then there occurred a vision.

This vision has an entirely different feeling about it from anything else I experienced in the whole LSD session. It still feels like a vision—as if a vision were actually given to me—it is so real. The resurrection garment of our Lord touched me. Yet you have to understand: it did not touch *me;* it touched all men and yet in touching all men it touched me. When it touched, several things happened at once, as they did many times during this experience. We all became very small—as small as a cell, as small as an atom. We all became very humble and bowed down. I was filled with peace and feelings of joy and love; I loved God completely. While this was happening, the touch of the garment was like a high voltage wire. Everything exploded, and it exploded us into the highest place there is—the place of absolute light. It was silent; there was no music; it was pure light. It was like being at the very center of the energy source. It was like being in God—not just in God's presence, but *in* God and participating in God.

This did not last long (although time means nothing during this experience), and we began the descent. It was not a descent into a world that had ever been known before; it was a descent into a world of very, very great beauty. During the singing of the choirs, during the Sanctus, the Glorias, and the Hosannas occasionally an oracle's voice could be heard: "Want nothing, want nothing." I can still hear that voice. It was followed by another voice saying: "Seek nothing, seek nothing."

During this central part of the session many other visions occurred, and I would like to share them with you. One major vision that I encountered was looking down through the earth to the foundations of the universe. I went down into the depths and discovered the secret that God is praised from the depths as well as from the heights. Also in the depths of the universe the light can be seen. In the depths of the universe are many prison cells; as I went through these cells, the cell doors opened, and the prisoners came forth praising God.

Another powerful vision in this session was that of a figure walking in a wide, beautiful river in a deep, broad valley. Easter lilies were growing up through the river's surface and the river was flowing quietly and gently. The valley was surrounded by very high mountains with many, many watersheds coming down into the valley floor. Into this scene comes the voice: "The river of life flows toward the mouth of God." I wanted very much to be in the river and cannot yet tell whether I was walking in the river or whether I was the river myself. The river moved and as it moved toward the mouth of God, hoards of persons and animals—all of creation—came down the watersheds and poured into the main stream of the river of life.

When my symphony began to come to an end, I felt myself rousing and being located back in the session room. I was still filled with awe and humility and peace and blessedness and joy. I distinctly had the sensation of having been with God in the energy center of the universe. I still have the feeling with me very strongly that all men are one and the river of life does flow into God and that there are no distinctions between people—friends or enemies, black or white, male or female—that we all are one.

Significance of Basic Perinatal Matrices in LSD Psychotherapy

For didactic reasons the basic perinatal matrices have been described here in the order of the corresponding phases of delivery during actual childbirth. It is necessary to emphasize, however, that in LSD therapy or in individual LSD sessions this natural chronological order is never maintained. Perinatal matrices occur in various patterns and combinations of sequences that show great interindividual and intraindividual variability. The polyform and multilevel configurations unfolding in this process are contingent on a number of variables, the most obvious of them being the personality of the subject and specific aspects of his past history, the type of clinical symptomatology involved or the lack thereof, the circumstances of his present life situation, the personality of the therapist or sitter, and the set and setting. In psycholytic therapy of severely disturbed psychiatric patients—especially psychoneurotics—it can take a long time and a great number of sessions to work through all the layers of traumatic experiences from their individual life history. When the psychodynamic level has been transcended and perinatal elements appear in the sessions, these patients usually first confront the "no exit" situation (BPM II). With an increasing number of sessions, the phenomena related to the death-rebirth struggle (BPM III) come to the foreground. Occasionally, brief episodes of rebirth (BPM IV) and of cosmic unity (BPM I) occur in this context. Finally, when the ego death and rebirth is experienced in a pure and final form, the pathway is opened to elements of the first perinatal matrix and to various clearly transpersonal dynamic structures. Following this, the phenomena related to the biological birth (BPM II, BPM III, and BPM IV) usually disappear from the sessions and do not recur when the LSD procedure is continued. All subsequent sessions consist almost exclusively of transpersonal experiences and have a definite religious and mystical emphasis.

In emotionally less disturbed individuals and "normal" subjects, positive ecstatic experiences related to BPM IV and BPM I can appear in the early sessions of the series, especially with the use of higher dosages. In these cases, the first hours of the sessions are usually dominated by BPM II and BPM III, and the remaining two matrices (BPM IV and BPM I) occur in the termination period. In psychedelic therapy the perinatal levels are frequently reached in the first sessions with normal subjects, with patients facing death from incurable diseases, and with most categories of psychiatric patients. It seems that the use of higher dosages, special preparation and therapeutic techniques, eyeshades, and stereophonic music can expedite and facilitate the occurrence of experiences of rebirth and cosmic unity.

The concept of the basic perinatal matrices is very useful for understanding the dynamics of LSD sessions involving the death-rebirth phenomena and of the corresponding postsession intervals. The governing function of these matrices is comparable to the role of the COEX systems on the psychodynamic level. The specific clinical implications of this concept will be discussed in detail in a separate book focusing primarily on practical aspects of LSD psychotherapy. In this context they will be only briefly outlined.

Activation of a particular perinatal matrix influences the way the subject experiences the persons present in his LSD session as well as his immediate physical environment; his perception is determined by the specific content of the matrix involved. The events that take place during the termination period of a session are of crucial importance for its outcome and for the nature of the postsession interval. If the subject is under the strong influence of one of the perinatal matrices at the time when the pharmacological action of the drug is wearing off, he can experience the influence of this matrix in a mitigated form for days, weeks, or months after the actual session has ended. These consequences are quite distinct and characteristic for each of the four perinatal matrices.

When the termination period of an LSD session is governed by BPM II and the subject stabilizes under its influence, the postsession interval is characterized by deep depression. In this situation, an individual is vexed by various highly unpleasant feelings; anxiety, guilt, inferiority, and shame seem to dominate his thinking about the past. His present life appears to be unbearable and fraught with problems that have no solution; and the future looks utterly hopeless. Life is devoid of any meaning, and there is an absolute inability to enjoy anything. The world is perceived as threatening, ominous, and without color. The subject feels that everything is closing in on him. Suicidal craving is not uncommon in this situation; it usually has the form of a wish to fall asleep or be unconscious, forget everything, and never wake up again. Persons in this state of mind have fantasies about taking an overdose of sleeping pills or narcotics, drinking themselves to death, inhaling illuminating gas, drowning in deep water, or walking into snow and freezing (suicide I). Typical physical symptoms accompanying this condition are headaches; oppression of the chest; breathing difficulties; various cardiac complaints; ringing in the ears; constipation; loss of appetite; and lack of interest in sex. Quite common are feelings of exhaustion and fatigue, drowsiness and somnolence, and a tendency to spend the entire day in bed in a darkened room.

Stabilization of an LSD session under the hegemony of BPM III results in feelings of intense aggressive tension associated frequently with strong but vague apprehension and anticipation of a catastrophe. Subjects in this state frequently liken themselves to "time bombs" ready to explode any minute. They oscillate between destructive and self-destructive impulses and are afraid of hurting other people or themselves. Typical is a high degree of irritability and a strong tendency to provoke violent conflicts. The world is perceived as a dangerous and unpredictable place, where one has to be constantly on guard and prepared to fight and struggle for survival. Painful awareness of one's real or imagined handicaps and limitations is combined with exaggerated ambitions and efforts to prove oneself. In contrast to the inhibited and tearless depression related to BPM II, the manifestations here resemble an agitated depression accompanied by emotional incontinence and psychomotor excitement. Suicidal thoughts and tendencies are quite frequent and follow a pattern distinctly different from that described for BPM II. Individuals in this state contemplate bloody and violent suicides, such as throwing oneself under a train, jumping from a window or cliff, harakiri, or shooting oneself (suicide II). Typical physical symptoms associated with this syndrome involve intense muscular tension, frequently resulting in tremors, twitches, and jerks; headaches; pains in various other parts of the body; nausea with occasional vomiting; intensification of intestinal activity and diarrhea; frequent urination or disturbances thereof; and profuse sweating. A characteristic manifestation in the sexual area is excessive augmentation of the libidinal drive, for which even repeated orgasms do not bring satisfactory relief. In male subjects, this intensification of sexual tension is sometimes associated with impotence and premature ejaculation; in females, with premenstrual emotional turbulence, dysmenorrhea, and painful genital cramps during intercourse (vaginismus).

Subjects whose LSD session terminates under the influence of BPM IV present a very different picture. The most remarkable aspect of this state is the often dramatic alleviation or even disappearance of previous psychopathological symptoms and a decrease of emotional problems of all kinds. Individuals feel that they have left the past behind and that they are capable of starting an entirely new chapter of their lives. Exhilarating feelings of freedom from anxiety, depression, and guilt are associated with deep physical relaxation and a sense of perfect functioning of all physiological processes. Life appears simple and exciting, and the individual has the feeling of unusual sensory richness and intense joy.

As far as BPM I is concerned, the individual can stabilize under the influence of its positive or negative aspects. In the former case, the postsession interval resembles the one described for BPM IV. All the feelings involved are, however, much deeper and are experienced in a religious or mystical framework. Subjects see new dimensions in the universe, have strong feelings of being an integral part of creation, and tend to regard ordinary things in everyday life—such as meals, walks in nature, playing with children, or sexual intercourse—as sacred. The experience of cosmic unity has an unusual therapeutic potential and can have lasting beneficial consequences for the individual. If the subject remains after an LSD session under the influence of the negative aspects of BPM I, he experiences various forms and degrees of emotional and physical distress associated with conceptual confusion. These difficulties are typically interpreted in a metaphysical framework, in occult, mystical, or religious terms. The above unpleasant condition is attributed to adverse forces of destiny, "bad karma," malefic astrological or cosmobiological influences, or various evil spiritual entities. In extreme cases, this condition can reach psychotic proportions. After the individual works through and integrates the experience, he assumes a tentative and metaphorical approach to his previous interpretations.

5 Transpersonal Experiences in LSD Sessions

Transpersonal experiences occur only rarely in early sessions of psycholytic therapy; they become quite common in advanced sessions after the subject has worked through and integrated the material on the psychodynamic and perinatal levels. After the final experience of ego death and rebirth, transpersonal elements dominate all subsequent LSD sessions of the individual. Occasionally, transpersonal experiences can occur in the culmination periods of the first high-dose session of psychedelic treatment.

Since transpersonal experiences represent a relatively new concept in psychology, the detailed discussion will be preceded by an attempt at their definition. The common denominator of this otherwise rich and ramified group of phenomena is the feeling of the individual that his consciousness expanded beyond the usual ego boundaries and limitations of time and space. In the "normal" or usual states of consciousness, an individual experiences himself as existing within the boundaries of his physical body, which separate him distinctly from the rest of the world. He is clearly aware of the space he occupies as a physical entity and also of its interfaces with the external world. This is usually referred to as one's body image. His perception of the environment is restricted by the physically determined range of his exteroceptors. Both the internal perception (interoception) and the perception of the environment (exteroception) are subject to specifiic space-time limitations. An individual can usually *experience* only those things happening at the present moment and in his present location; he can *recall* things that happened at another time and in another place, and *fantasize* or *anticipate* things that will happen in the future. The basic characteristic of transpersonal experiences is that one or several of these limitations appear to be transcended. In some instances, the subject experiences loosening of his usual ego boundaries, and his consciousness and self-awareness seem to expand and to include and encompass other individuals and elements of the external world. In other instances, the subject continues to experience his own identity but in a different form, at a different time, in a different place, or in a different context. In yet other cases, the subject experiences a complete loss of his own identity and a complete identification with the consciousness of another being or entity. Finally, in a rather large category of transpersonal experiences, the subject's consciousness appears to encompass elements that do not have any continuity with his usual ego identity and that cannot be considered simple derivatives of his experiences in the three-dimensional world.

On the basis of the above discussion, transpersonal experiences can be defined as "experiences involving an expansion or extension of consciousness beyond the usual ego boundaries and beyond the limitations of time and/or space." Transpersonal experiences cover such a wide range of phenomena and are so multifaceted that it is extremely difficult to find a suitable *principium divisionis* and present a simple and comprehensive system for their classification and systematic description. This problem can be approached from many different angles, all of which would yield interesting alternatives. For the purpose of this discussion, I have decided to use a system of classification based on the distinction of whether or not the content of a particular transpersonal experience consists of elements of the three-dimensional phenomenal world (or "objective reality") as we know it from our usual states of consciousness. Some transpersonal experiences involve phenomena, the existence of which has been generally accepted on the basis of consensual validation, empirical evidence, or scientific research. This is true, for example, for embryonal experiences, ancestral and phylogenetic memories, or elements of the collective unconscious. It is not the

content of the experience (the fact of one's embryonal development, genetic continuity with human and animal ancestors, or
belonging to a particular racial and cultural group) that is
unusual and surprising but the existence of these elements in the
human unconscious and the possibility of experiencing them
consciously in a vivid and realistic way. The category of transpersonal experiences of this sort can be further subdivided on the
basis of whether or not the extension of consciousness that they
entail can be understood in terms of alteration of the dimensions
of time or space.

There exists also a group of ESP phenomena that could be
classified as transpersonal experiences, the content of which is
understandable within the framework of "objective reality." In
the case of precognition, clairvoyance and clairaudience, "time
travel," out-of-body experiences, traveling clairvoyance, "space
travel," and telepathy, it again is not the content of the experiences that is unusual but the way of acquiring certain information or perceiving a certain situation that according to generally
accepted scientific paradigms is beyond the reach of the senses.

The second broad category of transpersonal experiences
would then involve phenomena that are not part of "objective
reality" in the Western sense. This would apply to such experiences as communication with spirits of deceased human beings
or with suprahuman spiritual entities, encounter or identification with various deities, archetypal experiences, etcetera.

The following tentative classification is based on the principle
described above:

TRANSPERSONAL EXPERIENCES

I. Experiential Extension within the Framework of "Objective Reality"

A. TEMPORAL EXPANSION OF CONSCIOUSNESS
Embryonal and Fetal Experiences
Ancestral Experiences
Collective and Racial Experiences
Phylogenetic (Evolutionary) Experiences
Past-Incarnation Experiences
*Precognition, Clairvoyance, Clairaudience, and "Time
Travels"*

B. SPATIAL EXPANSION OF CONSCIOUSNESS
 Ego Transcendence in Interpersonal Relations and the
   Experience of Dual Unity
 Identification with Other Persons
 Group Identification and Group Consciousness
 Animal Identification
 Plant Identification
 Oneness with Life and with All Creation
 Consciousness of Inorganic Matter
 Planetary Consciousness
 Extraplanetary Consciousness
 Out-of-Body Experiences, Traveling Clairvoyance and
   Clairaudience, "Space Travels," and Telepathy

C. SPATIAL CONSTRICTION OF CONSCIOUSNESS
 Organ, Tissue, and Cellular Consciousness

II. **Experiential Extension beyond the Framework of**
 "Objective Reality"
 Spiritistic and Mediumistic Experiences
 Experiences of Encounters with Suprahuman Spiritual
   Entities
 Experiences of Other Universes and Encounters with Their
   Inhabitants
 Archetypal Experiences and Complex Mythological Sequences
 Experiences of Encounters with Various Deities
 Intuitive Understanding of Universal Symbols
 Activation of the Chakras and Arousal of the Serpent Power
   (Kundalini)
 Consciousness of the Universal Mind
 The Supracosmic and Metacosmic Void

It is necessary to bear in mind that transpersonal experiences, especially in psychedelic sessions, do not always occur in a pure form. It was mentioned before that, for example, perinatal phenomena are frequently accompanied by certain types of transpersonal experiences, such as identification with other persons, group identification, some archetypal experiences, or encounters with various deities. Similarly, embryonal experiences can occur simultaneously with phylogenetic memories and with the experience of cosmic unity. These associations are rather constant, and they reflect deep intrinsic interrelations between various types of psychedelic phenomena as well as the multilevel nature of the LSD experience.

In what is to follow, each of the transpersonal experiences mentioned above in the synoptic list will be briefly described and some of them illustrated by typical clinical examples.

Experiential Extension within the Framework of "Objective Reality"

TEMPORAL EXPANSION OF CONSCIOUSNESS

Embryonal and Fetal Experiences

The first transpersonal phenomena that I observed or recognized in the course of early psycholytic therapy were embryonal and fetal experiences. Their existence represents a serious challenge to accepted scientific paradigms, although they are certainly the least controversial of the various transpersonal elements that emerge in LSD sessions. We have already briefly mentioned certain aspects of these experiences in relationship to BPM I, since they frequently occur in the context of the perinatal unfolding. In psychedelic or advanced psycholytic sessions, vivid, concrete episodes that appear to be memories of specific events from an individual's intrauterine development are rather common. Many of these involve instances of psychotraumatization resulting from various noxious and disturbing stimuli of a mechanical, physical, biological, or biochemical nature. Individuals reporting these relivings seem to be convinced that the fetus can subjectively experience not only gross disturbances of its existence, such as attempted abortions, penetrating and loud sounds, intense vibrations, and mechanical concussions, but also the distress associated with the mother's somatic condition when she is ill, exhausted, or intoxicated. Even more surprising are numerous independent claims that the fetus is aware of or shares its mother's affective states; subjects have reported in this connection fetal participation in the mother's anxiety attacks, emotional shocks, outbursts of aggression or hate, depressive moods, and sexual arousal, or, conversely, in her feelings of relaxation, satisfaction, love, and happiness. Another interesting aspect of this category of phenomena are accounts of the exchange of thoughts between the mother and child in the womb that have the form of a telepathic communication. While experiencing the various intrauterine states, many LSD subjects felt that, during their fetal existence, this multilevel communication with their mother made them keenly aware of being wanted and loved, or unwanted and resented. In the therapy of many psychiatric patients, this issue was of crucial importance, and subjects would spend much time in their sessions working it through. For those individuals who were twins, sharing the womb with a mate and rival appeared to be a difficult and complex problem that required much intricate psychological work in the sessions. Fetal distress, however, is not the only content of intrauterine experiences; equally frequent are episodes of positive oceanic feelings and blissful unity with the mother, accompanied by a nourishing exchange of physical, emotional, and spiritual energies as well as comforting thoughts and insights of transcendental relevance.

As in the case of the reliving of childhood and birth memories, the authenticity of recaptured intrauterine events is an open question. It seems, therefore, more appropriate to refer to them as experiences rather than memories. I would like to stress, however, that I have tried to be completely open-minded about these phenomena. Whenever it was possible, I have made attempts at objectively verifying such episodes, no matter how absurd these attempts might have appeared to my colleagues. This task was even more difficult than in the case of childhood memories. However, on several occasions, I was able to get surprising confirmations by independently questioning the mother or other persons involved; it should be emphasized that this was done with all the precautions necessary to avoid any contamination of the data. Another interesting aspect of these experiences that I found quite unusual was the fact that subjects, when discussing them, seemed to avail themselves of specific knowledge of embryology and the physiology of pregnancy that was far superior to their previous education in these areas. They have often accurately described certain characteristics of the heart sounds of the mother and child; the nature of various acoustic phenomena in the peritoneal cavity; specific details of positions, physical features, and behavior of the fetus; relevant facts about placentary circulation; and even details about exchanges between the maternal and fetal blood in the placentary villi. Sometimes, the descriptions of gravidity appearing in the accounts of LSD subjects reflect an awareness of and participation in the processes involved on the level of tissue physiology, cellular exchange, and biochemical reactions. Scientists from various disciplines, such as psychiatrists, psychologists, and biologists, who volunteered for the LSD training program expressed astonishment at how convincing and authentic these experiences could be. These same sophisticated subjects usually emphasized that experiences of this kind occurred in their sessions in spite of the fact that, before the sessions, they did not accept the possibility of prenatal memories; moreover, the existence of such phenomena was contrary to their presession scientific beliefs.

Sometimes, experiences of intrauterine existence depict very early stages of embryonal development. In this case, the emphasis usually is not on mother-fetus interaction or fetal reaction to external influences; rather, the individual focuses on growing tissues, the differentiation of various organs, and the biochemical processes involved in rapid growth. Insights experienced on this level are related to hereditary, spiritual, and cosmic factors codetermining the development of the embryo; they involve an awareness of genetic influences, cosmobiological and astrophysical energy fields, metaphysical forces, archetypical constellations, and the operation of karmic law.

It is evident from the above discussion that fetal and embryonal experiences occur in close connection with other types of transpersonal phenomena. Positive intrauterine experiences can be associated with feelings of cosmic unity, images of various blissful deities, and beneficent archetypes, especially those of the Great Mother and Mother Nature. Episodes of embryonal and fetal crises are accompanied by traumatic ancestral memories, visions of demons and wrathful deities, archetypical evil appearances, and negative past-incarnation experiences ("bad karma"). In addition, as has been suggested previously, elements of tissue and cellular consciousness are observed quite frequently in this context. Other typical concomitants of embryonal and fetal experiences are phylogenetic (evolutionary) memories. This liaison occurs even in unsophisticated subjects who know nothing about Ernst Haeckel's biogenetic law according to which the fetus repeats in its embryonal development (ontogenesis) the history of its species (phylogenesis) in an abbreviated and condensed way.

This section will be concluded by a short example illustrating the nature of intrauterine experiences; it is one of several observations in which the attempt at objective verification brought positive results. It involves part of an advanced LSD session of Richard, whose case was discussed earlier in connection with the COEX systems (see page 57).

In one of the sessions of his psycholytic series, Richard described what appeared to be a rather authentic intrauterine experience. He felt immersed in fetal liquid and fixed to the placenta by the umbilical cord. He was aware of nourishment streaming into his body through the navel area and experienced wonderful feelings of symbiotic unity with his mother. There was a continuity of circulation between them; life-giving liquid—blood—seemed to create a sort of magical link between him and her. He heard two sets of heart sounds with different frequencies that were merging into one undulating acoustic pattern. This was accompanied by peculiar hollow and roaring noises that he identified after some hesitation as those produced by gas and liquid during the peristaltic movements of his mother's intestines adjacent to the uterus. He was fully aware of his body image and recognized that it was very different from his adult one: his head was disproportionately large as compared with the body and extremities. On the basis of cues that he was not able to identify and explain, he diagnosed himself as being a rather mature fetus just before delivery.

In this state, he suddenly heard strange noises coming from the outside world. They had a very unusual echoing quality as if resounding in a large hall or coming through a layer of water. The resulting effect reminded him of the type of sound that music technicians achieve through electronic means in modern recordings. He finally concluded that the abdominal wall and fetal liquid were responsible for the distortion and that this was the form in which external sounds reach the fetus. He tried to identify what produced the sounds and where they were coming from. After some time, he could recognize human voices laughing and yelling and sounds that

162 / REALMS OF THE HUMAN UNCONSCIOUS

resembled carnival trumpets. Suddenly, the idea came to him that this must have been the fair held in his native village every year two days prior to his birthday. After having put together the above pieces of information, he came to the conclusion that his mother must have attended this fair in an advanced stage of pregnancy.

Richard's mother, when asked independently about the circumstances of his birth without being told about his LSD experience, volunteered among other things the following story. In the relatively dull life of the village, the annual fair was a rare excitement. Although she was in a late stage of pregnancy, she would not have missed this opportunity for anything in the world. In spite of strong objections and warnings from her mother and grandmother, she left home to participate in the festivities. According to her relatives, the noisy environment and excitement precipitated Richard's delivery. Richard denied ever having heard this story, and his mother did not remember having told him about it.

Ancestral Experiences

This category of transpersonal experiences is characterized by a strong sense of regression in historical time to periods preceding the subject's conception and his embryological development. The individual feels that his memory has transcended its usual limits and that he is in touch with information related to the life of his biological ancestors. Sometimes, such experiences are related to comparatively recent history and more immediate ancestors on the maternal or paternal side, such as parents or grandparents. In an extreme form, however, they can reach back many generations or even centuries. In general, the content of these phenomena is always compatible with the individual's racial background and cultural history. Thus, a Jewish subject may experience episodes from tribal life in Israel during Biblical times and develop a deep bond with his historical, religious, and cultural heritage. A person of Scandinavian origin may witness various scenes from the adventurous explorations and conquests of the Vikings with a great vividness of specific detail in regard to garments, weapons, jewelry, and naval technique. An Afro-American may relive sequences from the life of his African ancestors involving ordinary village life as well as rich festivities and rituals; on another occasion, he can relive traumatic events from the early history of slavery. Such experiences are usually associated with interesting psychological insights; the subject can relate these archaic elements to his present personality and become aware of their influence on his everyday behavior.

Ancestral experiences are multiform and complex. Sometimes, they involve actual reliving of short episodes from the life of one's ancestors or whole sequences that are specific and rich in concrete detail. In other instances, they follow the pattern of tuning in to the personality of a certain individual in one's biological lineage to the point of complete physical, emotional, and intellectual identification with this person. On occasion, ancestral experiences are of a much more diffuse and generalized nature; they can have the form of complex feelings concerning the psychological atmosphere and interpersonal relations in families, clans, and tribes, or that of intuitive insights into cultural attitudes, belief systems, family customs, traditions, superstitions, and prejudices. Some subjects have reported in this context that as a result of such experiences they have developed a new understanding of some of their personal problems and conflicts. They could trace them back to friction points, incompatibilities, and incongruences between their maternal and paternal lineages and realized that what was considered to have been primary intrapsychic problems were actually introjected and internalized conflicts between generations of their dead kinsmen.

There are two important characteristics of ancestral experiences that differentiate them from the following group, the collective and racial experiences. The persons with whom the individual identifies always belong to his own cultural group or to his possible biological lineage. A more important distinction is a certain experiential quality of ancestral experiences; they are accompanied by the subject's conviction that he is confronted with events that form a part of his own developmental line, as if he were reading his own genetic code.

One aspect of ancestral experiences deserves special attention; careful and unbiased study can occasionally reveal that they convey specific information that was unknown to the subject, and, in some instances, not even accessible to him at the time of the session. The mechanism involved is, at this point, quite obscure; none of the explanations available seems to cover all the unusual coincidences of this kind observed during my LSD work. The nature of this problem can be illustrated by the following typical example.

Nadja, a fifty-year-old psychologist, experienced in her LSD training session a very realistic identification with her mother and relived a scene that she considered to be a part of her mother's childhood. Here is her report of the relived event: "To my great surprise, my ego identity was suddenly changed. I was my mother at the age of three or four; it must have been the year 1902. I was dressed up in a starched, fussy dress and hiding underneath the staircase; my eyes were dilated like those of a frightened animal, and I felt anxious and lonely. I was covering my mouth with my hand, painfully aware that something terrible had just happened. I had said something very bad, was criticized, and someone roughly put their hand over my mouth. From my hideout, I could see a scene with many relatives— aunts and uncles, sitting on the porch of a frame house, in old-fashioned dresses characteristic of that time. Everybody seemed to be talking, unmindful of me. I had a sense of failure and felt overwhelmed by the unrealistic demands of the adults—to be good, to behave myself, to talk properly, not to get dirty—it seemed so impossible to please them. I felt excluded, ostracized, and ashamed."

Motivated by professional interest, Nadja approached her mother to obtain the necessary data about her childhood, which they had never discussed before. Reluctant to admit that she had had an LSD session, which her mother would have disapproved of, she explained to her that she had had a dream about her mother's childhood and wanted to know if it was true. No sooner had she started her story than her mother interrupted her and finished it in full accord with the reliving. She added many details about her childhood that logically complemented the episode experienced in the LSD session. She confessed to Nadja how ominous and strict her mother had been to her; she talked about her mother's excessive demands regarding cleanliness and proper behavior. This was reflected in her mother's favorite saying, "Children should be seen but not heard." Nadja's mother then emphasized how lonely she had felt during her whole childhood, being the only girl with two much older brothers, and how much she craved to have playmates. Her description of the house exactly matched Nadja's LSD experience, including the large porch and the steps leading up to it. She also mentioned the dresses covered by starched white pinafores that were characteristic of her childhood. According to the mother's narrative, Nadja's grandmother used to invite many relatives for family reunions on Sundays and made food for everyone.

A researcher studying transpersonal phenomena occurring in LSD sessions has to be prepared for many baffling observations and coincidences that can put to a serious test the existing scientific beliefs and instigate doubts about the validity of some widely accepted and shared basic premises. The following illustration is one of the most unusual coincidences that I have encountered during my LSD work. The phenomena involved have an ambiguous quality, since they have the combined characteristics of ancestral and past-incarnation experiences. This example shows clearly the complexity of this area of research. It is taken from the psycholytic treatment of Renata (see page 52).

In the advanced stage of Renata's psycholytic therapy, an unusual and unprecedented sequence of events was observed. Four consecutive LSD sessions consisted almost exclusively of scenes from a particular historical period. She experienced a number of episodes that took place in Prague during the seventeenth century. This time was a crucial period in Czech history; after the disastrous battle of White Mountain in 1621, which marked the beginning of the Thirty Years' War in Europe, the country ceased to exist as an independent kingdom and came under the hegemony of the Habsburg dynasty. In an effort to destroy the feelings of national pride and defeat the forces of resistance, the Habsburgs sent out mercenaries to capture the country's most prominent noblemen. Twenty-seven outstanding members of the nobility were arrested and beheaded at a public execution on a scaffolding erected on the Old Town Square in Prague.

During her historical sessions, Renata had an unusual variety of images and insights concerning the architecture of the experienced period and typical garments and costumes, as well as weapons and various utensils used in everyday life. She was also able to describe many of the complicated relationships existing at that time between the royal family and the vassals. Renata had never specifically studied this historical period, and special books were consulted in order to confirm the reported information. Many of her experiences were related to various periods in the life of a young nobleman, one of the twenty-seven members of the nobility beheaded by the Habsburgs. In a dramatic sequence, Renata finally relived with powerful emotions and in considerable detail the actual events of the execution, including this nobleman's terminal anguish and agony. On many occasions, Renata experienced full identification with this individual. She was not quite clear how the historical sequences were related to her present personality and what they meant. Despite her present beliefs and philosophy, she finally concluded that these experiences must have been relivings of events from the life of one of her ancestors.

Being an intimate witness of this personal drama, I shared Renata's bewilderment and confusion. Trying to decipher this enigma, I chose two different approaches. On one hand, I spent a considerable amount of time in an effort to verify the historical information involved and was increasingly impressed by its accuracy. On the other hand, I tried to apply a psychoanalytic approach to the content of Renata's stories in the hope that I would be able to understand them in psychodynamic terms as a symbolic disguise for her childhood experiences or elements of her present life situation. No matter how hard I tried, the experiential sequences did not make sense from this point of view, and I finally gave up on this problem when Renata's LSD experiences moved into new areas. Focusing on other more immediate tasks, I stopped thinking about this peculiar incident.

Two years later, when I was already in the United States, I received a long letter from Renata with the following unusual introduction: "Dear Dr. Grof, you will probably think that I am absolutely insane when I share with you the results of my recent private search." In the text that followed, Renata described how she had happened to meet her father, whom she had not seen since her parents' divorce when she was three years old. After a short discussion, her father invited her to have dinner with him, his second wife, and their children. After dinner, he told her that he wanted to show her his favorite hobby, which she might find of special interest. During World War II, it was required by the Nazis that every family present to the German authorities its pedigree demonstrating the absence of persons of Jewish origin for the last five generations. Preparing such a pedigree because of existential necessity, Renata's father became absolutely fascinated by this procedure. After he had completed the required five-generation pedigree for the authorities, he continued this activity because of his private interest, tracing the history of his family back through the centuries, thanks to the relatively complete system of birth records kept in the archives of parish houses in European countries. After dinner, the father showed Renata with considerable pride a carefully designed, ramified pedigree of their family, indicating that they were descendants of one of the noblemen executed after the battle of White Mountain. After having described this episode in the letter, Renata expressed her belief that highly emotionally charged memories can be imprinted in the genetic code and transmitted through centuries to future generations. The information obtained from her father only confirmed her previous suspicion, which was based on the convincing nature of the relived memories.

After my initial amazement in regard to this most unusual coincidence, I discovered a rather serious logical inconsistency in Renata's account. One of the experiences she had had in her "historical" LSD sessions was the reliving of the terminal anguish of the nobleman during his own execution. Physical death terminates, of course, the biological hereditary line; a dead person cannot procreate and "genetically" pass the memory of his terminal anguish to future generations.

Before completely discarding the information contained in Renata's letter as supporting evidence for the existence of ancestral memories, several facts deserve serious consideration. None of the remaining Czech patients, who had a total of over two thousand sessions, had ever even mentioned this historical period. In Renata's case, four consecutive LSD sessions contained, almost exclusively, historical sequences from this time. The unusual coincidence of these experiences with the results of her father's independent genealogical quest makes this clinical observation a rather difficult problem to interpret within the framework of traditionally accepted paradigms.

Collective and Racial Experiences

This category of transpersonal phenomena is related to C. G. Jung's concept of the collective and racial unconscious. The spontaneous emergence of such experiences in unsophisticated subjects who have not been exposed to Jungian ideas can be considered important supportive evidence and experimental confirmation of one of the most controversial aspects of Jung's analytical psychology. Subjects tuned in to these realms of the

Paintings from an advanced LSD session depicting archetypal material and elements of racial and collective unconscious. The author has never studied ancient cultures and could not relate these pictures to any known cultural area.

unconscious can go through brief episodes or long, elaborate sequences that take place in different countries and/or different centuries and depict various historical or contemporary cultures. These scenes can be experienced in the role of observer, but, more frequently, the subject identifies with one representative of the culture involved or with a greater number of them. This is typically associated with global as well as detailed insights concerning social structure, religious cosmology, forms of worship, moral code, specific characteristics of art, technological development, and many other aspects of these cultures.

Collective and racial experiences can be related to any country, historical period, and cultural tradition, although there seems to be a certain preference for ancient cultures and countries with highly developed religious, philosophical, and artistic traditions. Sequences related to Egypt, India, Tibet, China, Japan, Pre-Columbian Mexico and Peru, and ancient Greece tend to occur with surprising frequency. The choice of the cultures and their specific aspects seems to be quite independent of the subject's ethnic background, country of origin, cultural tradition, and even previous training, education, and interests. An Anglo-Saxon can, therefore, experience full identification with various periods in the history of Afro-Americans or North American Indians and develop, as a result, a new sensitivity to and awareness of racial problems. A person of Jewish heritage can tune in to the culture areas of the Far East and relive sequences from early China or Japan that enhance his understanding and appreciation of Buddhist or Taoist philosophy, Japanese music, the martial arts, and other aspects of these Oriental traditions. Similarly, an individual of Slavic origin can participate in the Asian conquests of Genghis Khan's Mongolian hordes, identify with African Bushmen or Australian Aborigines, and become a participant-observer in sacred ceremonies from those Central American Pre-Columbian cultures in whose religions bloody sacrifice and self-sacrifice were espoused.

The information communicated by these experiences is usually quite accurate and can be verified by consultation of archaeological and anthropological sources. It frequently encompasses specific esoteric details; in many instances, the degree of historical or ethnographic knowledge that emerges is clearly incongruent with the subject's previous education and level of information in these areas. On occasion, unsophisticated individuals have described details of Egyptian funeral services, including the form and meaning of various amulets and sepulchral boxes, the colors of funeral cones, the technology of embalmment and mummification, and the sequence of ritual procedures followed. One subject who experienced himself in one of his LSD sessions as an embalmer in ancient Egypt was able to describe the size and quality of the mummy bandages, materials used in fixing the mummy cloth, and the shape and symbolism of the four canopic jars and the corresponding canopic chests.* Other individuals gained an intuitive understanding of the functions of various Egyptian deities, the symbolism related to them, and the esoteric significance of the pyramids and the sphinx. In one instance, a subject who had experienced sequences from the life of old Parsees was able to describe not only the nature of their religion and their funeral practices but also specific technological details of the Zoroastrian *dakhmas* (towers of silence) in which the dead were devoured by vultures so that they would not contaminate the sacred elements of earth and fire. On other occasions, LSD subjects had interesting insights into Hinduism and Buddhism and manifested a deep understanding of their religious practices, as well as the symbolism of the painting and sculpture to be found in these religions. Many additional examples involving other cultures could be cited in this context.

Sometimes such experiences are accompanied by symbolic gestures or complex and elaborate sequences of motor activity that express or illustrate their content. It is not uncommon that in association with specific LSD experiences some subjects discover the meaning of various symbolic gestures *(mudras)* or spontaneously assume quite unusual postures *(asanas)* known

---

*"Canopic jars" is the name given to the series of four jars in which the organs of a deceased person were placed. Each jar was dedicated to one of four genii of the Egyptian underworld, was related to one of the cardinal points, and had the shape of the deity to whom it was dedicated. The man-headed jar (south) contained the stomach and large intestines; the dog-headed one (north), the small intestines; the jackal-headed (east), the lungs and heart; and the hawk-headed (west), the liver and gall bladder. The chests or coffers for canopic jars were made of wood and usually painted black.

from Hatha Yoga. In several instances, individuals enmeshed in elements of a certain culture felt a strong need to dance. Without any previous training or specific exposure to these cultures, they were able to perform complicated dance forms. Examples of such behavior observed in LSD sessions range from the !Kung Bushman trance dance and other African tribal rituals, Middle Eastern belly dancing, and whirling like the dervishes of the Sufi tradition, to Indonesian art forms as practiced in Java or Bali, and the symbolic dancing of the Indian Kathakali or Manipuri school.*

Collective and racial experiences can be combined with other types of transpersonal phenomena described later in this chapter. As suggested in the above discussion, they often involve a full identification with individual representatives of various cultures or elements of group consciousness. In their extreme form, they can encompass the consciousness of entire racial groups or the totality of the human race. Such experiential expansion of the individual to the consciousness of all mankind can approximate the Jungian archetype of the Cosmic Man. Some of these phenomena have the flavor of clairvoyance and clairaudience, traveling clairvoyance, or space and time travels. An important characteristic of collective and racial memories is the fact that the subject experiences them as insights into the diversity of cultural groups within the human race, illustrations of the history of mankind, or manifestations of the cosmic drama and divine play *(lila)*. In such a situation, a subject does not have the feeling that he is exploring his actual biological history—a quality essential for ancestral experiences—or that he is reliving scenes from his previous lifetimes, characteristic of past-incarnation experiences.

Phylogenetic (Evolutionary) Experiences

This type of experience involves a complete and quite realistic identification with animals on various levels of phylogenetic

---

*Kathakali dancing is performed along the Malabar coast; it expresses themes taken from Hindu mythological sources, such as the great epics *Mahabharata* and *Ramayana*, or later Puranas. The actors, magnificently dressed and painted, do not speak but mime the text. Manipuri dances are practiced in the little kingdom of Manipur in Assam. They have a very rich symbolic sign language used to communicate various stories from the life of the god Krishna and his beloved Radha.

development. As in the case of ancestral experiences, it is accompanied by a sense of regression in historical time; the subject will have a very vivid and convinced feeling that the animal specimens he identifies with are part of phylogenetic history and that he is exploring the evolution of the species in nature. The objects of identification are most frequently other mammals, birds, reptiles, amphibians, and various species of fish. Occasionally, they can be much less differentiated forms of life, such as insects, gastropods (various snails), brachiopods (shellfish), cephalopods (octopus and squid), and coelenterates (sea anemones and jellyfish). The subjective identification process occurring in phylogenetic experiences is rather complex and authentic; it can include size, body image, a variety of specific physiological sensations, particular emotions, and instinctual drives, as well as unusual perceptions of the environment.

Evolutionary memories have specific experiential characteristics that make them phenomena *sui generis;* they are distinctly different from human experiences and often seem to transcend the scope and limits of human fantasy and imagination. The individual can have, for example, an illuminating insight into what it feels like when a snake is hungry, when a turtle is sexually excited, when a hummingbird is feeding its young, or when a shark breathes through its gills. Subjects have reported that they have experienced the drive that sustains an eel or a sockeye salmon on its heroic journey against a river's flow, the sensations of a spider spinning his web, or the mysterious process of metamorphosis from an egg through a caterpillar and chrysalis to a butterfly.

Identification with other vertebrates can occasionally have specific physical concomitants that are accessible to an objective observer. Such experiences can be accompanied by unusual innervations of skeletal muscles, changes in neurological patterns, and sequences of motor activity that are not observed in man under normal circumstances. They appear to be related to the selective activation and automatic functioning of the so-called extrapyramidal system and other archaic neuronal pathways.

It is not uncommon for subjects reporting evolutionary experiences to manifest a detailed knowledge of the animals with whom they have identified—of their physical characteristics, habits, and behavior patterns—that far exceeds their education in the natural sciences. On occasion, subjects have accurately described courtship dances, complicated reproductive cycles, techniques of nest-building, patterns of aggression and defense, and many other zoological and ethological facts about the animals they have experienced in sessions. To illustrate this category we will use an example from an advanced LSD session of Renata, since the basic data of her case history were given earlier (page 52).

At one point in her session, Renata had a sense of complete identification with a female of a species of large reptiles that became extinct millions of years ago. She felt sleepy and lazy as she rested on sand by a big lake and basked luxuriously in the sun. While experiencing this in the session, she opened her eyes and looked at the therapist, who seemed transformed into a good-looking male of the same species; her feelings of laziness immediately vanished, and she experienced a strong sexual arousal and attraction. According to her description, these feelings did not have anything to do with human erotic and sexual excitement; it was a quite unique and specific "reptilian" interest in and attraction to the opposite sex. Any notion of the mouth, genitals, or other parts of the body that might interest her in a human partner was completely missing. She was absolutely fascinated by scalelike facets that she visualized on the side of the therapist's head. One large field of this sort seemed to have a shape and color that she found irresistible; it appeared to be radiating powerful sexual vibrations.

Since certain characteristics of this experience were so unusual and concrete, I decided to consult a good friend of mine who was a paleontologist educated in zoology and well acquainted with animal behavior. As I expected, he did not have any ethological information on the mating habits of antediluvian reptiles. However, he showed me passages in the zoological literature indicating that in certain contemporary reptiles particular distinctly colored areas on the head play an important role as triggers of sexual arousal.

Past-Incarnation Experiences

This is probably the most interesting and enigmatic category of transpersonal phenomena. Past-incarnation experiences consist of fragments of scenes, individual events, or entire, rather clear and logical sequences occurring at another place and time in history. In this, they resemble elements of the collective and racial unconscious and some ancestral experiences. The events involved, however, are very dramatic and are accompanied by an unusually intense emotional charge of a distinctly positive or negative quality. An essential characteristic of these phenomena is what could be called "a past-incarnation experiential quality." The subject participating in these dramatic sequences maintains his ego identity; although he experiences himself in another form, another place and time, and another context, he feels that he is basically the same individual entity as in his present existence. He also has a keen sense of being confronted with a *memory*, of reliving something that he has already seen and experienced. This *déjà vu* and *déjà vécu* flavor is specific; the individual feels and "knows" beyond any doubt that this experience is not related to or derived from anything in his present lifetime, and that it is a manifestation of one of his previous incarnations.

These experiences are not infrequent in advanced psycholytic sessions and occasionally can be observed in a first high-dose psychedelic session. Belief in reincarnation and familiarity with this concept is not a necessary prerequisite for their occurrence. They can be observed in sessions of scientists who previously considered this idea to be an absurd superstition of unsophisticated and uneducated individuals or a primitive cultural delusion shared by certain groups of religious fanatics in India. In several instances, subjects who have not been familiar with this concept had not only past-incarnation experiences but also complex and detailed insights into this area that were strikingly similar to those described in various religious and occult scriptures. In one case, an uneducated, unskilled laborer suffering from terminal cancer experienced in his session elaborate and illuminating insights into the mechanics of past incarnation and operations of the karmic law. He had done little reading in his life and claimed that he had not discussed these issues with anyone prior to his psychedelic session; in fact, he was at first embarrassed to share his experiences with the therapist, because he perceived them to be so strange and alien. Describing the content of the session, he was very tentative and apologetic and expected the therapist to think he was "out of his mind." The opening of this transpersonal area in his unconscious helped him face the grim reality of his life situation and ultimately meet death with equanimity.

Past-incarnation experiences usually entail one or several other persons; animals rarely appear as partners in such sequences. When they do, the subject feels that he became "karmically imprinted" on a scene in which he was killed by a tiger, bitten by a venomous snake, trampled to death by a wild elephant, or gored by a frenzied bull. Occasionally, the experiencer is the only protagonist in past life experiences. He might have to relive the bitterness, hatred, and envy that seemed to be connected with a painful and disabling disease or crippling accident in his previous incarnation. Subjects have also relived the anxiety and terminal agony associated with accidental death such as that occurring under a rock slide, the slow death in a swamp or quicksand, and immolation during a volcanic eruption and other conflagrations.

Karmic experiences fall into two distinct categories distinguished by the quality of the emotions involved. Some of them reflect highly positive affective associations with another person; most common of these are total mutual understanding, a nourishing and supportive exchange, a love bond, deep friendship, or spiritual partnership. The second group consists of scenes with strong negative emotional concomitants. The experiences belonging to this group cast subjects into past-life situations characterized by agonizing physical pain, bitterness, hatred and murderous aggression, inhuman terror and anguish, lustful passion, insane jealousy, or morbid greed and avarice. Many individuals describing such phenomena have felt that all the above negative emotions, intensified beyond a certain point, actually closely resemble each other. Accordingly, there exists a universal emotional pattern that represents the common denominator of all these emotions. It is a state of high emotional and biological arousal in which all the affective modalities converge, a "melting pot" of experiential qualities of an inhuman and unhuman nature, and a point where the bestial aspects of man reach metaphysical dimensions. More sophisticated individuals equated this undifferentiated arousal with *tṛṣṇa* or *tanha,* the thirst of flesh and blood that, according to Buddhist teachings, is the force that perpetuates the cycle of death and rebirth and is responsible for all suffering; it is this experience of unspecific affective activation that becomes imprinted as an unfinished gestalt which in subsequent lifetimes requires repetition and resolution. Such a karmic fixation occurring in LSD sessions cannot be worked through by the mere full reliving of all the painful emotions associated with a destructive karmic scene. To reach a satisfying completion, the experiencer has to transcend the event emotionally, ethically, and spiritually, rise above it, and finally forgive and be forgiven. LSD subjects have repeatedly stated that it does not seem to make a difference whether they were the oppressor or the victim in a negative karmic situation; it appears as though it is the dyadic traumatic pattern that is imprinted. On a deep level, the emotional state of the sadistic torturer is similar to that of the tortured, and the raging drive of the murderer fuses with the anguish of his dying victim. The inability to forgive and transcend one's suffering appears to be as conducive to karmic imprinting as actively performed injustice or violence.

The opening of the area of past-incarnation experiences in LSD sessions is sometimes preceded by complex instructions received through nonverbal means (i.e., on an intuitive level) that introduce the individual to the fact of reincarnation, make him recognize the responsibility for his past deeds, and present the law of karma as an important part of the cosmic order that is mandatory for all sentient beings. In addition to this more general information, such insights can encompass details that concern the mechanisms involved in the process of rebirth and the necessary prerequisites for karmic liberation. According to the reports of LSD subjects, the laws of reincarnation are closely related to, but virtually independent of, the subject's biological lineage and the genetic transfer of idioplasma. The assignment of an individual spiritual entity to a particular physical body occurs during conception according to its karmic past (referred to in the mystical literature as the akashic record); this choice bypasses the laws of heredity and genetics.

The resolution of a karmic pattern and liberation from the bonds it represents are associated with a sense of paramount accomplishment and triumph. Frequently, an individual feels that he has waited for and worked toward this event for many centuries; and that, even if he achieves nothing else in this lifetime, it has been fruitful and successful because in its course one of the karmic bonds was finally broken. The resolution of a single karmic pattern can thus result in feelings of indescribable bliss; the relevance of this event appears to be dictated by cosmic forces and is beyond the comprehension of the experiencer. On several occasions, it was accompanied by the experiential phenomenon of a gigantic "karmic hurricane or cyclone" blowing through the centuries and tearing karmic bonds related to scenes from various lifetimes that were secondary derivatives and repetitions of the original imprint resolved in the session. These phenomenological events bear a certain resemblance to some of the subjective experiences that accompanied the Buddha's efforts to achieve enlightenment.

It seems premature at this point to discuss the problem of the origin of these experiences and their ontological relevance. There is no doubt, however, that they represent the same phenomenon that has been described for centuries within such diverse religious, philosophical, and mystical frameworks as the cosmologies of certain African and Amerindian cultures, the Orphic cult and Plato's philosophy, early Christian thought, and several major religions of India—in particular, Hinduism, Buddhism, and Jainism.

Precognition, Clairvoyance, Clairaudience, and "Time Travels"

The most characteristic aspect of ESP phenomena in this group is the transcendence of the usual limitations of time and the resulting temporal extension of consciousness. Occasionally, LSD subjects report, particularly in advanced sessions of a psycholytic series, anticipation of events that will happen in the future. Sometimes, they witness complex and detailed scenes of future happenings in the form of vivid clairvoyant visions and can even hear the acoustic concomitants that are part of them; the latter range from ordinary sounds of everyday life, musical sequences, single words, and entire sentences, to noises produced by motor vehicles and various alarming acoustic signals (the sound of fire engines, ambulance sirens, or blowing car horns). Some of these experiences manifest various degrees of similarity with actual events occurring at a later time. Objective verification in this area can be particularly difficult. Unless these instances are reported and clearly documented during the LSD session, there is a great danger of contamination of data. Loose interpretation of events, distortions of memory, and the possibility of *déjà vu* phenomena during the perception of later occurrences are several of the major pitfalls involved. One general comment should be made in this context concerning the incidence of ESP phenomena in LSD sessions. Objective testing in the laboratory usually fails to demonstrate an increase of extrasensory perception as a standard and constant aspect of the LSD effect. States conducive to various paranormal phenomena and characterized by an unusually high incidence of ESP are, however, among the many alternative mental conditions that can be facilitated by this drug.

Another interesting element in this category is the experience of "time travel." Here the LSD subject is convinced that he can transcend the limitations of time at will and travel to any particular time period in a way not unlike that of science fiction's time machines. Such an individual can perceive a causal connection between his deliberate choice of such time periods and the subsequent subjective experiences. This is usually combined with a similar voluntary manipulation of the location of the events involved. The subject's feeling of making a free decision distinguishes these experiences from spontaneous, elemental, and uncontrollable reliving of episodes from childhood, ancestral experiences, or aspects of the collective and racial unconscious.

Spatial Expansion of Consciousness

Ego Transcendence in Interpersonal Relationships and the Experience of Dual Unity

This type of transpersonal phenomenon is characterized by a transcendence of the usual spatial limits of consciousness. The subject experiences various degrees of loosening and losing of his ego boundaries and merging with another person into a state of unity and oneness. In spite of feeling totally fused with the interpersonal partner, the individual always retains simultaneously the awareness of his own identity. In LSD sessions, this state of dual unity can be experienced with the therapist, sitter, family members, or other participating persons. It can also occur entirely in the inner space of the individual on a purely subjective level and be quite independent of the persons actually present during the session. Typical examples of this category are the symbiotic union between mother and child, the unitive fusion with a sexual partner (with or without the element of genital union), and the sense of oneness with a spiritual teacher in the guru-disciple relationship. The experiences of dual unity are accompanied by profound feelings of love and of the sacredness of the relationship involved.

Identification with Other Persons

In contrast with the preceding transpersonal group, here the subject feels a complete identification with another person and loses to a great degree the awareness of his own original identity. This identification is total and complex; it includes the body image, emotional reactions and attitudes, psychological characteristics, facial expression, typical gestures and mannerisms, postures, movements, and even the inflection of the voice. There are many different forms and levels of this experience. Thus, the reliving of traumatic childhood experiences involving more than one person is frequently characterized by simultaneous or alternating identification with all protagonists; this can give a transpersonal flavor to many otherwise typically personal experiences. In this connection, or independently, the subject can identify with his children, parents, and other close relatives, and with friends, acquaintances, and teachers. On other occasions, this process has involved prominent politicians, scientists, and artists, or typical representatives of various professional, ethnic, and racial groups. Equally common is identification with famous historical figures or religious teachers. The list of individuals who emerge in the sessions in this context would be very long; we will mention only a few of the famous personages who appear with unusual frequency. They are Albert Einstein, Richard Wagner, Ludwig van Beethoven, Leonardo da Vinci, Michelangelo, Galileo Galilei, Franz Kafka, Genghis Khan, Emperor Nero, Adolf Hitler, Joseph Stalin, Abraham Lincoln, John F. Kennedy, Saint Francis of Assisi, Saint Theresa, Jesus Christ, the Buddha, and Sri Ramana Maharishi.

Group Identification and Group Consciousness

This category is characterized by a further spatial expansion of consciousness; instead of identifying with individual persons, the subject manifests a global awareness of an entire group of people. The factor uniting and characterizing the members of such a group can be their race, nationality, cultural heritage, religion, profession, shared ideology, or destiny. In this way, a subject can experience the role of the Jews persecuted through the centuries, the Christians tortured and sacrificed by the Romans, the victims of the Spanish Inquisition, or the prisoners in Nazi concentration camps. One can feel the quality of the religious zeal of all the Moslems during their pilgrimage to Mecca, the devotion of the Hindus at the time of worship by the Ganges River, or the fanaticism of extremist religious sects, such as the Flagellants, the Snake Handlers, or the Russian Skopzy. In an LSD session, it is possible to experience the totality of suffering of all the soldiers who have ever died on battlefields since the beginning of history, the revolutionary fervor of all the Communists of the world obsessed by the idea of overthrowing the capitalist regimes, or the tenderness of all mothers loving their children and feeling concerned about their well-being. In these experiences, one can identify with whole social classes or castes, or the population of an entire country; in an extreme form of group identification, the subject can experience his consciousness expanding to encompass every member of the human race—indeed, all of humanity.

Animal Identification

These frequently occurring experiences are in many respects similar to the previously described phylogenetic memories. The identification with various animals is equally authentic and realistic and both categories can contain interesting and accurate information related to zoology, ethology, and animal psychology. The major difference between them is that simple animal identification is not accompanied by the sense of time regression and by the feeling that the individual is exploring the evolutionary lines of phylogenetic development.

It is important to distinguish genuine animal identification from the much more superficial autosymbolic animal transformations. The latter is related to the psychodynamic level of the unconscious and has a symbolic meaning and dynamic structure not dissimilar to those of dream images. The individual usually recognizes it as a cryptic message about his personality characteristics or his life situation and is open to a psychoanalytic approach to this phenomenon. An autosymbolic stylization into a predator, such as a tiger, lion, or black panther, can be deciphered as an expression of the subject's intense aggressive feelings. Transformation into a monkey can represent polymorphously perverted tendencies and an uninhibited indulgence in genital as well as pregenital pleasures. A strong sexual drive can be symbolized by a stallion or a bull; if it has a strong component of lust and promiscuity, it might be depicted by identification with a wild boar. A streak of masculine vanity and sexually tainted exhibitionism can be ridiculed by the autosymbolic representation of the subject as a noisy cock on the dunghill. The symbol of a donkey or ox is related to stupidity; a mule indicates stubbornness; and a hog can represent self-neglect, sloppiness, and moral flaws.

Genuine animal identification is a clearly transpersonal experience and has a primary quality: it is a phenomenon *sui generis* that cannot be derived from other unconscious material and interpreted symbolically. The three types of LSD experiences related to animals—animal autosymbolic transformations, animal identifications, and phylogenetic memories—each have their specific characteristics. Subjects who have encountered all three of these experiential varieties can easily distinguish among them.

Plant Identification

The instances of experiencing consciousness of various plant forms are in general much less frequent than those concerning animal life. An individual tuned in to this area has the unique feeling of witnessing and consciously participating in the basic physiological processes of plants. He can experience himself as a germinating seed, a leaf in the course of photosynthetic activity, or a root reaching out for water and nourishment. On other occasions, a subject might identify with the venus flytrap or other carnivorous plants, become plankton in the ocean, and experience pollination or cellular divisions occurring during vegetable growth. Subjects have also reported that they witnessed botanical processes on a molecular level; they were aware of the biochemical synthesis underlying the production of auxins, vegetable pigments, oils and sugars, aromatic substances, and various alkaloids.

The experiences of plant consciousness represent an interesting category of transpersonal phenomena. No matter how fantastic and absurd their content might seem to our common sense, it is not easy to discard them as mere fantasies. They occur independently in various individuals in advanced stages of treatment and have a very special experiential flavor that cannot be easily communicated in words. It is difficult to identify their source in the unconscious or explain them from some of the more usual unconscious material; also, the reason why the subject experiences them is often completely obscure.

Elements of plant consciousness can be accompanied by philosophical and spiritual ideation and insights. Several subjects, for example, have pondered over the purity and unselfishess of plant existence and have seen plant life as a model for ideal human conduct; unlike animals and man, most plants do not kill and do not live at the expense of other organisms. They are in direct contact with all four elements—earth, water, air, and fire (sun)—and their ability to transform cosmic energy is absolutely indispensable for life on this planet. Plants are uncontaminated by questions about purpose, awareness of goals, or concerns about the future; rather they seem to represent pure being in the here and now, the ideal of many mystical and religious schools. Not exploiting and hurting other organisms, most plants serve themselves as a source of food and bring beauty and joy into the life of others. Several individuals who have had experiences of plant consciousness felt that they now understood the relevance of scientific research concerned with plant sensitivity, as exemplified by the work of Sir Jagadis Chandra Bose in Calcutta and Darjeeling or the more recent experiments done by Cleve Backster.

Large trees known for their longevity, such as sequoias and redwoods, were experienced in the sessions as representing timeless and centered consciousness uninfluenced by the turmoils and upheavals in the external world. Other insights associated with similar experiences were related to the mystical connotations and deep religious significance of certain plants. The most salient examples of this sort are the symbolism of the lotus in Buddhism, the importance of corn in the cosmology of North American Indians, the deification of soma by the ancient Aryans, the use of mistletoe in Druid rituals, and, above all, the religions and cults built around psychedelic plants, exemplified by peyotl, Mexican sacred mushrooms, and *yajé*. On numerous occasions, these experiences had practical consequences; the fascination with the purity of the vegetable kingdom together with the aversion toward slaughter generated in perinatal sessions resulted in an appreciation of and interest in vegetarian diet.

Oneness with Life and with All Creation

In rare instances, an LSD subject can have the feeling that his consciousness has expanded to encompass the totality of life on this planet, including all humankind and the entirety of flora and fauna, from unicellular organisms to highly differentiated species. An individual can identify with the phylogenetic evolution of life in all its complexity and reach an intuitive understanding of the underlying biological laws. He can explore the factors that influence the origin of new species or are responsible for their extinction, and see the operation of Darwinian and Lamarckian forces determining the "survival of the fittest." Similar insights can be experienced in regard to the interaction of different life forms in all the permutations of their synergisms and antagonisms within the framework of planetary ecology. The consciousness of all living matter can also be associated with the exploration of the contradictions and conflicts intrinsic to life, with attempts to estimate the relative power of life's self-preserving forces versus self-destructive potentials, and with an assessment of the viability of life as a cosmic phenomenon. Experiences of this kind can result in an enhanced awareness of and sensitivity to ecological problems related to technological development and rapid industrialization.

Consciousness of Inorganic Matter

The experiential extensions of consciousness in LSD sessions are not limited to the world of biology; they can include macroscopic and microscopic phenomena of inorganic nature. Subjects have repeatedly reported that they experienced consciousness of the ocean, characterized by its timelessness, fluidity, all-encompassing and soothing quality, and paradoxical combination of immutability and dynamic change. On other occasions, they have identified with what they felt to be consciousness of fire, with its endless versatility, impermanence, propensity to create and destroy forms, and purifying potential. Rather common is a subjective awareness of the forces unleashed in natural catastrophes: the destructive as well as the creative, mountain-forming aspects of volcanic eruptions; the dynamic tension and moving masses involved in earthquakes; and the power of air currents in windstorms are just a few salient examples. Modern technological varieties of these experiences have also been described in the sessions. It is possible to explore the consciousness of a computer or identity with a flying jet, orbiting spaceship, and other modern inventions. Many LSD subjects have also stated that they experienced consciousness of a particular material; most frequently it was diamond, granite, gold, and steel. Similar experiences can reach even the microworld and depict the dynamic structure of the atoms, the nature of the electromagnetic forces involved, the world of interatomic bonds, or the Brownian dance of the molecules.

In the light of such phenomenological realms, LSD subjects often consider the possibility that consciousness is a basic cosmic phenomenon related to the organization of energy, and that it exists throughout the universe; in this context, human consciousness appears to be only one of its many varieties and outgrowths. Episodes of consciousness of inorganic matter can be accompanied by various insights of a philosophical and religious relevance; they can mediate a new understanding of animism and pantheism, of the parallels between spiritual states and material substances as described in alchemical writings, of Empedocles' doctrine of the four elements, or of the significance that water has in the Taoist teachings. For individuals who have been immersed in the consciousness of granite or that of volcanic processes, it was easy to comprehend why the Hindus see the Himalayas as a representation of reclining Shiva or why the Hawaiians worship the forces inherent in volcanic eruptions as the goddess Pele. Experiences of the consciousness of particularly stable, immutable, and durable substances are perceived as being high spiritual states involving an element of sacredness. Some subjects volunteered the insight that the Himalayas from the Hindu point of view, the granite sculptures of the Egyptians, or the Pre-Columbian golden statues did not really represent metaphors for deities or images thereof; they actually *were* the deities. It was the unchangeable, perennial, and undifferentiated consciousness of these materials that was worshiped because it differed so dramatically from the highly versatile, specifically focusing, and turbulent states of consciousness characterizing human beings.

Planetary Consciousness

This is a rare phenomenon usually occurring in advanced sessions of an LSD series. In this experience, the consciousness of the subject seems to encompass all aspects of this planet, including its geological substance, the inorganic materials on its surface, and the totality of life forms. From this point of view, the earth appears to be a complicated cosmic organism with the different aspects of geological, biological, cultural, and technological evolution on this planet seen as manifestations of an attempt to reach a higher level of integration and self-realization.

Extraplanetary Consciousness

Here, the subject experiences phenomena related to celestial bodies other than this planet and to astronomical events occurring in our solar system or outside it. Accounts of various LSD subjects mention in this context conditions on the surface of the moon, thermonuclear processes inside of the sun, the unusual physical circumstances on various planets, exploding supernovas, quasars and pulsars, and contracting large suns resulting in "black holes" in the universe. A special type of experience in this category is that of consciousness of interstellar space, reported on several occasions by various individuals. It is characterized by feelings of infinity and eternity, tranquillity, serenity, purity, and unity of all opposites. It seems to have its spiritual counterpart in the experience of the void described later in this chapter.

LSD subjects sophisticated in mathematics and physics have occasionally reported that many of the concepts of these disciplines that transcend rational understanding can become more easily comprehensible and be actually experienced in altered states of consciousness. These illuminating insights involve such theoretical systems as non-Euclidean geometry, Riemann's geometry of an n-dimensional space, Minkowski's space-time, and Einstein's special and general theories of relativity. The relativity of time and space, the curvature of space, the idea of an infinite but self-enclosed universe, the interchangeability of matter and energy, various orders and degrees of infinities, zeros of different magnitudes—all these difficult constructs of modern physics and mathematics were on occasion understood and actually subjectively experienced in psychedelic sessions.

Out-of-Body Experiences, Traveling Clairvoyance and Clairaudience, "Space Travels," and Telepathy

This group of ESP experiences can be understood in terms of an extension of consciousness beyond the usual spatial limits. The sensation of leaving one's body is a frequent occurrence in LSD sessions. Some individuals have experienced themselves completely detached from their physical bodies, hovering above them or watching them from another part of the room. Occasionally, the subject can also lose the awareness of the physical setting of the session and his consciousness moves into various experiential realms and subjective realities that appear to be entirely independent of material reality. Less frequently, this experience has the form of traveling clairvoyance and clairaudience, in which the individual feels himself moving to another place in the physical world and can give a detailed description of the situation he encounters. Attempts to verify such extrasensory perception sometimes bring interesting results.

In rare instances, the subject has the feeling that he can actively control such a process, transcend the usual limitations of space, and travel at will to any location he chooses. The following is an example of such a "space travel" from a training session of a psychiatrist. It illustrates the nature of these phenomena and also shows the difficulties that can occur if the subject tries to experiment on the interface of two realities and put his experience to a rigid test.

The first three hours of my LSD session were experienced as a fantastic battle between the forces of Light and Darkness; it was a beautiful illustration of the passage from the ancient Persian Zend Avesta describing the fight between the armies of Ahura Mazda and Ahriman. It was fought on all conceivable levels—in the cells and tissues of my body, on the surface of our planet throughout history, in the cosmic space, and on a metaphysical, transcendental level. Occasionally, I had a rather convincing feeling that the battle I was witnessing and experiencing had something to do with the relationship between matter and spirit, in particular with the entrapment of spirit in matter.

After this battle was over, I found myself in a rather unusual state of mind; I felt a mixture of serenity and bliss with the naïve and primitive faith of the early Christians. It was a world where miracles were possible, acceptable, and understandable. I was preoccupied with the problems of time and space and the insoluble paradoxes of infinity and eternity that baffle our reason in the usual state of consciousness. I could not understand how I could have let myself be "brainwashed" into accepting the simple-minded concept of one-dimensional time and three-dimensional space as being mandatory and existing in objective reality. It appeared to me rather obvious that there are no limits in the realm of spirit and that time and space are arbitrary constructs of the mind. Any number of spaces with different orders of infinities could be deliberately created and experienced. A single second and eternity seemed to be freely interchangeable. I thought about higher mathematics and saw deep parallels between various mathematical concepts and altered states of consciousness.

In this situation, it suddenly occurred to me that I do not have to be bound by the limitations of time and space and can travel in the time-space continuum quite deliberately and without any restrictions. This feeling was so convincing and overwhelming that I wanted to test it by an experiment. I decided to try traveling to the city of my birth, which was several thousand miles away. After visualizing the direction and the distance, I set myself into motion and tried to fly through space to the place of destination. This effort resulted in an experience of flight through space at an enormous velocity, but to my disappointment, I wasn't getting anywhere. I stopped this activity and reconsidered the situation; I could not understand that the experiment would not work in spite of my convincing feeling that such space travel was possible. Immediately, I realized that I was still under the influence of my old concepts of time and space. I continued thinking in terms of directions and distances and approached the task accordingly. All of a sudden it occurred to me that the proper approach would be to make myself believe that the place of the session was actually identical with the place of destination. When I approached the task in this way, I experienced peculiar and bizarre sensations. I found myself in a strange, rather congested place full of vacuum tubes, wires, resistors, and condensers. After a short period of confusion, I realized that I was trapped in a TV set located in the corner of the room of the apartment in my native city where I had spent my childhood. I was trying, somehow, to use the speakers for hearing and the tube for seeing. Suddenly, I understood that this experience was a symbolic expression ridiculing the fact that I was still hung up on my previous beliefs concerning space and matter. The only way of transmitting images at long distances that was conceivable and acceptable for me was based on the use of electromagnetic waves, as in television broadcasting. Such a transmission, of course, is restricted by the velocity of the waves involved. At the moment when I realized and firmly believed that I could operate in the realm of free spirit and did not have to be restricted even by the velocity of light or other types of electromagnetic waves, the experience changed rapidly. I broke through the TV screen and found myself walking in the apartment of my parents. I did not feel any drug effect at that point, and the experience was as sober and real as any other experience of my life. I walked to the window and looked at the clock on the street corner; it showed a five-hour difference from the time in the time zone where the experiment took place. In spite of the fact that this difference reflected the actual time difference between the two zones, I did not find it convincing evidence. I knew the time difference intellectually and my mind could have easily fabricated this experience.

I felt I needed a much more convincing proof of whether or not what I was experiencing was "objectively real" in the usual sense. I finally decided to perform a test—to take a picture from the wall and later check in correspondence with my parents if something unusual had happened at that time in their apartment. I reached for the picture, but before I was able to touch the frame I was overcome by an increasingly unpleasant feeling that it was an extremely risky and dangerous undertaking. I suddenly felt the uncanny influence of evil forces and a touch of something like "black magic"; it seemed as if I were gambling for my soul. I paused and started analyzing what was happening. Images from the world's famous casinos were flashing in front of my eyes—Monte Carlo, the Venetian Lido, Las Vegas, Reno. . . . I saw roulette balls spiraling at intoxicating speeds, the mechanical movements of slot machines, dice jolting on the green surface of the gambling tables during a game of craps, scenes of gamblers involved in baccarat, and the flickering lights of the keno panels. This was followed by scenes of secret meetings of statesmen, politicians, army officials, and topnotch scientists. I realized that I had not yet overcome my egocentrism and could not resist the temptation of power. The possibility of transcending the limitations of time and space appeared to be intoxicating and dangerously seductive. If I could have control over time and space, an unlimited supply of money appeared to be guaranteed, together with everything that money can buy. All one had to do under those circumstances was to go to the nearest casino, stock market, or lottery office. No secrets would exist for somebody controlling time and space at will; he could eavesdrop on summit meetings of political leaders and have access to top-secret discoveries. This would open undreamed-of possibilities for controlling the course of events in the world.

I started understanding the dangers involved in my experiment. I remembered passages from different books warning against toying with these powers before the individual overcomes his ego limitations and reaches spiritual maturity. There was, however, something that appeared even more relevant. I found out that I was extremely ambivalent in regard to the outcome of my test. On one hand, it seemed extremely enticing to be able to liberate oneself from the slavery of time and space. On the other hand, it was obvious that something like this had far-reaching and serious consequences and could not be seen as an isolated experiment in the voluntary control of space. If I could get confirmation that it was possible to manipulate the physical environment at a distance of several thousand miles, my whole universe would collapse as a result of this one experiment, and I would find myself in a state of utter metaphysical confusion. The world as I knew it would not exist any more; I would lose all the maps I relied on and felt comfortable with. I would not know who, where, and when I was and would be lost in a totally new, frightening universe, the laws of which would be alien and unfamiliar to me.

I could not bring myself to carry through the intended experiment and decided to leave the problem of the objectivity and reality of the experience unresolved. This made it possible for me to toy with the idea that I had conquered time and space, while at the same time it allowed me, in case the whole thing became too frightening, to see the entire episode as one of many peculiar deceptions due to the intoxication of my brain by a powerful psychedelic drug. The moment I gave up the experiment, I found myself back in the room where the drug session took place.

I never forgave myself for having wasted such a unique and fantastic experiment. The memory of the metaphysical horror involved in this test makes me doubt, however, that I would be more courageous given a similar chance in the future.

Occasionally, telepathic experiences can be observed in psychedelic sessions. The firm feeling of an LSD subject that he can read the minds of the persons present in the session or that he can tune in to people in other parts of the world is more frequently a self-deception than an objectively verifiable fact. Besides gross distortions and misinterpretations, there are, however, situations that are strongly indicative of genuine extrasensory perception. Accordingly, an LSD subject can be unusually accurate in his awareness of the sitter's ideation and emotions without even looking at him. Two individuals who have sessions at the same time can share many ideas or have parallel experiences without much verbal communication and interchange. In exceptional cases, a claim made by an LSD subject about telepathic contact with a distant person can be supported by objective evidence obtained by independent investigation.

SPATIAL CONSTRICTION OF CONSCIOUSNESS

Organ, Tissue, and Cellular Consciousness

In this type of experience, the individual's consciousness seems to be confined to areas smaller than the usual body image; in most instances, it involves the parts of the subject's body and physiological processes that under normal circumstances are not accessible to awareness. Such phenomena thus combine a spatial constriction of consciousness with its functional extension. Subjects in this state have the sense of tuning in to the consciousness of various organs or tissues of their body. They can witness the action of the pacemaker in the heart, the contractions of cardiac musculature, and the opening and closing of the heart valves. In a similar way, it is possible to observe hepatic function and the resulting production and collection of gall, the digestive processes and resorption in the gastrointestinal tract, or, for that matter, the function of any other organ. In this state, consciousness often seems to regress all the way to the cellular level or even subcellular processes. On occasion, LSD subjects have stated that they experienced themselves as neurons in their own brains, white and red blood corpuscles, uterine epithelium, or germinal cells. The commonly reported experience of identification with the ovum and sperm at the time of conception belongs to this category. Another interesting phenomenon is the conscious exploration of the cellular nucleus and the genes in the chromosomes; this can be combined with the feeling of "reading one's DNA code." As in the case of other transpersonal experiences, episodes of organ, tissue, and cellular consciousness can be associated with many concrete insights; various details concerning anatomy, histology, physiology, and chemistry of the body found in the accounts of such experiences often reveal a level of information that the subjects did not have before the sessions. Some of the phenomena in this category bear a close resemblance to various scenes in the movie *Fantastic Voyage;* references to this film are frequently found in the descriptions of such LSD experiences.

The following excerpt from an LSD training session of a psychiatrist has several good examples of experiences of cellular and tissue consciousness.

The most interesting sequences of this session were yet to come. My consciousness became less and less differentiated, and I started experiencing a strange excitement that was dissimilar to anything I have ever felt in my life. The middle part of my back was generating rhythmical impulses, and I had the feeling of being propelled through space and time toward some unknown goal; I had a very vague awareness of the final destination, but the mission appeared to be one of utmost importance. After some time I was able to recognize to my great surprise that I was a spermatozoid and that the explosive regular impulses were generated by a biological pacemaker and transmitted to a long flagella flashing in vibratory movements. I was involved in a hectic super-race toward the source of some chemical messages that had an enticing and irresistible quality. By then I realized that the goal was to reach the egg, penetrate it, and impregnate. In spite of the fact that this whole scene seemed absurd and ridiculous to my sober scientific mind, I could not resist the temptation to get involved in this race with all seriousness and full expenditure of energy.

Experiencing myself as a spermatozoid competing for the egg, I was conscious of all the processes involved. What was happening had the basic characteristics of the physiological event as it is taught in medical schools; there were, however, many additional dimensions that were far beyond anything that one could produce in fantasy in a usual state of mind. The consciousness of this spermatozoid was a whole autonomous microcosm, a universe of its own. There was a clear awareness of the biochemical processes in the nucleoplasm; in a nebulous atmosphere I could recognize the structure of the chromosomes, individual genes, and molecules of DNA. I could perceive their physiochemical configuration as being simultaneously elements of ancestral memories, primordial phylogenetic forms, nuclear forms of historical events, myths, and archetypal images. Genetics, biochemistry, mythology, and history seemed to be inextricably interwoven and were just different aspects of the same phenomenon. This microworld of the spermatozoid was at the same time influenced and governed by some forces modifying and determining the outcome of the race. They seemed to have the form of karmic, cosmobiological, and astrological force-fields.

The excitement of this race was building up every second, and the hectic pace seemed to increase to such a degree that it resembled the flight of a spaceship approaching the speed of light. Then came the culmination in the form of a triumphant implosion and ecstatic fusion with the egg. During the sperm race my consciousness was alternating between that of the sperm heading toward its destination and that of the egg with a vague but strong expectation of an overwhelming event. At the time of the conception these two split units of consciousness came together, and I was both germinal cells at the same time. Strangely enough both units involved seemed to interpret the same event in terms of individual success as well as joint triumph. Both of them achieved their mission—the sperm that of penetration and implosion, the egg that of incorporation. A single act involving two participants and resulting in total satisfaction on both sides. I felt that here was an ideal model, not only for the cooperation of the male and the female principle in adult sexual activities but for interpersonal situations in general. The task seemed to be to arrange the circumstances in such a way that all parties involved interpret the outcome as their personal success. I saw at that time how the complexity and multitude of the existing interpretive frameworks would make something like this possible.

After the fusion of the germ cells the experience continued, still in the same hectic pace set by the sperm race. In a condensed and accelerated way, I experienced embryogenesis following conception. There was again the full conscious awareness of biochemical processes, cellular divisions, and tissue growth. There were numerous tasks to be met and critical periods to overcome. I was witnessing the differentiation of tissues and formation of new organs. I became the branchial arches, the pulsating fetal heart, columns of liver cells, and cells of the intestinal mucous membrane. An enormous release of energy and light accompanied the embryonal development. I felt that this blinding golden glow had something to do with biochemical energy involved in the precipitous growth of cells and tissues. At one point, I had a very definite feeling of completion of the fetal development; this was experienced again as a great accomplishment— individual success as well as triumph of the creative force of nature.

Even when I returned to my usual state of consciousness, I had the feeling that this experience would have a lasting effect on my self-esteem. No matter what my life trajectory will be, I have already had two distinct successes—having won the sperm race in a multimillion competition and completed successfully the complicated task of embryogenesis. Although my reason forced me into a condescending smile while I was thinking these ideas, the emotions behind them were strong and convincing.

Experiential Extension beyond the Framework of "Objective Reality"

Spiritistic and Mediumistic Experiences

These rare experiences closely resemble phenomena known from spiritistic seances and occult literature. The LSD subject can, for example, suddenly enter a state similar to a mediumistic trance; his facial expression is strikingly transformed, his countenance and gestures appear alien, and his voice is dramatically changed. He can speak in a foreign language, write automatic texts, and produce obscure hieroglyphic designs or draw strange pictures and unintelligible squiggles. Other experiences from this category can have the form of encounters with astral bodies or spirit entities of deceased persons, as well as extrasensory communication with them. Some of these phenomena have the characteristics of spirit possession as described in a number of medieval sources or by anthropologists studying religious practices and beliefs of various cultures.

The following episode from an advanced LSD session of a psycholytic series at the Psychiatric Research Institute in Prague is an example of a profound and shattering spiritistic experience. It was observed in the course of therapy of Dana, a neurotic patient briefly mentioned earlier (see page 65).

In one of her sessions Dana was reliving an extremely painful traumatic episode from her childhood. Her father was hospitalized for many years in a mental institution for a severe psychotic condition. When she was ten years old, he suffered a cerebral haemorrhage and was discharged from the hospital to die at home. Dana had to witness the deterioration of her father and was at his bedside at the time of his terminal agony. In the LSD session, she literally regressed to this situation and became a frightened little girl watching the death struggle of her father. At first she watched his terminal agony, but later started experiencing agony herself; in full identification with her father, she approached the moment of physical death. When they had transcended the boundary between life and death in this peculiar dual unity, she went into a state of almost uncontrollable panic. It was not possible to communicate with her for at least two hours.

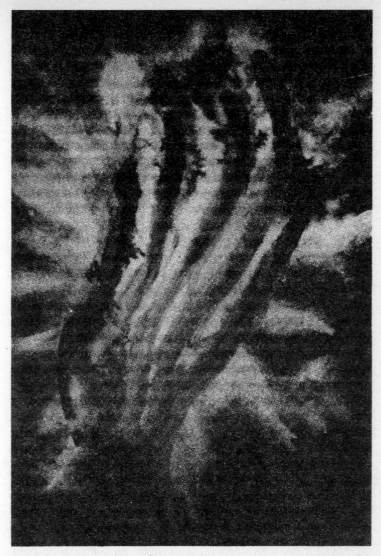

A painting reflecting Dana's "spiritistic" experience in one of her LSD sessions. She relived her father's terminal agony, which she had witnessed as a child; after being an observer, Dana experienced full identification with her father in this situation. Having passed through the moment of death, she found herself in an uncanny universe filled with fluorescent ether. Souls of deceased people were suspended in space and communicated with her telepathically. When she looked at her hand, she saw on it the superimposed astral hand of her dead father.

When contact was re-established, she was able to describe her experience in retrospect: "After we crossed the threshold of life and death, I found myself in an uncanny and frightening world. It was filled with fluorescent ether of a strangely macabre nature. There was no way of assessing whether the space involved was finite or infinite. An endless number of souls of deceased human beings were suspended in the luminescent ether; in an atmosphere of peculiar distress and disquieting excitement, they were sending me nonverbal messages through some unidentifiable extrasensory channels. They appeared unusually demanding, and it seemed as if they needed something from me. In general, the atmosphere reminded me of the descriptions of the underworld that I had read in Greek literature. But the objectivity and reality of the situation was beyond my imagination—it provoked a state of sheer and utter metaphysical horror that I cannot even start describing. My father was present in this world as an astral body; since I entered this world in union with him, his astral body was as if superimposed over mine. I was not able to communicate with you [the therapist] at all, and it seemed pointless anyway. I was sure that you knew as little about this uncanny world as I did, and you could not, therefore, be of any help. It was by far the most frightening experience of my life; in none of my previous LSD sessions did I encounter anything that would come close to it."

Experiences of Encounters with Suprahuman Spiritual Entities

The ancient theme of an encounter and interaction with spirit guides, teachers, and protectors is one of the most valuable and rewarding transpersonal experiences in LSD sessions. The subject perceives these beings as suprahuman or spiritual entities existing on higher planes of consciousness and higher energy levels. Only exceptionally is this experience accompanied by an actual image or communication in verbal form. Sometimes, the spirit guides are a source of light or energy with or without concomitant vibrations of a high frequency; usually, the individual only senses their presence and receives messages, instructions, and explanations through various extrasensory channels. Typically, the ego identity of the subject is preserved, and he relates to these entities as separate from himself; it is possible, however, to experience various degrees of fusion or even full identification with them.

Spirit guides appear in the sessions in various capacities; sometimes they give an explanation of what is happening or advice in regard to the desirable approach to the LSD experience. On other occasions, they accompany the individual through various difficult experiences, like Vergil in Dante's *Divine Comedy,* giving him intellectual and spiritual support, or even creating shields of positive energy that protect him from the destructive influences of evil entities. Such guides can also give specific directives and suggestions concerning the subject's present life situation or the general course of his life. Sometimes, these spiritual helpers remain unrecognized; at other times, the subject identifies them as various aspects of his higher self or as discarnate religious teachers and enlightened beings, such as Sri Ramana Maharishi, Ramakrishna, Sri Aurobindo, Gandhi, or Jesus Christ.

The phenomenology of this experiential category has been dramatically described by John C. Lilly in his book *The Center of the Cyclone.*[12] In his account, Lilly shares with the reader his powerful encounters with two guardians from higher planes of consciousness who played an important role in various critical periods of his spiritual search.

Experiences of Other Universes and Encounters with Their Inhabitants

The strange and alien worlds that LSD subjects discover and explore in this type of experience seem to have a reality of their own, although not within the range of our cosmos; they appear to exist in other dimensions, in universes coexistent with ours. The individual can encounter entities who have bizarre physical forms, operate on the basis of some incomprehensible laws, and have metabolic and physiological processes completely different from our own. They are perceived as obviously intelligent creatures, but their ideational and emotional characteristics do not resemble anything known to man. On several occasions, LSD subjects reported contacts or encounters with flying saucers and other types of extraterrestrial spacecrafts. Sometimes, they were seen as visitations from remote parts of our universe or as astral expeditions from other dimensions and parallel worlds. Such alien universes experienced in LSD sessions can be much smaller or infinitely bigger than ours and can be governed by unfamiliar forms of energy. Having been through these extraordinary cosmic adventures, individuals have likened them to the most ingenious science-fiction stories ever written. Some subjects have referred to Jonathan Swift's *Gulliver's Travels;* others have compared them to various sequences of the American television series "Star Trek."

Archetypal Experiences and Complex Mythological Sequences

An important group of transpersonal experiences in LSD sessions are phenomena for which C. G. Jung has used the terms primordial images, dominants of the collective unconscious, or archetypes. They repeatedly occur in sessions of both those subjects familiar with this concept and naïve individuals without any previous exposure to Jungian ideas. In its broadest sense, the term "archetype" can be used for all static patterns and configurations, as well as dynamic happenings within the psyche that are transindividual and have a universal quality. Such a delineation and definition of archetypes would apply to many categories of phenomena described in this chapter. Here, we will discuss only the group of transpersonal experiences of an archetypal nature that represent generalized biological, psychological, and social types and roles.

An LSD subject can, for example, experience full identification with the archetypes of the Martyr, Fugitive, Outcast, Enlightened Ruler, Tyrant, Fool, Good Samaritan, Wise Old Man, Avarice, Vicious Spoiler, Ascetic, or Hermit. These experiences are closely related to, but not identical with, the elements of group consciousness described earlier. In the latter, the subject feels simultaneously identified with all individual members of a particular group; these archetypical experiences represent personified concepts of the roles involved (i.e., all the Jews as compared with the Jew). Archetypal phenomena of this kind can reflect various levels of abstraction and different degrees of generalization. In some of the most universal archetypes, the subject can identify with the roles of the Mother, Father, Child, Woman, Man, or Lover. Many highly universalized roles are felt as sacred, as exemplified by the archetypes of the Great

Mother, the Terrible Mother, the Earth Mother, Mother Nature, the Great Hermaphrodite, or Cosmic Man. Archetypes representing certain aspects of the subject's personality, such as the Shadow, Animus and Anima, or Persona, are also rather common in advanced LSD sessions. The images of the Golden Age and Dark Age, as well as the vision of the flow of all the consecutive Hindu yugas, can be mentioned as examples of rich, extensive, and generalized archetypes.

Sometimes, instead of experiencing the individual and usually static archetypal images described above, LSD subjects participate in legendary, mythological, or fairy-tale themes and complex sequences. Some of these have rather simple and ordinary motifs, such as those of the evil stepmother and the battered stepdaughter, the good brother and bad brother, and great love endangered by unfortunate circumstances or intrigues. Others are much more specific and unusual; here belong the motifs of eternal damnation found in the stories of Tantalus, Sisyphus, Prometheus, Ahasuerus, or the Flying Dutchman, the theme of the birth or death of the hero, legends of man's ambition and his thirst for knowledge as exemplified by the stories of Daedalus and Icarus or Faust, and the myth of the superhero accomplishing difficult labors or saving and liberating an imprisoned and endangered woman. Not infrequently, unsophisticated subjects have reported stories that strongly resemble ancient mythological themes from Mesopotamia, India, Egypt, Greece, Central America, and other countries of the world. These observations closely parallel C. G. Jung's descriptions of the appearance of relatively unknown but distinctly archetypal themes in the dreams of children and unsophisticated patients, as well as in the manifest symptomatology of some schizophrenics.

Experiences of Encounters
with Various Deities

This category is closely related to the previous one. In a strictly Jungian sense, encounters with various deities and/or identification with them would be considered archetypal experiences. However, those professionals acquainted with Jung's theories who volunteered for LSD sessions seemed to distinguish clearly between the archetypes in the form of generalized roles and universal prototypes and experiences involving concrete deities related to specific cultures. Sometimes, subjects are familiar with the gods or demons they are experiencing and can give them specific names and assign them to the corresponding cultural areas. On other occasions, they can give detailed descriptions of the visions involved or even draw them and identify the culture of origin. It is then up to the therapist to obtain the necessary information and assess the degree of accuracy of the insights involved. There also exist situations in which the identity of such an appearance remains obscure or uncertain, in spite of the combined efforts of the subject and the therapist to clarify it.

Most deities appearing in LSD sessions fall into two rather sharply defined categories: the first group includes those that are associated with the forces of light and good; the second is comprised of deities of darkness and evil. Typical representatives of blissful and beneficent divinities are Isis and Osiris, Ahura Mazda, Apollo, Boddhisattva, and Krishna; examples of wrathful deities would be Set, Hades, Ahriman, Kali, Moloch, Astarte, Huitzilopochtli, or Satan. In serial LSD sessions, these deities usually appear for the first time in the perinatal phase; in that context, the images of those gods representing dark forces are associated with the birth agony of BPM II and III; blissful divinities then accompany the ecstatic experiences of BPM I and IV. Later on, such images of deities occur independently, either in the form of static visions or as part of the mythological sequences mentioned in the previous section. Occasionally, LSD subjects witness entire cosmological dramas, such as the battle between the forces of Ahriman and Ahura Mazda, the war between the gods and titans, the fall of Lucifer and other angels, various versions of the creation of the world, the Biblical Deluge, and the Last Judgment or Armageddon.

Subjects experiencing an encounter with various blissful and wrathful deities usually have very powerful emotional reactions ranging from ecstatic rapture and divine bliss to metaphysical terror and feelings of insanity. However, most individuals do not have the feeling that they are confronted with the Supreme Being or the ultimate force in this universe.

Intuitive Understanding of
Universal Symbols

Visions of various universal symbols form an important part of LSD sessions. They can occur independently or in association with various other types of transpersonal phenomena. The experiences of universal symbols are followed or accompanied by an intuitive understanding of various levels of their esoteric meaning. Many individuals undergoing LSD treatment have had visions of complicated geometrical compositions closely resembling Oriental mandalas; some subjects were even able to draw them and gave quite detailed explanations of what was meant by various aspects of their design. It is rather common for individuals who are in no way familiar with Oriental and mystical literature to offer interpretations of universal symbols in accord with the pertinent esoteric texts. The most frequent symbols observed in the sessions were the cross, the six-pointed star of David, the Indoiranian swastika, the ancient Egyptian ankh (Nile cross or *crux ansata*), the lotus flower, the Taoist yin-yang, the Hindu sacred phallus (Shiva lingam), the diamond and other jewels, the Buddhist wheel of death and rebirth, and the circle (frequently appearing as the archetypal gigantic snake Ouroboros devouring its tail).

We have mentioned elsewhere that as a result of LSD sessions some subjects have developed insights into entire systems of esoteric thought. Thus, individuals unfamiliar with the cabbala have had experiences described in the Zohar and Sepher Yetzirah and have demonstrated a surprising familiarity with cabbalistic symbols. Others spontaneously played with the transcendental meaning of numbers and came to conclusions that were parallel with Pythagorean algebra or numerology. Subjects who had previously ridiculed astrology and had a condescending attitude toward alchemy discovered deeper meaning in these systems and gained a deep appreciation of their metaphysical relevance. Such new understanding was also observed in regard to various ancient forms of divination, such as the I Ching and Tarot.

Activation of the Chakras and
Arousal of the Serpent Power (Kundalini)

Many experiences from transpersonal LSD sessions bear a striking resemblance to phenomena described in various schools of Kundalini yoga as signs of the activation and opening of individual chakras.* These parallels do not exist only for experiences of a positive nature; the phenomenology and consequences of mishandled or poorly integrated LSD sessions is very similar to the complications occurring in the course of unsupervised and amateurish Kundalini practices.** Those subjects familiar with Indian philosophies and religions often make specific references to the Serpent Power, various chakras, and to Tantric practices. Intellectual knowledge of this area is not, however, a necessary prerequisite for these experiences; they can occur in completely naïve individuals. In such cases, these persons have been able to give surprisingly detailed descriptions of similar experiential sequences and sometimes even of the corresponding theoretical systems without, of course, using the specific Sanskrit terms. In general, the chakra system seems to provide very useful maps of consciousness that are of great help in understanding and conceptualizing many unusual experiences in LSD sessions. Detailed discussion of these interesting parallels would be beyond the scope of this chapter and has to be reserved for a future publication.

An extremely rare and extraordinary experience that can occur in advanced LSD sessions is that of the arousal of the Kundalini in the sacral part of the spinal cord and the upward flow of spiritual energy, with the sequential activation of all the chakras. In its complete form this process can result in a pro-

---

*Chakras (a Sanskrit term for "wheels") are hypothetical centers of radiation of primal energy *(prana)* roughly corresponding to certain levels of the spinal cord and certain body organs. Most systems distinguish seven chakras: (1) root chakra *(muladhara)*, (2) genital chakra *(svadhisthana)*, (3) navel chakra *(manipura)*, (4) heart chakra *(anahata)*, (5) throat chakra *(vishuddha)*, (6) brow chakra *(ajna)*, and (7) crown chakra *(sahasrara)*. The flow of prana is mediated by one central conduit *(sushumna)* and two lateral conduits *(ida* and *pingala)*.

**Gopi Krishna describing the history of his spiritual search in *Kundalini: The Evolutionary Energy in Man,* [7] gives numerous examples of the adverse side effects of naïve experimentation of this sort.

found transcendental experience of an ecstatic and integrative nature related to the highest chakra, the thousand-petal lotus.

I would like to mention in this connection a very interesting discussion that followed my presentation describing the parallels between LSD experiences and Indian religions at the First International Conference for Scientific Yoga in New Delhi, India, December 1971. The audience of over two hundred persons represented many different spiritual orientations existing in contemporary India, including several groups of Tibetan Buddhists who had fled from Tibet after the Chinese invasion. The discussants seemed to converge on the fact that, of all the systems of yoga, Kundalini yoga bears the closest resemblance to LSD psychotherapy. Both techniques mediate an instant and enormous release of energy, produce profound and dramatic experiences, and can bring impressive results in a relatively short time. On the other hand, they involve the greatest risk and can be quite dangerous if they are not practiced under careful supervision and responsible guidance.

Consciousness of the Universal Mind

This is one of the most profound and total experiences observed in LSD sessions. Identifying with the consciousness of the Universal Mind, the individual senses that he has experientially encompassed the totality of existence. He feels that he has reached the reality underlying all realities and is confronted with the supreme and ultimate principle that represents all Being. The illusions of matter, space, and time, as well as an infinite number of other subjective realities, have been completely transcended and finally reduced to this one mode of consciousness which is their common source and denominator. This experience is boundless, unfathomable, and ineffable; it is existence itself. Verbal communication and the symbolic structure of our everyday language seem to be a ridiculously inadequate means to capture and convey its nature and quality. The experience of the phenomenal world and what we call usual states of consciousness appear in this context to be only very limited, idiosyncratic, and partial aspects of the over-all consciousness of the Universal Mind. This principle is totally and clearly beyond rational comprehension and yet even a short experiential exposure to it satisfies the subject's intellectual, philosophical, and spiritual craving. All of the questions that have ever been asked seem to be answered, and there is no need to question any further.

The best approximation to understanding the nature of this experience is to describe it in terms of the concept of *Saccidananda* that occurs in Indian religious and philosophical writings. This composite Sanskrit word consists of three separate roots: *sat* means existence or being; *cit,* awareness and intellect; and *ananda,* bliss. The formless, dimensionless, and intangible principle that an individual can perceive as the Universal Mind is characterized by infinite existence, infinite awareness and knowledge, and infinite bliss. Any descriptions and definitions, however, necessarily use words that we associate with the phenomena of the three-dimensional world; they are, therefore, incapable of conveying the essence of this ultimate transcendental principle. Discussing experiences of this nature, subjects have frequently commented on the fact that the language of poets, although still highly imperfect, seems to be a more adequate and appropriate tool for this purpose. One understands why so many great seers, prophets, and religious teachers have resorted to poetry, parable, and metaphor in order to share their transcendental visions.

The experience of consciousness of the Universal Mind is closely related to that of cosmic unity described earlier but not identical with it. Its important concomitants are intuitive insights into the process of creation of the phenomenal world as we know it and into the Buddhist concept of the wheel of death and rebirth. These can result in a temporary or enduring feeling that the individual has achieved a global, nonrational, and transrational understanding of the basic ontological and cosmological problems that beset existence.

The Supracosmic and Metacosmic Void

The last and most paradoxical transpersonal phenomenon to be discussed in this context is the experience of the supracosmic and metacosmic Void, of the primordial emptiness, nothingness, and silence, which is the ultimate source and cradle of all existence and the "uncreated and ineffable Supreme." The terms supra- and metacosmic used by sophisticated LSD subjects in this context refer to the fact that this Void appears to be both supraordinated to and underlying the phenomenal world. It is beyond time and space, beyond form or any experiential differentiation, and beyond polarities such as good and evil, light and darkness, stability and motion, and agony and ecstasy.

The Void also involves transcendence of our ordinary concept of causality. On occasion, LSD subjects have reported that they have witnessed the emergence of *Saccidananda* from the Void as the first formulation thereof, or contrariwise, its return into the Void and disappearance. This phenomenon has not been associated with the disqualifying feelings of absurdity which one would experience in usual states of consciousness while considering the possibility of something originating out of nothing or vanishing without traces. Similarly, the fact of something's happening without a precedent, sufficient cause, or initiating impulse is not questioned by the subject on this level. No matter how paradoxical it might seem, the Void and the Universal Mind are perceived as identical and freely interchangeable; they are two different aspects of the same phenomenon. The Void appears to be emptiness pregnant with form, and the subtle forms of the Universal Mind are experienced as absolutely empty.

Significance of Transpersonal Experiences in LSD Psychotherapy

Understanding the dynamics of transpersonal experiences is important for LSD psychotherapy since certain transpersonal phenomena have specific consequences for postsession intervals. The mechanism involved is similar to that described for COEX systems on the psychodynamic level or the BPM on the perinatal level. After an LSD session that has involved transpersonal elements, the individual seems to remain under the influence of the dynamic structure that dominated the termination period of that particular session.

For example, following an LSD experience in which an individual has not resolved episodes of severe embryonal crises, he can experience for days or months various difficult symptoms; the nature of the problems depends on the specific fetal distress involved. They can be panic anxiety, paranoid feelings, or anticipation of a disaster if attempted abortion is the event in question; or nausea, gastrointestinal distress, and feelings of being poisoned in the case of toxic influences during pregnancy. Exceptionally, the subject may continue to experience elements of the symbiotic union with the mother projected on the therapist (or sitter); his ego boundaries may be loose and precarious, and it may be difficult for him to differentiate his own feelings and thoughts from those of the therapist. The subject may form the delusional conviction that he can read the therapist's mind and that the latter in turn has access to his thoughts. He may suspect the therapist of trying to influence him telepathically or through hypnosis. As will be discussed in detail in the forthcoming book on the practical aspects of LSD psychotherapy, episodes of this sort are frequent in the psycholytic treatment of schizophrenics. Conversely, if the subject is coming down from a session in which he was tuned in to the feelings of oceanic bliss associated with undisturbed embryonal existence, the postsession interval is usually characterized by relaxation, joy, and serenity. An individual in this situation will feel that the world is a safe and friendly place to be. In the case of phylogenetic memories and animal identification, unusual and often bizarre anatomical and physiological feelings and sensations that formed an integral part of these phenomena in the LSD session can persist for various periods of time following the actual LSD exposure.

Past-incarnation experiences activated and unresolved in LSD sessions can have a very powerful effect on the individual in the postsession interval. The specific content of a karmic pattern often influences the person's perception of himself, of his present life situation, and of his social network; it also modifies his behavior in the direction dictated by the content of the past-incarnation experience. Conversely, the resolution of a karmic gestalt in an LSD session can be followed by very beneficial changes in the subject and his interpersonal field. The simplification, clarification, and improvement of interpersonal and situational problems after such a reliving is sometimes dramatic. In some instances, such changes involve circumstances in which the individual was not instrumental in any conceivable material way and which could not, therefore, be directly influenced by him and his new state of mind. Thus, various specific changes have occurred in the life and behavior of other people who were, according to the subject's description, part of a particular karmic pattern that has been worked through in an LSD session. Such individuals were not present in the session or aware of it, and sometimes they were not even a part of the subject's immediate life situation; they were at various distant places, and there was no real contact between them and the subject. The time of specific changes in their lives coincided exactly with the manifestation, unfolding, and resolution of the karmic pattern in the LSD session. These unusual coincidences observed in LSD work involving past-incarnation experiences seem to indicate that events in the sessions are part of a broader pattern, the scope of which transcends the energy field of the individual. One has to think in this connection about C. G. Jung's concept of synchronicity.[10] It seems that Jung's approach can be useful in many instances of transpersonal phenomena, where the application of the principle of causality obviously fails to bring satisfactory answers. One more observation should be mentioned in this context. The subject who has experienced activation of a strong karmic pattern without its final resolution can end up painfully aware of its utmost relevance; he can have the feeling of being crushed by the burden of "bad karma" and preoccupied by a desire to undo the painful consequences of his past deeds. In a similar fashion other types of transpersonal phenomena have consequences for the free intervals between LSD sessions.

The experience of dual unity with another person can persist in the form of deep sympathy, empathy, love, and understanding. The most salient examples of this phenomenon have been observed between spouses and sexual partners whose intimate life was transformed after such an experience in the direction of oceanic and tantric sex.

A similar situation can be observed in the case of archetypal experiences. When a strong archetype dominates the termination of a session, its influence on the individual can continue after the effect of the drug has worn off. The subject's perception of himself, his behavior, and his environment can be strongly influenced by its specific content. If such an archetypal structure has the form of a specific deity, demon, or other individual entity, the resulting condition can be indistinguishable from a possession state. Here the subject can have the feeling that the entity in question has taken over and controls his thoughts, emotions, and behavior.

Many transpersonal experiences also have a strong influence on the individual's values, attitudes, and interests. Thus, experiences of the collective and racial unconscious can generate a sensitivity to the needs and problems of another culture and create a deep appreciation for its religion, art, and life philosophy. Elements of animal and plant consciousness can increase an individual's love of nature and make him more responsive to ecological problems. Profound transcendental experiences, such as the activation of the Kundalini or consciousness of the Universal Mind or of the Void, in addition to having a very beneficial effect on the subject's physical and emotional well-being, are usually central in creating in him a keen interest in religious, mystical, and philosophical issues, and a strong need to incorporate the spiritual dimension into his way of life.

Transpersonal Experiences and Contemporary Psychiatry

Having defined transpersonal experiences and discussed their most important representatives as they occur in LSD sessions, we will make a few general comments about their place in modern psychiatry and psychotherapy. The situation in regard to these phenomena is actually very similar to that of the perinatal experiences described earlier. It certainly is not the first time behavioral scientists and mental health professionals have been confronted with transpersonal experiences, nor is the use of psychedelic substances the only framework in which they can be observed. Many of these experiences have been known for centuries or millennia. Descriptions of them can be found in the holy scriptures of all the great religions of the world, as well as in written documents of countless minor sects, factions, and religious movements. They have also played a crucial role in the visionary states of individual saints, mystics, and religious teachers. Ethnologists and anthropologists have observed and described them in aboriginal sacred rituals, ecstatic and mystery religions, indigenous healing practices, and rites of passage of various cultures. Psychiatrists and psychologists have been seeing transpersonal phenomena, without identifying and labeling them as such, in their everyday practice in many psychotic patients, especially schizophrenics. Historians, religionists, anthropologists, and experimental psychiatrists and psychologists have been aware of the existence of a variety of ancient as well as modern techniques that facilitate the occurrence of transpersonal experiences; they are the same procedures that were described earlier as conducive to the emergence of the perinatal elements.

In spite of the frequency of these phenomena and their obvious relevance for many areas of human life, surprisingly few serious attempts have been made in the past to incorporate them into the theory and practice of contemporary psychiatry and psychology. The attitude of most professionals has oscillated among several distinct approaches to these phenomena. Some professionals have been only marginally acquainted with various transpersonal experiences and have more or less ignored them. These individuals feel that such phenomena do not really have much practical or theoretical relevance, and they have turned their attention to other areas of psychology and psychopathology which they consider important for the understanding of the human mind in health and illness.

For another large group of professionals, transpersonal phenomena are clearly too bizarre to be considered within the framework of variations of normal mental functioning. Any manifestation of this sort is then readily labeled psychotic, whether it occurs in a schizophrenic patient, in a normal subject after the ingestion of a psychedelic drug, in an individual who has spent several hours in a sensory-deprivation tank, in a Zen student during a sesshin, or in mystics and religious teachers of the stature of Sri Ramana Maharishi, Sri Aurobindo, or Jesus. From this point of view, there is no practical reason to study the nature and dynamics of these phenomena and no major heuristic breakthroughs should be expected from such an undertaking. This approach necessarily involves a value judgment— namely, the assumption that transpersonal phenomena are irreconcilable with "normal mental functioning" and should, therefore, be suppressed. Once science discovers the secret of effective therapy for psychosis, it will be possible to eradicate globally all such symptoms of mental dysfunction in a way not dissimilar to episodes of malaric fever. A practical consequence of this type of reasoning is a tendency to use tranquillizers in the treatment of all persons who have transpersonal experiences; the rationale involved is to control at least the symptoms when the cause of the pathological process itself still defies science.

Yet another group of professionals has manifested definite interest in various aspects of the transpersonal realm and made serious attempts at theoretical explanations and conceptualizations. They have not, however, acknowledged the uniqueness of this category or the specific characteristics of such phenomena. In their approach, transpersonal experiences have been explained in terms of old and widely accepted paradigms; in most instances, they are reduced to biographically determined psychodynamic phenomena. Thus, intrauterine experiences (as well as the perinatal elements) appearing in dreams and free associations of many patients are usually treated as mere fantasies; various religious thoughts and feelings are explained from unresolved conflicts with parental authority; experiences of cosmic unity are interpreted as indications of primary infantile narcissism; some archetypal images are seen as a symbolic disguise for the subject's father or mother figure; and past-incarnation experiences are considered a reaction formation to one's fear of impermanence and death, or a wishful compensatory fantasy reflecting dissatisfaction with various aspects of the individual's present existence.

Only a few rather exceptional professionals have shown a

genuine interest in and appreciation of transpersonal experiences as phenomena of their own right. These individuals have recognized their heuristic value and their relevance for a new understanding of the unconscious, of the human potential, and of the nature of man. Among these, William James, Roberto Assagioli, Carl Gustav Jung, and Abraham Maslow deserve special notice.

The scientific and popular interest in psychedelic drugs triggered by the discovery of LSD has brought the problem of transpersonal experiences into a new focus. Observations made in LSD sessions of patients and experimental subjects as well as in individuals involved in illicit self-experimentation clearly demonstrate the limitations of the old approaches to the understanding of transpersonal realms. In addition, large numbers of professionals have had the chance to experience transpersonal phenomena in their own training sessions and have recognized their unusual and specific nature. This set of data was one of the major heuristic streams that converged into transpersonal psychology as a new and separate discipline.

During the many years of my research in LSD psychotherapy, I have spent thousands of hours observing and analyzing transpersonal phenomena in the sessions of others as well as in my own. At present, there is little doubt in my mind that they represent phenomena *sui generis* which originate in the deep unconscious, in areas that have been unrecognized and unacknowledged by classical Freudian psychoanalysis. I am convinced that they cannot be reduced to the psychodynamic level and adequately explained within the Freudian conceptual framework. In this context, I have frequently heard an objection against the material emerging in LSD sessions that deserves special attention. Some professionals who have had access to material from LSD psychotherapy have expressed the opinion that the differences in the experiences of subjects can be explained in terms of the high suggestibility of the LSD state and implicit or explicit indoctrination by the therapist. According to this criticism, a psychoanalytically oriented LSD therapist tends to get from his patients Freudian experiences, whereas an individual with a Jungian orientation sees mostly archetypal material. There is no doubt that the therapist is an important factor in LSD psychotherapy and that he can facilitate certain types of experiences. It is also true that it is generally possible to *interpret* the same content in both Freudian and Jungian terms. I believe, however, that the psychodynamic and transpersonal levels have their own specific characteristics and independent existence and cannot be reduced to each other. If a Freudian and a Jungian therapist interpret the same experience differently, each in his own terms, one of them has necessarily failed to understand the nature of the material involved. One interpreter was very probably neglectful or not aware of certain phenomenological and experiential characteristics of the experience and/or ignored the context in which it occurred. Careful analysis that takes all these factors into consideration makes it almost always possible to identify the nature of a certain phenomenon and the level of the unconscious on which it originates.

The history of my own LSD research can be used as an argument against the above objection that the specific differences in LSD experiences are due to indoctrination by the therapist. I started my own clinical experiments with LSD as a member of the Prague psychoanalytic group and a convinced Freudian. My *a priori* disbelief in Rankian concepts was further reinforced by what I learned in medical school about the myelinization of the cerebral cortex.* Although I found C. G. Jung's writings an inexhaustible source of fascinating information on human culture, I shared the view of many Freudians that his concepts were a manifestation of mythomania with little, if any, scientific relevance. In psycholytic LSD sessions, all my subjects sooner or later transcended the narrow psychodynamic framework and moved into perinatal and transpersonal realms. This happened in spite of my intense effort and need to understand the events in the sessions in psychodynamic terms. It was the everyday observation of transpersonal experiences over many years that finally forced me to expand my theoretical framework. During this process, I recognized not only the theoretical

---

*A frequent objection against the existence of intrauterine or birth memories is the reference to the immaturity of the brain of the newborn and the incomplete myelinization of the cortical neurons.

relevance of the transpersonal realm but also its immediate clinical importance. These broader implications of LSD research were summarized in my recent article entitled "Theoretical and Empirical Basis of Transpersonal Psychology and Psychotherapy: Observations from LSD Sessions."[8] This area will be discussed in detail in a future volume.

I will conclude this section with a short clinical example that illustrates some of the points in the above discussion.

Several years ago I was called as consultant to a patient hospitalized for a psychotic breakdown triggered by LSD. He was on high dosages of Melleril and was seen regularly by a psychoanalytically oriented psychotherapist. In spite of an enormous investment of time and energy on the part of the clinical staff, essentially no therapeutic progress had been made during the six months since his admission. The patient told me that he had been discussing with his therapist the content of his twenty-five unsupervised LSD sessions from the past, as well as some of the unusual experiences that he had been having in everyday life since his last session, which precipitated his psychotic breakdown. He complained that the therapist did not understand the nature of the phenomena they were discussing and did not really know what he [the patient] was talking about. The patient felt no respect for this therapist, considered him ignorant, and did not develop a workable relationship with him. The patient's general impression about the therapeutic procedure was that it was as if "somebody entirely blind was trying to lead a one-eyed person who had a serious problem with eyesight of his only eye." He felt that he had gotten lost and shipwrecked while exploring areas of the mind that the therapist did not know anything about and did not even believe existed.

A brief discussion revealed that in his early sessions the patient had had many aesthetic and psychodynamic experiences, but his more recent sessions were predominantly perinatal and transpersonal in nature. The problem that triggered his psychotic episode seemed to have been his inability to face the ego death. During therapeutic interviews, his therapist was making constant efforts to interpret in Freudian terms many mystical, religious, and archetypal phenomena from the patient's LSD sessions. Where this was not possible he labeled them simply as psychotic, which essentially excluded them from further discussions.

For many hours the discussions with the therapist revolved around a vision that the patient had had in his last LSD session; he referred to it as a scene of worshiping the Cosmic Phallus. It occurred in a typically Jungian framework, was associated with a number of archetypal experiences, and had a definite religious and mystical emphasis. To save myself a long and complicated description, I will mention only that the symbolic vision in question appeared to be closely related to the Hindu concept of Shiva lingam. The analyst made numerous attempts to convince the patient that his vision clearly indicated a traumatic exposure to an adult male's penis at some time during his childhood; he kept suggesting that he must have seen his father naked and that in the LSD session this experience became transformed into the image of the Cosmic Phallus. When the patient did not accept this interpretation, the therapist spent many hours in frustrating attempts to analyze his alleged resistance.

When, in our discussion, I recognized and acknowledged the transpersonal nature of this symbol and talked about it in the appropriate context, the patient soon developed a positive relationship, proved to be interested in therapeutic work, and was rather cooperative. He was willing to undergo an LSD session with careful preparation and supervision to work through the underlying problem; after this session his clinical symptomatology improved to the extent that he could be discharged from the hospital.

6 Multidimensional and Multilevel Nature of the LSD Experience

In the preceding text, the phenomenology of the LSD state has been dissected and itemized for didactic purposes and the discussion has focused on separate levels of the unconscious and individual types of experiences manifested in the sessions. At this point, it is necessary to re-emphasize the complexity and the multidimensional nature of the LSD reaction, describe some of its general characteristics, and approach it more holistically. For theoretical and practical purposes, it is important to understand the way in which different levels of the unconscious exteriorized in the session are related to the personality of the subject, his present life situation, and his psychological problems, as well as to the general context in which such a session takes place. One must also be aware of all the variables determining the nature and course of the LSD experience and of the major sources of its experiential material.

The content of LSD sessions is always highly specific for the subject and expresses in a condensed symbolic dramatization the psychophysiological, emotional, intellectual, philosophical, and spiritual problems most relevant at the time of the session. This is particularly obvious for sessions of a psychodynamic nature, where the LSD experiences are more or less directly related to the individual's present life circumstances and past biographical data. However, similar specificity can be demonstrated for various aspects of perinatal experiences and even transpersonal phenomena. This is true not only for ancestral and racial memories but also for archetypal dynamics and past-incarnation sequences. All these seem to have immediate relevance for the subject as a complex psychobiological and social entity and to be meaningfully related to his present life situation. There are some exceptions to this rule; certain advanced transpersonal phenomena, such as the experience of the Universal Mind or the Void, are of such a high degree of generality that they are applicable to the problems of the individual only in the broad and unspecific form of philosophical or spiritual guidelines.

A very important principle influencing the selection of unconscious elements for exteriorization and conscious representation in a particular LSD session is the definite preference for material with a strong emotional charge. It seems that the unconscious elements that are at the time connected with the most intense negative or positive affect will be activated by the drug, emerge into consciousness, and become the manifest content of the LSD experience. This specific affinity of LSD for emotionally highly charged dynamic structures has significant diagnostic and therapeutic implications. Because of this unusual property, LSD can be used as a kind of "inner radar" that scans the unconscious, identifies the areas of high affective tension, and brings them to the open. It helps the patient and the therapist to distinguish relevant material from the trivial and unimportant, establish proper hierarchies of priorities, and recognize the most urgent areas for therapeutic work. The phenomenology of LSD sessions thus reflects the key problems of the subject and exposes the roots and sources of his emotional difficulties on the psychodynamic, perinatal, and transpersonal levels. This can happen in a direct, immediate way that is self-evident and does not require any further clarification or interpretive work. At other times, the relevant connections are at first not obvious. In such cases, it is necessary to use free associations or explanatory comments by the subject in a way not dissimilar to psychoanalytic interpretation of dreams. Through the use of this approach in the session or especially during subsequent analysis of the material in question, it is usually possible to decipher the ingenious structure of the symbolic language of the LSD state. An individual's associations to various aspects of his LSD session can lead in a surprisingly short time to the most relevant unconscious material.

Freud once said of dreams that they were the *via regia* or royal way to study the unconscious; to an even greater degree this seems to be true for the LSD experience.

This unusual propensity of LSD to represent selectively important conflict-laden emotional themes can be illustrated in the case of Otto, in whom the phenomenology of a high-dose session was limited to a single manifestation.

Otto was a thirty-one-year-old technician with a schizoid personality and many unusual interests. He was admitted to our department because of severe depressions, excessive consumption of alcohol, bouts of anxiety, and a tendency to bizarre ideation. His first LSD session followed a long period of intense medication with Niamid, an antidepressive drug from the group of monoaminooxidase inhibitors; it was discontinued only three days before the session. As we discovered later, long premedication with Niamid enormously increases resistance to LSD and makes the person almost immune to its effects.* Otto had only one very brief, unusual experience during the entire session day although the dose of LSD was successively increased to 350 micrograms. In spite of the fact that the session was rather disappointing and uneventful, the postsession analysis of this isolated phenomenon brought interesting results.

During the preparation for this session, Otto repeatedly talked about his two recurring anxiety dreams. In the first one, he was being prosecuted and tried because he had murdered a man by cutting off his head; Otto had a suspicion that the victim might have been his father. In the second dream, a stranger approached him and started touching his genitals; at first, this man was just gently stroking his penis; later he began to wring and crush his testicles. Otto was afraid that these dreams might be indications of a latent sexual abnormality and asked for a checkup in regard to possible homosexuality.

As mentioned above, Otto had failed to respond to a very high dose of LSD; the only perceptual change that he had noticed during the entire session was a very vivid, concrete, and realistic feeling that

---

*Our short and casual paper on this finding,[9] which we considered theoretically interesting but quite marginal to our research efforts, aroused an unexpected response. Although the article was published in a rather obscure journal, we received within several weeks literally hundreds of requests for reprints from military centers from all over the world. This made us realize that the use of LSD was being seriously considered for other purposes than the intensification and acceleration of psychotherapy.

his hands were transformed into his father's hands. For reasons that he did not understand at first, he found this experience very frightening and felt a deep need to understand the nature and source of his fear. He was asked to focus on the phenomenon of the transformation of his hands and report his associations. After much hesitation and with strong affective involvement, Otto painfully and reluctantly described the tormenting incestuous problems that he had had for many years in the relationship with his mother. This issue was particularly precarious after his father's death, at which time it had become the dominant theme in Otto's life. According to his descriptions, his mother's behavior toward him was very seductive and sexually stimulating. She insisted on sharing a double bed with him, used every opportunity for intimate physical contact, and systematically blocked his efforts to get married. She also repeatedly suggested that they live together for the rest of their lives and offered to care for his young illegitimate child. With further discussion, it emerged that the only symptom in Otto's LSD session expressed in a condensed form many of the deep conflicts he had in regard to aggression, sex, and incest. The hands played a crucial role as instruments in a sexual relationship that had not and must never reach the level of genital union. The transformation of Otto's hands into those of his father's expressed his wish to substitute for his father in sexual activities. It represented a bridge to his mother and legitimized the approach to her as an erotic object, while still respecting the incest taboo in regard to actual intercourse. The hands were an important component in both recurring dreams; this connection revealed Otto's strong ambivalence toward his father as being one important root and determinant of his truncated LSD experience. The feelings involved ranged from the need to be approached sexually by his father (caressing of the penis) to violent murderous impulses (parricide by decapitation) and castration fears with autopunitive elements (crushing of the testicles). Otto's excessive and guilt-laden masturbation represented the link between the dream themes and the hand transformation in the LSD session. At this point, Otto had sudden insights into some of his unusual habits, particularly in regard to his collecting bizarre and peculiar items. In the course of many years, he had put together a most extraordinary museum occupying several rooms of a storage house. Its dark walls harbored a unique mixture of archaic hand organs, calliopes, and various music machines; animated figures and other ingenious automata; and skulls and skeletons resting on a black velvet background. The highlight of this panopticum was, however, a collection of wax imitations exhibited on dark shelves in a twilight atmosphere. The most important items of this little private Madame Tussaud museum were wax heads of famous murderers, together with casts of arms and hands damaged by vitriol, lightning, or tortures of the Spanish Inquisition. Other models showed genitals disfigured by syphilis, chancroid, and cancer. In addition to all these associations, Otto remembered that during his entire childhood his father had always put enormous emphasis on hands and the imperative necessity of keeping them neat, clean, and in good shape. The material uncovered during this discussion increased considerably Otto's self-understanding and was very helpful in his subsequent therapy.

One more aspect of the LSD reaction should be reemphasized at this time—namely, its enormous complexity and the number of variables and determinants that are involved and can play an important role. Knowledge and awareness of these elements is essential for every therapist and guide. The present picture of what is happening in the sessions is very far from the original concepts of early experimenters who saw the LSD experience as a result of a simple interaction between the drug and the physiological processes in the brain. Observations made over several decades of LSD research have clearly indicated that, in addition to the basic pharmacological effects of the drug, numerous nonpharmacological (or extrapharmacological) factors have to be taken into consideration for a more complete understanding of the LSD state. In the following text, we will briefly review the most important areas the LSD therapist must be aware of, because they function in different combinations as potential sources of experiential material or as factors modifying the LSD reaction.

Environmental Stimuli and Elements of the Setting

The setting is an extremely important variable that can have a powerful influence on the nature of the LSD experience. It makes a great difference whether the session takes place in a busy laboratory milieu, in a comfortable homelike environment, in a sterile medical setting with white coats and syringes, or in a place of great natural beauty. Each of these settings tends to activate and facilitate the emergence of quite different matrices from the unconscious of the subject.

Also, various particularized external stimuli can codetermine the character and course of the LSD session, sometimes in a rather decisive way. Thus, a picture on the wall or in a book, photographs of close relatives, a glimpse of the shape and color of a certain piece of furniture, scenery briefly seen from the window, or a look at the toilet bowl during a physiological break in the session can trigger very specific sequences of experiences. Equally powerful in this sense are acoustical stimuli, such as a certain piece of music, the ringing of the telephone in the session room, the singing of a bird or barking of a dog, sounds of a jet plane or ambulance, as well as the monotonous buzzing of electrical appliances or laboratory gadgets. An especially power-ful and complex stimulus from this category can be a single word, sentence, or a longer verbal communication coming from the therapist or accidentally overheard during the session. At times, other sensory modalities can be involved; pain associated with an injection, the pressure of a belt or a tight collar, holding of the hand or other forms of physical contact, the temperature in the room, a breeze or a draft, all these can become signifi-cant determinants of an LSD experience. The same is true of gustatory and olfactory stimuli; the taste of food or beverages, as well as various odors and distinct fragrances, can have a rather strong influence on the subject. Some internal stimuli coming from various organs of the body can be included here, since they have a similar function; thus, hunger, thirst, and the urge to urinate or defecate may initiate specific experiences.

Even more relevant are various stimuli of an interpersonal nature; the outlook, clothing, and demeanor of the persons who are present in the session or briefly visit the subject, as well as the way they interact, can become critical determinants for the LSD experience.

Personality of the Therapist and the Therapeutic Situation

The personality of the therapist (sitter), his concept of the LSD session, and his specific approach to it, as well as the nature of his interaction with the subject are among the crucial variables determining the LSD experience. Besides the therapeutic relationship and the current transference problems, many other factors related to treatment can be important sources of material for the session. The general atmosphere in the therapeutic facility, the nature of the patient's relationships with the nurses and fellow patients, the specificities of recent situational factors, and the information exchanged between the patients have the potential to shape certain aspects of the LSD experience.

Present Life Situation

The circumstances of the subject's life situation at the time of his session are a factor the significance of which should not be underestimated. The most frequent source of experiential material for LSD sessions from this category are strongly emotionally charged and conflict-laden relationships, particularly those involving marked dependence and ambivalence. In some individuals, it can be with members of their family of origin; in others, the major focus might be on erotic, sexual, and marital relationships or problems with children. Current conflicts with employers and supervisors, coworkers and subordinates, and other difficulties in the professional area are another common theme in this group. Occasionally, economic, legal, or political problems can be instigative.

Past Life History

This is a very broad category covering a rather large time span and encompassing a variety of important events and problems from childhood, school years, adolescence, postadolescence, and adulthood. Some of them are traumatic; others reflect positive past experiences with parents, friends, or sexual partners; periods of personal success and happiness; encounters with elements of natural beauty; and exposure to artistic creations of high aesthetic quality.

Early Childhood and Infancy

This group includes biographical events from early stages of the developmental history; they are of a very basic nature and are associated with a strong negative or positive emotional charge. Most of them are related to the frustration or satisfaction of primitive instinctual needs of the child; this category was discussed in detail earlier in the context of core experiences of COEX systems.

Biological Birth and the Perinatal Period

Many LSD subjects refer to the circumstances of their biological birth as the deepest source of many agonizing as well as ecstatic experiences in the sessions. The varieties of physical, emotional, and psychological concomitants of the birth process have been discussed in the chapter on perinatal phenomena. A word of caution should be repeated in regard to the elements of this category and of the following ones: it remains to be established whether they are symbolic products of the unconscious or reflect events that once existed in objective reality.

Embryonal and Fetal Existence

This area becomes particularly significant in advanced stages of LSD psychotherapy. The re-enactment of events from various periods of intrauterine development of the fetus include embryonal crises, blissful aspects of fetal existence, and factual illustrations of embryological processes.

Transindividual (Transpersonal and Transhuman) Sources

As we have discussed earlier, much of the material occurring in LSD sessions cannot be adequately explained by biographical data and the biopsychological history of the individual. At the present time, this fact is quite enigmatic, and no satisfactory explanation can be offered for the mechanisms involved. When such material appears in LSD sessions, it has the form of ancestral and phylogenetic sequences; identification with other people, animals, and inorganic material; or of archetypal images; collective and racial memories; and past-incarnation experiences. From a medical point of view, we could also refer in this context to infraindividual sources, as when an LSD subject describes experiences of consciousness of individual organs, tissues, and cells of his own body.

To illustrate the complexity and multidimensional dynamic nature of the LSD experience, we will now complement the above synoptic survey of the individual levels and sources of material with concrete clinical examples. Although each of them is specially selected to focus on material from one particular level, elements from other levels are always simultaneously present. This overlapping of levels is a typical and essential feature of the LSD experience.

We were able to learn a great deal about the significance of *environmental and situational stimuli* in the early years of experimenting with LSD, when the nature and complexity of the drug reaction was insufficiently understood and the conditions for the sessions were far from optimal. I will describe here one of the most drastic external interferences in an LSD session I have ever witnessed.

One of the treatment rooms in the Psychiatric Research Institute in Prague was equipped with a one-way mirror when we started using it for LSD therapy. At that time, two eager but not very sensitive psychology students were interning in our department. One day, when I was running an LSD session with Armida, a young female patient with borderline psychotic symptomatology, they combined a disciplinary trespass with a serious technical error. Without permission from the patient or myself, they decided to watch the LSD session through the one-way screen. Ignorant of the fact that the proper use of this device required darkness in the observer's room, they left the lights on while uncovering the rear side of the mirror. As a result, their ghostlike images appeared on the screen in the treatment room. Armida saw them, and she reacted with a combination of panic and extreme rage. For over an hour, she screamed, yelled, and flailed around, rolling on the floor; during this time, I had virtually no contact with her. After she calmed down and rapport was re-established, Armida was able to explain what had happened. When she had looked into the mirror, the whole scene suddenly changed into a frightening forest. The ghostlike figures of the psychologists were transformed into two aggressive young men with whom she had had a very traumatic experience at the age of seventeen. During the time when she was agitated and unable to communicate, she was totally absorbed in reliving this incident. According to her description, the two scoundrels exploited her naïveté and lured her into a dark forest. Helping each other, they successively raped her in spite of her desperate resistance. As a result of this incident, Armida contracted gonorrhea, which had a chronic course and caused her much gynecological trouble. The biological and emotional sequelae of this event contributed considerably to the problems of her sexual life.

Thus, the real circumstances of the session provided a massive and dramatic external stimulus; the latter was, however, transformed in the sense of an old traumatic experience, and, in turn, triggered the reliving thereof.

The importance of the *therapeutic relationship* as a major determinant of the content of an LSD session can be clearly demonstrated in the first session of Charlotte, a twenty-three-year-old nurse. Several years before her LSD therapy, she was hospitalized in a locked ward of a state mental hospital for a stuporous condition that was diagnosed as schizophrenia simplex. After discharge, she had systematic psychotherapy over a period of several years preceding her first LSD experience. During this time, she successively manifested symptoms of obsessive compulsive neurosis and conversion as well as anxiety hysteria. Important elements in her development were a cool and rigid family milieu without understanding of her needs and virtually no emotional support from her parents. The atmosphere at home was dominated by unrealistic religious demands and was particularly hostile to sexual manifestations of any kind. At the time of the session, Charlotte was completely isolated, and the therapist was her only emotional resource. She manifested a very intense transference and was preoccupied by the idea of breaking the artificial and professional framework of the therapeutic relationship, changing it into an erotic one, and integrating it into her life. This problem strongly influenced the content and nature of her first LSD session.

At the beginning of this session, Charlotte became aware of the strength of her emotional attachment to the therapist and was questioning whether he was interested in her only as a patient or whether "real human interest" was involved. She could not tolerate the idea that he had other patients and did not belong entirely to her. Moreover, the very fact of her being in the role of a patient seemed hardly acceptable. Suddenly, she looked at her body and with a peculiar smile made the comment, "I have the feeling that there is nothing *on* me . . . I mean, there is nothing *to* me; at least nothing you would be interested in. I don't mean anything to you." Shortly afterward, the tendency revealed in the preceding Freudian slip of the tongue fully emerged. Charlotte experienced herself as a beautiful nude model, and the therapist was transformed into a frivolous and lighthearted bohemian painter. The treatment room became a cozy and untidy Montmartre atelier. At that moment, everything seemed beautiful, and Charlotte felt extremely happy. This brief romantic interlude was brutally interrupted by visions of devils and infernal fire on the walls. When Charlotte looked at the therapist she imagined that his tongue was growing and saw his face becoming darker; she then perceived him as a devil with terrifying eyes and little horns on his forehead.

Later, Charlotte hallucinated a ravishingly beautiful woman with a black mask. She expressed her wish to be equally attractive, irresistible, and inaccessible, so that no man could resist her. When she looked at the therapist with a teasing expression and he did not respond to the cryptic seductive message, she saw the wall full of dull-looking oxen. To make sure that he understood this time, she apologized for her visions, stressing that they were involuntary and should not be taken personally. Next the entire room was filled with emblems and coats-of-arms of nobility* composed of various love symbols, such as kissing doves, hearts, embracing couples, and stylized male and female genitals in union.

Shortly afterward, Charlotte envisioned numerous images of personified, bespectacled owls, sitting in a library filled with cobwebs and antique leather-bound volumes. They looked very funny and absurd, like caricatures of scientists. When she looked at the therapist, she burst out laughing, because he was also transformed into one of those learned birds. The visions of this symbolic aviary did not last long; soon the treatment room changed into a space laboratory where everything seemed cold and artificial. Plastic and metal surfaces and long cables dominated the scene (a dim-witted person who does not get the message promptly is referred to in a Czech idiom as having "long cables"). The therapist appeared to be dressed in the

---

*The patient later explained that she knew the Hungarian meaning of the word *gróf*, which (like the German *Graf*) denotes a member of the nobility.

protective space suit of a cosmonaut, "safe from any changes of temperature and external influences." In the scene that followed, the therapist was transformed into a nosy, pipe-smoking detective who looked like Sherlock Holmes himself. The room was being filled with pipe smoke; Charlotte commented that soon nobody would be able to see anything and enjoyed the prospect of such privacy. Not getting an encouraging response, she hallucinated donkeys with big ears and stupid expressions in their eyes. She again emphasized that she did not produce these visions on purpose and that nobody should feel offended by them. The last transformation of the therapist in this session was into a provincial barber dressed in a dirty white coat.

All the aforementioned phenomena are related to the patient's transference problems and have a clearly ambivalent character. Charlotte's feeling that she did not have anything on and that there was nothing to her expresses in a condensed way her desire to change the therapeutic situation into an erotic one and, at the same time, her concern that she was not attractive enough to be interesting to the therapist. The next scene is a wishful erotization of the situation. Instead of a doctor with his patient, there is a messy atelier, a lively artist, and his nude model. The pictures of the sexualized coat-of-arms is another variation of the same theme. The scenes involving devils have a complicated ambivalent meaning. In regard to Charlotte's strict religious upbringing, they symbolize punishment for forbidden wishes; on the other hand, they are expressions of unleashed instinctual tendencies of a sexual and aggressive nature (the devil as seducer). The visions of owls are an ironical reaction to the fact that the therapist did not respond to her overt seductive maneuvers and maintained an objective and "scientific" attitude. According to Charlotte's associations, the experience involving the space lab reflects her perception of the therapist's coolness and inaccessibility and the sort of protective outfit that he used against her coquetry. The astronaut's voyage to the stars symbolizes Charlotte's fantasies concerning the future scientific career of the therapist. Many of the visions in the session also express Charlotte's dissatisfaction, irony, and criticism of the psychiatrist's lack of understanding of and response to her erotic signals. This includes the visions of oxen, asses, owls, and long cables in the lab. The transformation of the therapist into a barber represents another attack on the therapeutic role by redefining the function of the white coat, a common symbol of the medical profession. The discussion of this session and detailed analysis of its content proved very helpful in identifying and resolving the transference problems so vividly manifested in its content.

On occasions, even a single image in an LSD session, if thoroughly analyzed, can be an important source of information about the transference process. We can use as an illustration one brief experience from Charlotte's second session. This example also shows the intricate dynamic structure of the LSD phenomena on the psychodynamic level.

At one point Charlotte opened her eyes and saw a speck of lint on the rug illusively transformed into a funny-looking mouse with unusually large ears; it was dressed as a pilot and was sitting astride a helicopter. Subsequent analysis using the patient's associations revealed the auto-symbolic character of this image. The mouse represented Charlotte and the complexity of her feelings in regard to the session and the transference situation. Earlier in the session, Charlotte had used several maneuvers to drive the therapist into various complementary roles; he had responded with certain therapeutic countermeasures. She did not like this approach and had the feeling that it resembled the play of a cat and mouse. Immediately afterward, she thought about the novelty of LSD therapy and felt like a laboratory animal on whom a new drug was being tested. During her nurse's training, she had often seen experimental mice in such a role. As she was mulling over these ideas, Charlotte began to sweat profusely; a Czech idiom used for this condition is "sweating like a mouse." At the time when the lint changed into the mouse-pilot, the idea of a mouse as a symbol for herself was thus already strongly overdetermined by several independent trends of thought. Before the lint was illusively transformed, Charlotte watched it and associated it with her low self-esteem: "I feel very funny, as if I am an absolute zero, a nothing, like that lint over there, waiting for the vacuum cleaner." In our discussion after the session, Charlotte also shared interesting associations to the symbol of the helicopter. The two directions that characterize its flight, namely upward and forward, symbolized to her the trajectory of a successful life career; the helicopter represented the therapist from whom she expected help in realizing this aim. This composite image reflected Charlotte's ambivalence in the transference relationship. On one hand, she felt inadequate and expected help and support; on the other hand, she wished to manipulate and control. This was expressed in the ambiguous role of the mouse who was a passenger of the helicopter but at the same time functioned as its pilot.

The mouse/helicopter symbol was based on actual elements of the treatment situation, such as lint on the floor, the testing of a new drug, and excessive sweating; at the same time, it reflected Charlotte's life feelings and problems in the therapeutic relationship. In addition, several connections were later traced to important childhood experiences—especially to her phobia of storms and strong wind.

The above clinical example can be used to demonstrate a general principle that deserves special notice. Free associations to Charlotte's auto-symbolic image clearly indicated that individual experiential elements in psychodynamic LSD sessions are sensory or motor exteriorizations of important "nodal points" of the unconscious dynamics. These points occupy the "crossroads" of several association chains connecting areas with emotionally strongly charged unconscious material. Detailed analysis shows that the elements selected for manifest representation (mouse and helicopter in Charlotte's case) are quite regularly those which allow for condensed symbolic expression of a greater number of relevant emotional themes. These individual themes then participate in the resultant manifest experiences in a *pars pro toto* fashion; in other words, each of them is represented by the partial component that they all share. It is often found that the same image or element expresses several significant and often conflicting themes and tendencies of the subject. At the same time, it is also meaningfully related to various aspects of the environment and the treatment situation.

The importance of the *present life situation* for the content and course of LSD experiences can be shown in the case of Peter, whose basic biographical data were given earlier (page 49).

During his entire childhood, Peter suffered from severe emotional deprivation; as a result, he craved affection and maternal love in his adult life. In one of the early LSD sessions of his psycholytic series, there was a long, unusual episode characterized by joyful Christmas scenes alternating with tragic funeral sequences. When he looked out of the window, Peter saw a fairy tale–like winter landscape (the session took place on a sunny November day at least a month before the advent of snow) and the treatment room had "Christmas acoustics." He visualized and smelled his favorite dishes that used to be served on Christmas Eve when he was a child; he heard Christmas bells and the sounds of Christmas carols, and saw scenes depicting traditional yuletide customs performed in his native village. The therapist changed into a magnificent, richly lighted and decorated Christmas tree with various children's toys hanging from its branches.

During the alternating tragic episodes, the atmosphere was very sad and heavy. In a spot on the wall, Peter saw a funeral cortege with many people clad in black and following a hearse. Trivial sounds from the environment that were perceived earlier as capricious Christmas chimes now sounded like death bells. The opaque lamp became a large, ominous-looking phosphorescent skull. Another psychiatrist present in the room looked as if he were dying of a serious illness and he seemed to have the livid color of a corpse. Finally, he was transformed into a skeleton with a scythe, the traditional symbol of the Grim Reaper.

This sequence was rather unclear until it was analyzed with the help of Peter's associations. During his whole life, he had been attracted to maternal women, attempting to get the affection he had missed in the relationship with his own mother. The latter was now eighty years old, and he expected her death any day. The LSD session took place six weeks before the Christmas holidays, during which he planned to visit his mother and spend some time with her. Peter thought of this visit as his last chance to see his mother alive. In his fantasies, he anticipated that she would give him on this occasion a warm hug and kiss and allow him to put his head on her lap. Thus, the idea of the imminent death of his mother was intimately linked with the Christmas atmosphere and the theme of blissful reunion.

Although the material in this sequence reflected the problems of Peter's current life situation, the deepest roots of the themes involved could later be traced to basic perinatal matrices; the imminence of death and the funeral motifs were related to BPM II and the element of union with the mother to BPM I.

The multilevel overdetermination of a single experience in an LSD session by *material from various periods of an individual's past history* can be illustrated by the following clinical example.

Paul was a thirty-two-year-old chemist admitted to our department after an unsuccessful suicide attempt, with the diagnosis of severe character disorder, drug addiction, and alcoholism. He was addicted to fenmetrazine (Preludine), an antiappetite drug with psychostimulant properties. In the past, he kept increasing the initially prescribed dosage of 25 milligrams three times a day until his average daily consumption amounted to about 1500 milligrams. At that time, he developed symptoms of an acute paranoid psychosis with panic anxiety, multiple acoustic hallucinations, and delusions of persecution. After several days spent in a Kafkaesque world, running and hiding from imagined persecutors, he attempted to kill himself and was brought to our institute.

In one of his LSD sessions, Paul had the intense feeling that his body was shrinking and becoming progressively more and more emaciated. Using the technique of free association, we could reconstruct the ideational and emotional content of this experience. Some of the associations led us to the circumstances that precipitated Paul's drug addiction. During prolonged inactivity following the fracture of his leg, Paul became quite obese. He was very unhappy about his appearance and the desire to lose weight rapidly was the main reason he started using fenmetrazine. As a result of this medication, he was actually losing weight drastically.

Another chain of associations linked this experience with Paul's feelings about his father. Paul was born of a mixed marriage; during World War II, his Jewish father spent several years in a Nazi concentration camp, and he himself was persecuted and frequently humiliated. As the war progressed, he used to watch the transportation of starved prisoners in cattle cars; on these occasions, he always thought about his father, concentration camps, and the tragic destiny of the Jews. This very painful and traumatic period of his life represented one important root of the experience of emaciation in the LSD session.

Additional associations led to Paul's overinvestment in the cultivation of his intellect and to his fear of aging, decrepitude, and death. Paul's brilliance was his major asset and his primary compensatory tool. He had an insatiable intellectual hunger and was continually tortured by the feeling that he was aging too quickly. One of his most terrible nightmares was related to his failure and inability to live up to his ambitions and the lack of time to achieve all his goals. Experiencing emaciation in his LSD session, he had on several occasions the strong feeling that he was undergoing accelerated aging and was actually mutating into a decrepit senile man. The most frightening aspect of this experience was the realization of the loss of intellectual functioning that characterizes senile dementia. Thus, the experience of becoming emaciated was also an expression of the most significant fears of his life. Subsequent sessions showed that, in addition, the experience of shrinking also involved an element of age regression into a major traumatic memory of his early childhood.

Paul's experience could be used as another illustration of the exteriorization of nodal points of unconscious dynamics in LSD sessions. In this case, a single experiential theme (shrinking and emaciation) seemed to represent and express many relevant traumatic areas and periods of his life.

The next example involves experiences from a more advanced session of a psycholytic series. The most obvious sources of its content are *traumatic experiences from childhood*, but there is a strong participation of *perinatal elements* (BPM III).

Dana, a thirty-eight-year-old high-school teacher with a doctorate in philosophy, had suffered for many years from a complicated neurosis. Her symptoms included suicidal depressions, bouts of free-floating anxiety, hysterical seizures, and various psychosomatic manifestations; however, the most paralyzing problem was an obsessive-phobic attitude toward her daughter. For eight years, ever since the girl was born, Dana had been experiencing strong impulses to hurt her—stab her with a knife, throw her out of the window, or strangle her. This alternated with a panicky fear that something bad could happen to the child; every elevation of fever was perceived as a possible symptom of fatal illness; the baby bottles, plastic nipples, and diapers were never clean enough to insure the elimination of all dangerous bacteria, and every absence from home was seen as a potentially serious hazard. In addition, Dana, as a person of high moral standards, was vexed by agonizing guilt and self-accusations because of her destructive tendencies against her own daughter.

One of Dana's LSD sessions was completely dominated by monstrous, blasphemous distortions of religious themes. The most sacred elements were contaminated by "obscene" and brutal biology. She saw, for example, scenes of the crucifixion in which Christ's face was disfigured, his fingers were changed into bloody claws, and he was urinating from the cross; mangy, dirty rats were running over

A series of pictures reflecting monstrous, blasphemous distortion of the most sacred religious themes and their contamination by "obscene" biology. The patient was flooded by similar images in an LSD session in which she was working through specific traumatic childhood experiences and elements of the birth trauma.

A picture showing the resolution of the problems illustrated by the preceding drawings. The spiritual element symbolized by Jesus is rising above biology (stomach, intestines, genitals, bladder, and human embryos) and separated from it. The patient's hands are reaching for the Black Sun, the "inner reality" that is even "beyond Christ."

Calvary desecrating this holy place with saliva, feces, and urine. After several hours of experiences of this kind, she relived a traumatic event from her adolescence; this was the first concrete and personal example of a situation from her life which involved confusion of religion and "obscene" biology. Her boy friend, a divinity student who appeared on the surface to be a pious and rigidly religious person, exhibited toward her what she considered to be perverse sexual behavior. Later, after excessive resistances were reduced, the session was dominated by reliving traumatic childhood memories. When she was ten, her psychotic father suffered a cerebral hemorrhage and was kept at home in spite of his rapidly deteriorating physical and mental condition. In the LSD session, Dana had to re-experience and suffer through many scenes in which, as a young girl, she saw her father neglecting basic aspects of hygiene. Severely decompensated as a result of his psychotic process and organic brain damage, he frequently performed various physiological functions in her presence. The father was a religious fanatic who had holy pictures, little altars, and various liturgical objects in every room of the house. Many of the scenes relived in Dana's LSD session showed her father's uninhibited behavior in this overly religious setting; this had been an important source for the confusion of religion and biology in the session.

The deepest roots of this intimate fusion of religious feelings and "obscene" biology were later found in the experiences related to BPM III. On the perinatal level, the feelings of identification with Christ and his suffering and the element of spiritual death and rebirth were accompanied by biological reliving of the birth trauma, with the emphasis on its brutality, monstrosity, and obscenity. Simultaneously with her own birth, Dana also relived the birth of her daughter. She found the source of her aggression toward this child in the feelings that she experienced during early stages of her delivery, at a time when the uterine cervix is still closed and the mother and child are inflicting pain on each other. After full reliving and integration of this memory, Dana could experience for the first time in her life genuine maternal feelings free from aggression, guilt, and anxiety.

Toward the end of her LSD session, Dana had the vision of a purified and radiant Jesus separated from biology; this was associated with genuine Christian feelings and a new intuitive understanding of Christ's message. At the same time, she felt that there was something even beyond Christ, and she used for this principle the symbol of the Black Sun. Dana's description of this transcendental symbol resembled in many ways the concept of Atman in Hinduism.

The last example is a description of an advanced LSD session of Michael, a nineteen-year-old schizophrenic student who was the youngest person we treated with psycholytic therapy. He was the brother of Eva, a hysterical patient who also participated in LSD therapy; the condensed history of both siblings was presented earlier in the section dealing with the authenticity of relived childhood memories (page 66). In spite of very serious clinical symptomatology, Michael was able to make rapid therapeutic progress; he moved relatively quickly through the psychodynamic and perinatal stage of his treatment to transpersonal levels. The following outline is of his thirty-second session, which he had shortly before termination of therapy.

The session started with a feeling of "pure tension" that was building up to higher and higher levels. When the tension was transcended, Michael had an experience of overwhelming cosmic ecstasy; the universe seemed to be illuminated by radiant light emanating from an unidentifiable supernatural source. The entire world was filled with serenity, love, and peace; the atmosphere was that of "absolute victory, final liberation, and freedom in the soul." The scene then changed into an endless bluish-green ocean, the primordial cradle of all life. Michael felt that he had returned to the source; he was floating gently in this nourishing and soothing fluid, and his body and soul seemed to be dissolving and melting into it. The experience had a distinct Indian undertone; he asked the therapist whether this state of unity of the individual self with the universe was described in Indian religious scriptures. He saw numerous visions of Hindu worship, mourning ceremonies on the Ganges River, and Indian yogis practicing in the monumental setting of the Himalayas. Without having had any previous knowledge of Hatha Yoga, Michael intuitively assumed several of the classical body postures (asanas) because they seemed best suited to his present state of mind.

This ecstatic condition was suddenly interrupted and the sense of harmony deeply disturbed. The water in the ocean became amniotic fluid, and Michael experienced himself as a fetus in the womb. Some adverse influences were endangering his existence; he had a strange, unpleasant taste in his mouth, was aware of poison streaming through his body, felt profoundly tense and anxious, and various groups of muscles in his body were trembling and twitching. These symptoms were accompanied by many terrifying visions of demons and other evil appearances; they resembled those on religious painting and sculpture of various cultures. After this episode of distress passed, Michael re-experienced his own embryological development, from the fusion of the sperm and egg through millions of cell divisions and processes of differentiation to a whole individual. This was accompanied by an enormous release of energy and radiant light. The sequences of embryonal development were intermingled with phylogenetic flashbacks showing the transformation of animal species during the historical evolution of life.

Toward the end of the session, Michael returned to the feelings of fusion and melting in the ocean alternating with identification with the entire universe. On this general background, he had numerous visions of ancient Egypt, with pyramids, royal tombs, majestic granite sculptures, and various deities and mythological figures. These ecstatic visions continued until late at night; the last vision in the session was a triumphant cruise of an Egyptian princess with her elaborate retinue on the Nile River.

The following day, Michael was in the calmest, most joyful, and most balanced emotional condition he had experienced in his entire life. After this session, his psychotic symptoms never reappeared. Several years later, he got married and left Czechoslovakia. He has been able to take full responsibility for himself and his family and to cope successfully with all the hardships associated with the life of an emigrant.

We will conclude this discussion of the multilevel and multidimensional nature of the LSD experiences with several remarks that have direct bearing on the use of this drug for personality diagnostics and the therapy of emotional disorders. Clinical applications of the theoretical principles outlined in this volume will be discussed in detail in the forthcoming book focusing primarily on practical aspects of LSD psychotherapy.

Many of the examples used in this chapter clearly illustrate that LSD activates emotionally important material in different areas and on various levels of the personality; the resulting multiple overdetermination of the manifest content is one of the most characteristic features of the LSD experience. It has been a common observation in LSD therapy that patients present several relevant, mutually overlapping, and logically consistent interpretations of a single symbolic experience. However, in the case of complex sequences, one of the levels is usually in the center of the experiential field and "in the spotlight" of consciousness. Additional levels can be tangentially alluded to in the periphery of the perceptual stream while the main theme is unfolding; at other times, they are revealed by systematic analysis after the session with the use of the patient's free associations, or emerge spontaneously in subsequent LSD sessions. The variables determining the depth of the prevailing level are the personality of the subject, the facilitating influence of the therapist, the dosage of LSD, the intensity of the emotional charge connected with the material involved, the degree of resistance and strength of the defense system, the set and setting, and the number of previous LSD exposures. The latter factor deserves special explanation because of its significance for understanding the nature of the LSD reaction, the inter- and intraindividual variability of the content of the sessions, and the dynamics of LSD psychotherapy.

Different subjects are in very different situations at the time when they have their first LSD session. Some of them are heavily defended against unconscious material from any level; others have easy access not only to psychodynamic phenomena but also to perinatal and even transpersonal experiences. In the process of consecutive LSD sessions, the major experiential focus tends to shift, by and large, from abstract and psychodynamic elements to the problems of death and rebirth, and eventually to various transpersonal sequences. Advanced LSD sessions are usually dominated by mystical and religious themes and are all transpersonal in nature; elements of the levels worked through in earlier sessions do not reappear in this stage. In a series of LSD sessions, these consecutive shifts of focus from one level of the individual's unconscious to another are accompanied by corresponding changes of the personality structure, emotional sets, values, attitudes, belief systems, and often the entire world view. The understanding of this process and its specific dynamics forms the basis for sensitive guidance and optimal utilization of the therapeutic and growth potential of the LSD procedure.

Epilogue
Bibliography
Index

Epilogue

I am presenting this book to my professional colleagues and to the general public with somewhat mixed feelings and not without hesitation. I am fully aware how unusual and surprising some of its sections must seem to a reader who has not had a firsthand experience with psychedelics or some other type of altered state of consciousness. I know from my own personal development how difficult it was for me to consider seriously and accept the implications of some of the quite extraordinary observations from LSD sessions. I had resisted the influx of the revolutionary new data that I was exposed to in my everyday clinical work and kept trying to explain them within the accepted theoretical frameworks, until my tendency to defend traditional ways of thinking was defeated and overwhelmed by an avalanche of indisputable clinical facts. Whenever I violated the boundaries of tradition, conventional thinking, and commonly shared assumptions, it was only because rather convincing evidence made the old concepts incomplete, unsatisfactory, implausible, or untenable. I would like to emphasize in this context that I did not indulge in iconoclastic pleasure in opposing the existing concepts and theories. On the contrary, having been rather conservative by nature, I experienced a considerable amount of discomfort when the accepted systems proved inadequate. I had to suffer through a long period of rather unpleasant conceptual chaos, with a painful lack of any meaningful guidelines. This lasted until I developed a broader theoretical framework that seemed to introduce new order into the research data and made possible a simplifying integration and synthesis of the most important observations.

Looking for an appropriate form to communicate my findings, I rejected what seemed to be a tempting alternative, namely censoring or truncating some of the most unusual observations in order to avoid disapproval and harsh criticism. In addition to being personally and professionally dishonest, such an approach would have defeated the very purpose for which this book was written. It seemed important to share the data in their true form, including the challenge that they represent to our common sense and to scientific thinking. I have therefore decided to take the risk of attacks, fierce criticism, and possible ridicule for the sake of integrity and accurate reporting.

I do not anticipate that it will be easy for the reader to accept the ideas expressed in this book; it is reasonable to expect that the skepticism of others in regard to the data will not be less acute than that which I experienced myself. The most conclusive confirmation or rejection of the presented material will have to come from similar studies conducted by other researchers. Theoretically, of course, the research described in this book is replicable, even if the present political and administrative situation in regard to drug investigations makes such a task rather difficult. Indirectly, the validity of the presented concepts can be tested in the situation of the uncontrolled experiment happening on a large scale in the contemporary United States, namely the unsupervised use of psychedelic drugs. The persons who have taken LSD and those mental-health professionals who have worked with such individuals will be able to judge to what extent the described cartography of the unconscious is congruent with their experience. Another indirect way of testing the new conceptual framework is to apply it to various states in which the activation of the unconscious material is induced by powerful nondrug techniques. Numerous examples can be found in religious scriptures, mystical writings, and anthropological books and journals, as well as in contemporary literature on experiential psychotherapeutic techniques and laboratory mind-altering procedures.

The significance of the LSD observations transcends the

framework of psychiatry and psychology and extends to many other scientific disciplines. It is far beyond the capacity of a single individual to outline and evaluate all the implications and consequences of the findings in their entirety. Detailed study of psychedelic phenomena would require a long-term systematic team cooperation of experts from diverse disciplines, such as psychology, psychiatry, neurophysiology, neuropharmacology, ethnobotany, modern physics, zoology, ethology, genetics, internal medicine, obstetrics and gynecology, anthropology, history of art, theology, philosophy, and comparative study of religion and mythology.

At the present time, the future of psychedelic research is problematic, and it is uncertain whether it will be possible to replicate the study of serial LSD sessions described in this book. In any case, it will undoubtedly take a long time before such studies will be completed and will generate new data. In the meantime, I would like to offer the material on which this book is based for detailed analysis to every serious researcher who finds it of interest from the point of view of his own discipline. In turn, I would appreciate any critical comments and suggestions from the specialists of various disciplines that would help to clarify the findings described in this volume.

Bibliography

1. Arcamone, F. "Production of Lysergic Acid Derivatives by a Strain of Claviceps Paspali Stevens and Hall in Submerged Culture." *Nature.* 187 (1960): 238.

2. Cohen, S. "Side Effects and Complications." *Journal of the Nervous and Mental Diseases.* 130 (1960): 30.

3. Fanchamps, A. "Des drogues magiques des Aztèques à la thérapie psycholytique." *Acta Psychotherapeutica.* 10 (1962): 372.

4. Freud, A. *The Ego and the Mechanisms of Defense.* London: Hogarth Press, 1937.

5. Freud, S. "From the History of an Infantile Neurosis." *Collected papers,* vol. 3. London: Institute of Psychoanalysis and Hogarth Press, 1924.

6. Freud, S. "The Aetiology of Hysteria." *Collected papers,* vol. 1. London: Institute of Psychoanalysis and Hogarth Press, 1924.

7. Gopi Krishna, *Kundalini: The Evolutionary Energy in Man.* Berkeley, Calif.: Shambala Publications, 1970.

8. Grof, S. "Theoretical and Empirical Basis of Transpersonal Psychology and Psychotherapy: Observations from LSD Research." *Journal of Transpersonal Psychology.* 5 (1973): 15.

9. Grof, S., and Dytrych, Z. "Blocking of the LSD Reaction by Premedication with Niamid." *Activitas nervosa superior.* 7 (1965): 306.

10. Jung, C. G. "Synchronicity: An Acausal Connecting Principle." *Collected works,* vol. 8. Princeton, N.J.: Bollingen Series. Princeton University Press, 1960.

11. Leuner, H. *Die experimentelle Psychose*. Berlin, Göttingen, Heidelberg: Springer Verlag, 1962.

12. Lilly, J. C. *The Center of the Cyclone*. New York: The Julian Press, Inc., 1972.

13. Maslow, A. H. *Toward a Psychology of Being*. Princeton, N.J.: D. van Nostrand Co., Inc., 1962.

14. Maslow, A. H. "A Theory of Metamotivation: The Biological Rooting of the Value Life." In *Readings in Humanistic Psychology*, edited by A. J. Sutich and M. A. Vich. New York: The Free Press, Ltd., 1969.

15. Pahnke, W. N., and Richards, W. E. "Implications of LSD and Experimental Mysticism." *Journal of Religion and Health*. 5 (1966): 175.

16. Rank, O. *The Trauma of Birth*. New York: Harcourt Brace, 1929.

17. Stoll, W. A. "LSD, ein Phantastikum aus der Mutterkorngruppe." *Schweizer Archiv für Neurologie und Psychiatrie*. 60 (1947): 279.

18. Stoll, A., Hofmann, A., and Troxler, F. "Ueber die Isomerie von Lysergsäure und Isolysergsäure." *Helvetica Chimica Acta*. 32 (1949): 506.

19. Varella, G., Vazquez, A., and Toroella, J. "Probable existencia de la LSD-25 en la infección por Toxoplasma Gondii." *Revista del Instituto de salud y Enfermedades tropicas (Mexico)*. 16 (1956): 29.

Index

abortions, reliving of, 141
Abraham and Isaac, 132
abstract LSD experiences, 3, 13,
    33, 34–43
Adonis, 142
adrenaline derivatives, 15–
    16
adrenochrome, 15–16
adrenolutine, 15–16
aesthetic LSD experiences, 3,
    13, 33, 34–43
African tribal rituals, 171
afterimages, 34–35
Ahasuerus, 199
Ahura Mazda and Ahriman,
    143, 187, 200
akashic record, 176
alchemy, 201
alcoholism, 98
ambrosia, 143
ancestral experiences, 107,
    162–67
anguish, resolution of, 176
animal identification, 101, 180–
    181
animal transformations, 181
animism, 185
ankh, 201
apocalyptic outlook, 116

Apollo, 200
archetypal experiences, 100,
    108, 109, 113, 171, 198–
    199, 208
Aristotelian logic, 106
Armageddon, 125, 200
Assagioli, Roberto, 33, 211
Astarte, 132, 200
astral bodies, contact with, 194–
    196, 197–98
Atlantis, 125
Atman-Brahman union, 143,
    235
atropine, 13
Augeas, 131
Aurobindo, 197
authenticity of LSD-evoked
    memories, 64–70. *See also*
    LSD research, verification
    of
axial reflexes, 61
Aztec religion, 128, 131, 132,
    142

Babinksi reflex, 61
Babylonian religion, 130
bacchanalia, 132
Backster, Cleve, 183

Bateson, Gregory, 64
Báthory, Elizabeth, 128
Beethoven, Ludwig van, 180
belly dancing, 171
benactyzine, 13
Bindrim, Paul, 99*n*
bioenergetics, xiv, 99*n*
biofeedback, xiv
birth trauma: relation to death
    fear, 95–96, 117; relation
    to later childhood trauma,
    72, 76; reliving of, 51, 56–
    60, 68–73, 80, 96–98, 108–
    109, 114, 232–33, 235–36;
    spiritual counterpart of,
    101–104. *See also* perinatal
    matrices, basic, BPM II
black magic, 189
Black Mass, 132, 133
Black Sabbath, 132
Boddhisattva, 200
body image, changes of, 10, 60
Borgia, Cesare, 128
Bosch, Hieronymus, 120, 146
Bose, Jagadis Chandra, 183
bowels, effect of trauma on, 71,
    79–80
BPM I–IV. *See* perinatal
    matrices, basic
Braque, Georges, 37
Bridge of Sighs, 146
Buddha, the, 109, 113, 120,
    132, 177, 180
Buddhism, 99, 119, 131, 170,
    176, 177, 183, 201, 204

cabbala, 201
Camus, Albert, 118
cancerophobia, 52–57

cancer patients, LSD therapy
    for, x, xv
"cardboard" world, 117
cardiovascular system, effect of
    trauma on, 71, 79–80
carnival atmosphere, 130
Casanova, Jacopo, 130
castration, fear of, 141
catastrophic awareness, 124–25,
    184
Céline, Louis Ferdinand, 118
Center of the Cyclone, The (Lilly),
    197
chakras, 202
childhood memories, reliving
    of, 60–65, 68–73, 78, 232–
    233, 235–36
chimaera, 142
Christ. *See* Jesus
Christian religious traditions,
    119, 177
circumcision, reliving of, 141
clairaudience and clairvoyance,
    177–78, 186–87
Claviceps paspali, 7
COEX_systems (systems of
    condensed experience),
    46–94, 205; contrasted
    with individual memories,
    70–71; definition of, 46–
    49; determining function
    in LSD reaction, 81, 150;
    exterioration of, 88–91;
    external stimulation of,
    90–91; formation of, 73–
    74; governing influence of,
    92–93; LSD activation of,
    77–88, 92; negative core
    of, 61–64; origin and
    dynamics of, 61–77;
    positive core of, 64, 110;
    resolution of, 93–94
Cohen, Sidney, 2

collective unconscious, 100, 107, 155, 167–71, 198

color, LSD experience of, 34–35

conception, consciousness of, 191–93

conflagrations, 175

consciousness constriction, 191–193

consciousness expansion, 13, 154, 158–90

coprophagia, 130n

coprophilia, 130n

core experience: repetition of, 75–76; significance of, 68–73, 78–79, 91–92. *See also* COEX

Cortes, Hernando, 128

Cosmic Man, 171, 199

cosmic unity, 101, 105–109, 113, 114, 139, 153, 160, 185–87, 204, 235

cosmobiological cycles, 144

counterculture, xi–xii, 5

crux ansata, 201

Daedalus, 199

Dali, Salvador, 120

Damocles' sword, 117

Dante Alighieri, 120, 197

Darwinian insights, 107, 183–184

Dass, Baba Ram, 107n

David, star of, 201

death: emotional preparation for, x, xv; fear of, 95; LSD experience of, 194–96; perinatal experience of, 95–96; relation to birth trauma, 95, 124; sexual associations with, 54, 124, 129

death-rebirth experience, 101, 124, 130, 139–40, 150, 176. *See also* perinatal experiences, basic, BPM IV

deities, encounters with, 107–108, 109, 199–200

déjà vu, 174, 178

delirogens, 13

delusions, 12

demons, 109

depression, 11

dimethyl- and diethyltryptamine, 15

Dionysus, 134, 142

Divine Comedy (Dante), 120, 133, 197

Don Juan, 130

Dostoevski, Fëdor, 120

Dracula, 128

dreams, 217

drug addiction, 98

Druid rituals, 183

dual unity, 178–79, 194–96, 207

Duchamp, Marcel, 37–40

Dürrenmatt, Friedrich, 82

dysmenorrhea, 152

dyspnea, 97

Dytrych, Zdeněk, 23

Echidna, 142

ecological awareness, 183–84

ecstasy, 106, 108, 110, 113, 125, 129, 134, 203

Ego and the Mechanisms of Defense, The, 83n

ego death and rebirth, 101, 106, 114, 139, 141, 149

ego identity, 174, 179, 196

ego transcendence, 178–79

Egyptian religion, 170, 185

Einstein, Albert, 180, 186
El Greco, 133
Elkes, Joel, ix
embryonal experiences, 107,
    108, 109, 155, 158, 222
emotional disorders, LSD
    therapy for, 236–37
Empedocles, 185
encounter groups, xiv, 99*n*
energy, cosmic organization of,
    184–85
engulfment, cosmic, 101, 121
Ensor, James, 120
entoptic (intraocular)
    phenomena, 34–35
epilepsy, 32
erogenic zones, 104, 111, 122,
    135, 145
ESP, 156, 178, 186–87, 190
euphoria, 11
evolutionary memories, 101,
    107, 114, 156, 161, 171–
    173
existentialist crisis, 117–18
exteroception, 154
extraplanetary consciousness,
    185–86

Fantastic Voyage, 191
Faust, 199
Faust (Goethe), 133
feces, association with birth and
    sex, 115, 130*n*
fire, initiation by, 131
"flashbacks, 91, 93
Flying Dutchman, the, 199
flying saucers, 197
Foundations' Fund for
    Research in Psychiatry,
    New Haven, ix
Francis of Assisi, Saint, 180
Freud, Anna, 83*n*

Freud, Sigmund, 44, 45, 68, 70,
    217
Freudian theory, 100–101, 104,
    211–14
Fromm-Reichmann, Frieda, 22

Galileo Galilei, 180
Gandhi, Mohandas K., 197
genetic code, 191
Genghis Khan, 128, 180
geometry, non-Euclidean, 186
George, Saint, 142
Gestalt therapy, xiv, 99*n*
God, identification with, 106
Goethe, Johann von, 133
Gogh, Vincent van, 133
Golgotha, 147
Good Friday, 142
Gopi Krishna, 202*n*
Gothic architecture, 133
Gotterdämmerung (Wagner), 131
Goya, Francisco, 120
Grail, 142
Grandier, Urbin, 130
Greek religious traditions, 119,
    132, 196
grof, etymology of, 225*n*
group consciousness, 180
guilt, 119, 139, 152, 176–77
Gulliver's Travels, 198
guru-disciple relationship, 179

Hades, 200
Haeckel, Ernst, 161
Haggard, Rider, 131
Halifax-Grof, Joan, xv
Harpies, 131
Hatha Yoga, 170–71, 235
Hawaiian religious concepts, 185
Hecate, 132
Heidegger, Martin, 118

hell, experience of, 101, 116, 119, 120, 123
Hercules, 131
Herculeum, 125
Herod, 142
Himalayas, sacred nature of, 185
Hinduism: concepts, 99, 107n, 113, 177, 185, 199, 235; traditions, 119, 143, 170, 171n, 201
hippie movement, xi, 5
Hitler, Adolf, 128, 180
Hofmann, Albert, 1, 7–8
Huit Clos (Sartre), 118
Huitzilopochtli, 132, 142, 200
Human Encounter with Death (Grof and Halifax-Grof), xv
Hydra, 142

Icarus, 199
I Ching, 201
identification with other persons, 179
idioplasma, 176
Indian religions, LSD experience compared with, 203
Indoiranian swastika, 201
Indra, 143
Inquisition, 129
interoception, 154
intraocular phenomena, 34–35
intrauterine life, 105–14, 158–162
ischemia, 129n
Isis and Osiris, 142, 143, 200

Jainism, 177
James, William, 211
Jesus, 119–20, 132, 142, 147, 180, 197, 233

John of the Cross, Saint, 119
Journey to the End of the Night, The (Céline), 118
Jung, Carl Gustav, 33, 167, 198, 199, 207, 211, 212

Kafka, Franz, 180
Kali, 132, 141, 200
Kama-Mara, 132
kamikaze phenomenon, 128
Kandinski, Wassily, 35
karma, 109–10, 153, 160, 173–177, 206–207
Kathakali dancing, 171n
Kennedy, John F., 180
Kierkegaard, Søren, 118
Klimt, Gustav, 35
Knittel, John, 82
Krishna, 171n, 200
Kundalini, 202
Kundalini: The Evolutionary Energy in Man (Gopi Krishna), 202n
Kung Bushman trance dance, 171

Lamarckian insights, 183–84
Last Judgment, 120, 200
latency period, 8–9, 16, 111
Léger, Fernand, 37
Leonardo da Vinci, 133, 180
Leuner, H., 46n
life, search for meaning in, 114, 120
Lilith, 132
Lilly, John C., 197
Lincoln, Abraham, 180
lotus, 183, 201, 203
LSD (diethylamide of d-lysergic acid): chemical structure of, 7; dosage of, 8, 21–22, 24, 28–31, 98, 111;

LSD (diethylamide of d-lysergic acid) (*continued*): hallucinogenic properties of, 7–8; history of, 1–6; methods of administration, 8; methods of production, 7; psychotomimetic use of, 1–2; public attitudes toward, x–xi, 4–6, 239; resistance to, 28–31; therapeutic potential of, ix, x, xv, 2–3, 18–20; toxicity level of, 8

LSD experiences: abstract and aesthetic, 3, 13, 33, 34–43; belated reoccurrence of ("flashbacks"), 91, 93; consciousness changes, 13; determinants of, 80, 219–224, 237; emotional changes, 11; emotional relevance of, 216, 236–37; levels or types of, 33 (*see also* abstract LSD experiences; perinatal LSD experiences; psychodynamic LSD experiences; transpersonal LSD experiences); multilevel nature of, 14, 16–17, 26–28, 100, 215–237; mystical, 3–4, 13–14, 24, 239; non- and extrapharmacological analysis of, 219–37; onset of, 8, 34; past life history's effect on, 221, 229–31; perceptual changes, 10, 34–43; pharmacological analysis of, 26–32, 237; philosophical and spiritual dimensions of, xv, 203; physical symptoms of, 9–

LSD experiences (*continued*): 10, 27; present life situation's effect on, 221, 228–29; professional attitudes toward, xii–xiii, 5–6, 239; psychodynamic analysis of, 17–20, 93, 237; psychomotor changes, 12–13; range of, 8–9, 16–17, 27; setting of, 219–20; sexuality changes, 13; similarity to schizophrenia, 1–2, 15–16; similarity to yoga, 203; thought changes, 11–12; time and space distortion, 10–11

LSD research: heuristic aspects of, xv, 25–33, 210–14; public attitudes toward, xi–xii; purpose of, ix, xiv–xv; verification of, 64–65, 69–70, 112, 159, 178, 187, 190, 222

LSD therapy: COEX systems manifested in, 60, 77–88; emotional disorders treated in, 24–25, 236–37; procedure used in, xv, 21–22; professional attitudes toward, xi, 211–14, 239; selection of subjects for, 20–21, 25; theory of, 25, 239–40; therapist's role in, xi, 24, 211–12, 220–21, 224–28

Lucifer, 200

lysergic acid, amides of, 7

lysis, 20n

Mahabharata, 171n

Maharishi, Ramana, 180, 197

mandala, 201

Manipuri dances, 171n
Maria Theresa, 130
Mary, mother of Jesus, 142
Mary Magdalene, 130
Maryland Psychiatric Research
    Center, 23–24
Maslow, Abraham H., 33, 107,
    140, 211
Matisse, Henri, 35
Mayan religion, 132
Medusa, 142
memory mechanisms, 110–11,
    121, 134–35, 145
mescaline, 8, 15
Michelangelo, 180
Minkowski, Hermann, 186
Mithra, 142
"model psychosis" theory, 1, 2,
    16, 17
Moloch, 132, 141, 200
Mondrian, Piet, 35
morning-glory seeds, 7
Moses, 132
mother, archetypes of, 101,
    143, 160, 198–99
mother-child conflict, 115
mother-child cooperation, 124
muscular tension, 71, 79–80,108
music, LSD enhancement of, 40
mydriasis, 27
mystical union: feelings of
    relation to human
    personality, 95; relation to
    LSD experience, xiii, 13–
    14, 24, 110, 239; relation
    to psychoses, 110

natural phenomena, relation to
    perinatal matrices, 144
n-dimensional space, geometry
    of, 186
nectar, 143

Nero, 128, 180
Nibelungenring (Wagner), 133–
    134
Nietzsche, Friedrich, 134
Nile cross, 201
No Exit (Sartre), 118
"no exit" situation, 101, 116,
    118–19, 120, 137, 149
Nordic mythology, 143

"objective reality," 155–57, 187,
    189, 194–205
obsessive-compulsive neurosis,
    28–31, 48, 52, 61, 98–99,
    224–28
oceanic state of consciousness,
    13, 105, 207
Olmec religion, 132
ololiuqui, 7
Olympus, 143
oneness with life, feeling of,
    183–84
optical illusions, 34–43
Orpheus, 142
Orphic cult, 177
Osmond, Humphrey, 24
Ouroboros, 201
out-of-body experiences, 186–
    190

Pahnke, Walter N., 107
pantheistic religious feeling,
    113, 185
Paradise, visions of, 114
paranoia, 110, 121
Parsees, 170
Parsifal (Wagner), 133
past-incarnation experiences,
    173–76, 206
peak experiences, 107, 140
Pele (Hawaiian goddess), 185

perinatal experiences:
accessibility of, 98–99;
basic characteristics of, 95–
98; relation to individual
and transpersonal
psychology, 99–100;
relationship to LSD
research, 33, 222
perinatal matrices, basic (BPM
I–IV), 100–104, 149, 205;
BPM I, 104–15, 138, 139,
144–45, 149, 150, 152–53,
200, 229; BPM II, 107,
115–23, 144–49, 150, 151,
152, 200, 229; BPM III,
106, 123–37, 140, 141,
144, 149–52, 200, 231–35;
BPM IV, 138–49, 150,
152, 200
perinatal traumatization, 72, 76
Persephone, 142
Perseus, 142
personality diagnostics, LSD use
in, 236–37
Petronius, 122
Phineus, 131
Phipps Clinic, Baltimore, ix
phylogenetic experiences, 101,
107, 114, 155, 161, 171–73
physical traumas, 100–101
Picasso, Pablo, 37
Pizarro, Francisco, 128
planetary consciousness, 185
plants, identification with, 181–
183
Plato, 177
Pledge, The (Dürrenmatt), 82
Poe, Edgar Allan, 120, 133
Pompeii, 125
Poppaea, 130
Prague-Krč, 15
prana, 202n
precognition, 177–78

Pre-Columbian spiritual
concepts, 185
primal union with the mother,
104–15
*Principles of Intensive
Psychotherapy* (Fromm-
Reichmann), 22n
Prometheus, 199
pseudohallucinations, 10, 16
psilocybin, 8, 15
psychedelic, invention of term, 24
psychedelic movement, xi
psychedelic therapy, definition
of, 24. *See also* LSD
therapy
Psychiatric Research Institute,
Prague, x, 18–23, 194–96,
223
psychiatric training, LSD use in,
1, 110, 111–15, 122–23,
135–37, 164–65, 187–90,
192–93
psychodynamic LSD
experiences, 33, 42, 44–94
psychodynamics, 17–20, 93,
104
psycholytic therapy, definition
of, 20n. *See also* LSD
therapy
Puranas, 171n
purgation, 139, 152
purgatory, 132, 133
Pythagorean teachings, 201

Quetzalcoatl, 142

racial experiences, 167–71
Radha, 171n
Ramakrishna, 197
Ramayana, 171n
Rank, Otto, 98

Rankian concepts, 100–101, 212
Rasputin, Grigori E., 130
rebirth, experience of. *See* death-rebirth experience
regression, 60
Reichian therapy, 99*n*
relativity, theories of, 186
religious experiences. *See* mystical union, feelings of
religious symbols, blasphemous distortion of, 231–35
Riemann, Georg F., 186
Rivea corymbosa, 7
Rousseau, Jean Jacques, 139
Rubens, Peter Paul, 133

Saccidananda, 204–205
sacrifice, religious, 128, 131–32
sadomasochism, 124, 125–30, 132–33
Salome, 128
salvation, sense of, 139
Sandison, Ronald A., 20*n*
Sandoz laboratories, 7
Sartre, Jean Paul, 118, 122
Satan, 200
Satanic Mass, 132, 133
satiation, 111, 145
scatological struggle, 124, 130
schizophrenia, 1–2, 15–16, 110, 235
Scientific Yoga, 203
scopolamine, 13
seasons of the year, relation to perinatal matrices, 144
Seneca, 122
sensory isolation, xiv
sensory overload, xiv
Sepher Yetzirah, 201
Serpent Power, 202
Set (Egyptian deity), 142, 200

set and setting, definition of, 14*n*
Seurat, Georges, 35
sex: oceanic, 13, 207; in religious ceremonies, 130, 132–33; satanic, 13; tantric, 13, 207
sexual feelings, 104, 124, 129
sexual impotence, 152
She (Haggard), 131
Shiva, 141, 185
Shiva lingam, 201
Sisyphus, 199
Skopzy, 128
Sobotkiewicz, Julia, 23
Sodom and Gomorrah, 125, 132
space travel, 186–90
Sphinx, 132, 142
Spinoza, Baruch, 113
spirit guides, encounters with, 196–97
spiritistic experiences, 194–96
spiritual search. *See* mystical union, feelings of
Spring Grove State Hospital, Baltimore, ix, 23–24
Stalin, Joseph, 128, 180
"Star Trek," 198
statoacoustic eroticism, 135
stereophonic music, 9, 22, 24
Stoker, Bram, 128*n*
Stoll, W. A., 7
sucking reflex, 61
suffocation, feelings of, 124, 129
Sufi religious traditions, 171
suicide, 116, 122, 129*n*, 151, 152
swastika, 201
Swift, Jonathan, 198
symbiotic union with the mother, 123–37; termination of, 137–49
synaesthesia, 40

synchronicity, 207
synergism with the mother,
    123–37

tanha, 176
Tannhäuser (Wagner), 133
Tantalus, 199
tantric sex, 207
tantric yoga, 202
Taoism, 114, 139, 185, 201
Tarot, 201
telepathy, 159, 186–87, 190
Tepes, Vlad, 128
"Theoretical and Empirical
    Basis of Transpersonal
    Experience" (Grof), 213–
    214
Theresa, Saint, 180
Theseus, 142
Thor, 143
Tibetan religious figures, 109
time travel, 178, 188–90
titanic struggle, 124–25, 129
Totaleinsetzung, 50n
"toxic psychosis" theory, 16, 19,
    25–26
toxoplasmosis, 7
transcendence of space, 101,
    107
transference, 83, 89–90, 91
transpersonal LSD experiences,
    33, 99–100, 101, 157–204,
    222–23; definition of,
    154–55; examples of, 157–
    204; professional attitudes
    toward, 208–14;
    therapeutic significance of,
    205–208; types of, 156–57
transpersonal psychology, 211–
    214
transphenomenal dynamic
    governing systems, 46n

Trauma of Birth, The (Rank), 98n
traumatic experiences: effect on
    specific body organs, 71,
    79–80; reliving of, 61–64,
    78, 84–87, 100–101, 231–
    235; types of, 74. *See also*
    birth trauma
Troxler, F., 7
trsna, 176
Typhon, 142

umbilical crisis, 141
unitive fusion, 179
universal consciousness, 113
universal mind, 203–205, 216
Upanishads, 106n, 114, 143
urine, association with birth and
    sex, 124, 130n
urogenital apparatus, effect of
    trauma on, 71, 79–80
urolagnia, 130n

vaginismus, 152
Valhalla, 143
Van Gogh, Vincent, 35
Vedic tradition, 143
vegetative symptoms, 16–17,
    27
Venice, 146
Vergil, 197
Via Mala, 82
Void, the, 204–205, 216
Vojtěchovský, Miloš, 15
volcanic ecstasy, 125, 134

Wagner, Richard, 131, 133, 180
Wain, Louis, 37
Walpurgis Night, 133
War of the Worlds (Wells), 125
Wells, H. G., 125

Yahweh, 132
yin-yang, 201
yoga, 170–71, 202, 203, 235

Zen Buddhism, 139

Zend Avesta, 143, 187
Zohar, 201
Zola, Émile, 120
Zoroastrian religious customs,
170

A Note About the Author

DR. STANISLAV GROF began his research into psychedelic drugs in his native Czechoslovakia in 1956. From 1967 to 1973 he continued this work in the United States as Chief of Psychiatric Research at the Maryland Psychiatric Research Center in Baltimore, where he also served as Clinical and Research Fellow at Johns Hopkins University. He is the author of over fifty articles in the field, which have appeared in professional journals and books over the past eighteen years. Dr. Grof has lectured on the subject of LSD research and its implications in a number of European countries, Iceland, England, Canada, Japan, India, and the United States. He serves on the editorial board of *The Journal of Transpersonal Psychology, The Journal for the Study of Consciousness, Synthesis,* and *Psychedelic Review.* He is presently scholar-in-residence at The Esalen Institute in Big Sur, California.